STRIKEFORCE

TRUST ME

FEATURING:

ERIC BROOKS, A.K.A.
BLADE
HALF MAN, HALF VAMPIRE.
OCCASIONAL AVENGER.
CONSTANT BAD ████.

ALDRIF ODINSDOTTIR, A.K.A.
ANGELA
ASGARDIAN PRINCESS STOLEN
FROM THE CRADLE, RAISED AS
AN ANGELIC ASSASSIN. HER
RIBBONS WILL BEAT YOU UP.

MONICA RAMBEAU, A.K.A.
SPECTRUM
TURNS INTO ANY FORM OF
ENERGY ALONG THE
ELECTROMAGNETIC SPECTRUM.
ONCE LED THE AVENGERS.
DON'T GIVE HER ████ ABOUT IT.

BUCKY BARNES, A.K.A.
THE WINTER SOLDIER
CAPTAIN AMERICA'S FORMER
SIDEKICK TURNED BRAINWASHED
RUSSIAN SPY TURNED HERO.
GOT A FANCY METAL ARM,
NOT AFRAID TO USE IT.

JESSICA DREW, A.K.A.
SPIDER-WOMAN
CHILDHOOD EXPERIMENTS GAVE HER
SPIDERY SUPER-POWERS, INCLUDING
PHEROMONE MANIPULATION. NOW A
SUPER HERO AND A MOM. DIDN'T NEED
A MAN TO GET PREGNANT, CERTAINLY
DOESN'T NEED YOU.

BILLY KAPLAN, A.K.A.
WICCAN
DREAM CHILD OF THE SCARLET WITCH
AND THE VISION. DESTINED TO
SOMEDAY BECOME THE SENTIENT LIFE
FORCE OF THE UNIVERSE. CURRENTLY
STILL FIGURING OUT HOW TO DO HIS
OWN LAUNDRY.

DAIMON
HELLSTROM
SON OF SATAN. R.I.P.

STRIKEFORCE VOL. 1: TRUST ME. Contains material originally published in magazine form as STRIKEFORCE (2019) #1-5. First printing 2020. ISBN 978-1-302-92009-8. Published by MARVEL WORLDWIDE, INC., a subsidiary of MARVEL ENTERTAINMENT, LLC. OFFICE OF PUBLICATION: 1290 Avenue of the Americas, New York, NY 10104. © 2020 MARVEL No similarity between any of the names, characters, persons, and/or institutions in this magazine with those of any living or dead person or institution is intended, and any such similarity which may exist is purely coincidental. **Printed in Canada.** KEVIN FEIGE, Chief Creative Officer; DAN BUCKLEY, President, Marvel Entertainment; JOHN NEE, Publisher; JOE QUESADA, EVP & Creative Director; TOM BREVOORT, SVP of Publishing; DAVID BOGART, Associate Publisher & SVP of Talent Affairs; Publishing & Partnership; DAVID GABRIEL, VP of Print & Digital Publishing; JEFF YOUNGQUIST, VP of Production & Special Projects; DAN CARR, Executive Director of Publishing Technology; ALEX MORALES, Director of Publishing Operations; DAN EDINGTON, Managing Editor; SUSAN CRESPI, Production Manager; STAN LEE, Chairman Emeritus. For information regarding advertising in Marvel Comics or on Marvel.com, please contact Vit DeBellis, Custom Solutions & Integrated Advertising Manager, at vdebellis@marvel.com. For Marvel subscription inquiries, please call 888-511-5480. **Manufactured between 1/3/2020 and 2/4/2020 by SOLISCO PRINTERS, SCOTT, QC, CANADA.**

10 9 8 7 6 5 4 3 2 1

TRUST ME

TINI HOWARD
WRITER

GERMÁN PERALTA (#1-4) & JACOPO CAMAGNI (#5)
ARTISTS

JORDIE BELLAIRE (#1),
MIROSLAV MRVA (#2) & GURU-eFX (#3-5)
COLOR ARTISTS

MARCO RUDY
BIRGIT FLASHBACK ART (#3)

MAX FIUMARA & DAN BROWN
WINTER SOLDIER FLASHBACK ART (#4)

MARIKA CRESTA & DAN BROWN
HELLSTROM FLASHBACK ART (#4)

STACEY LEE & DAN BROWN
SPIDER-WOMAN FLASHBACK ART (#4)

VC'S JOE SABINO
LETTERER

ANDREA SORRENTINO & DEAN WHITE (#1-2),
ANDREA SORRENTINO & MATTHEW WILSON (#3)
AND **JUAN JOSÉ RYP & MATTHEW WILSON** (#4-5)
COVER ART

JAY BOWEN
LOGO DESIGN

SARAH BRUNSTAD
ASSOCIATE EDITOR

WIL MOSS
EDITOR

COLLECTION EDITOR **JENNIFER GRÜNWALD**   VP PRODUCTION & SPECIAL PROJECTS **JEFF YOUNGQUIST**
ASSISTANT MANAGING EDITOR **MAIA LOY**   BOOK DESIGNER **JAY BOWEN**
ASSISTANT EDITOR **CAITLIN O'CONNELL**   SVP PRINT, SALES & MARKETING **DAVID GABRIEL**
EDITOR, SPECIAL PROJECTS **MARK D. BEAZLEY**   EDITOR IN CHIEF **C.B. CEBULSKI**

1

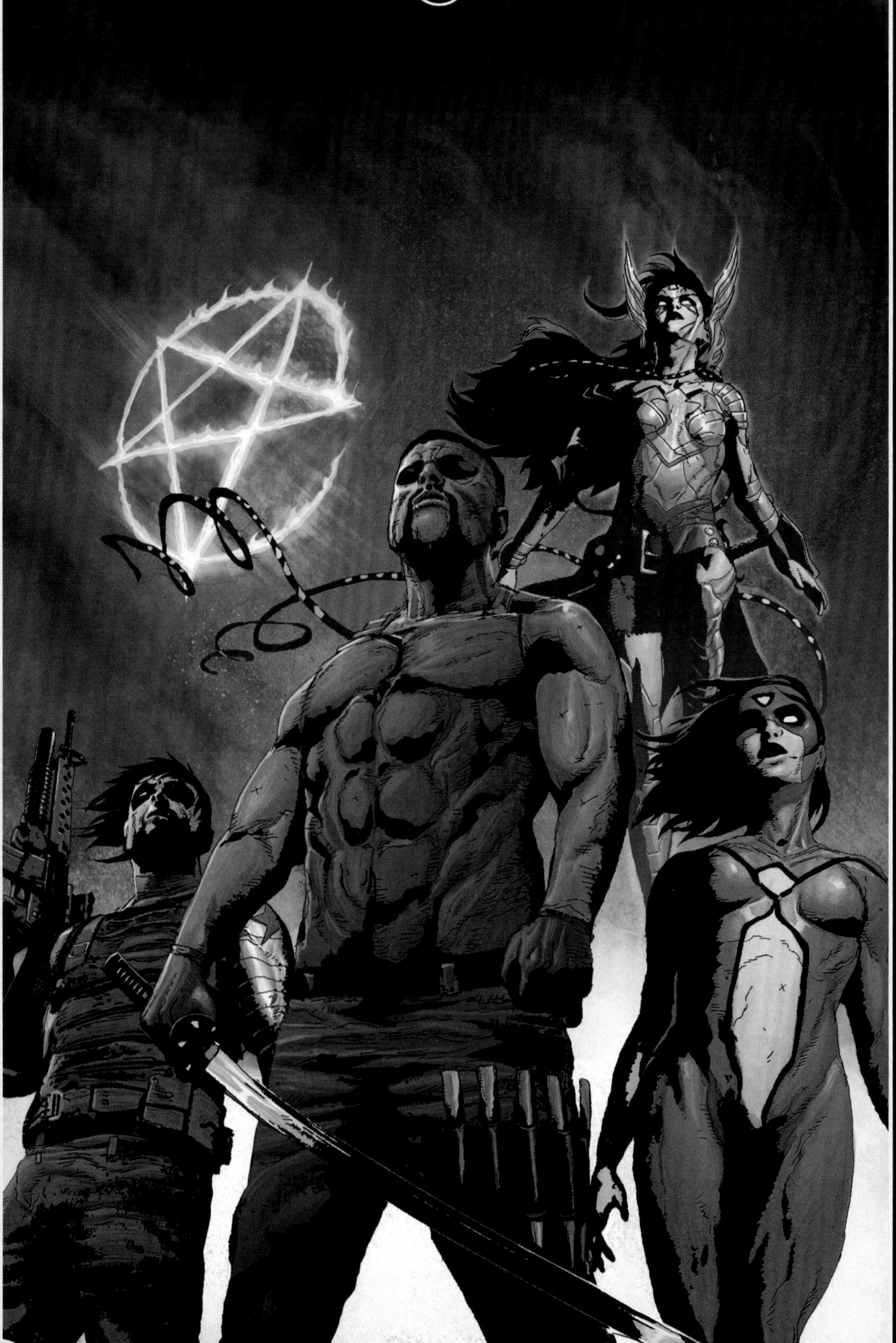

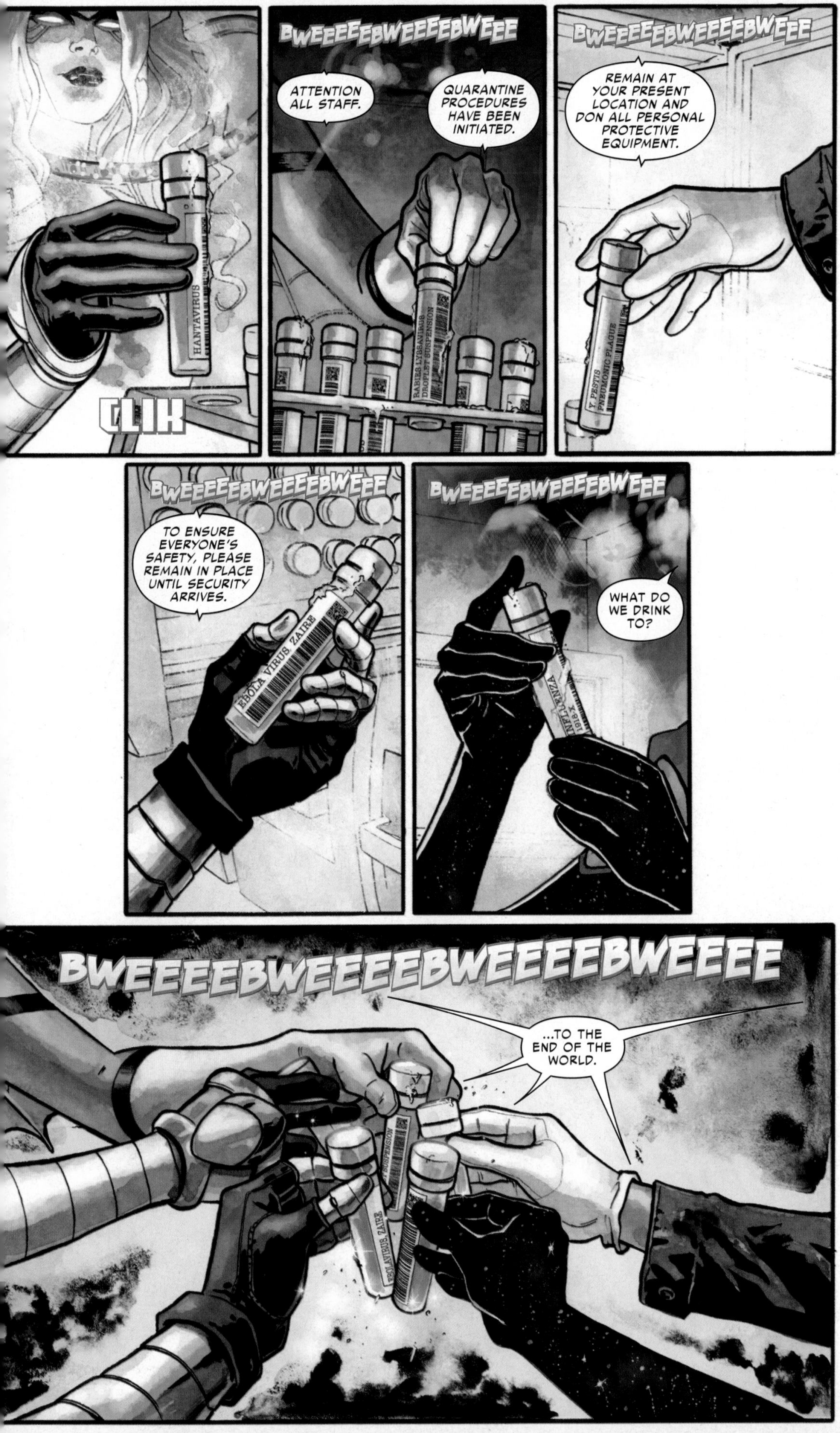

HANTAVIRUS
CLIK
BWEEEEEBWEEEEEBWEEE
ATTENTION ALL STAFF.
QUARANTINE PROCEDURES HAVE BEEN INITIATED.
RABIES LYSSAVIRUS DROPLET SUSPENSION
BWEEEEEBWEEEEEBWEEE
REMAIN AT YOUR PRESENT LOCATION AND DON ALL PERSONAL PROTECTIVE EQUIPMENT.
Y. PESTIS PNEUMONIC PLAGUE
BWEEEEEBWEEEEEBWEEE
TO ENSURE EVERYONE'S SAFETY, PLEASE REMAIN IN PLACE UNTIL SECURITY ARRIVES.
EBOLA VIRUS, ZAIRE
BWEEEEEBWEEEEEBWEEE
WHAT DO WE DRINK TO?
INFLUENZA 1918-X
BWEEEEBWEEEEEBWEEEEE
...TO THE END OF THE WORLD.

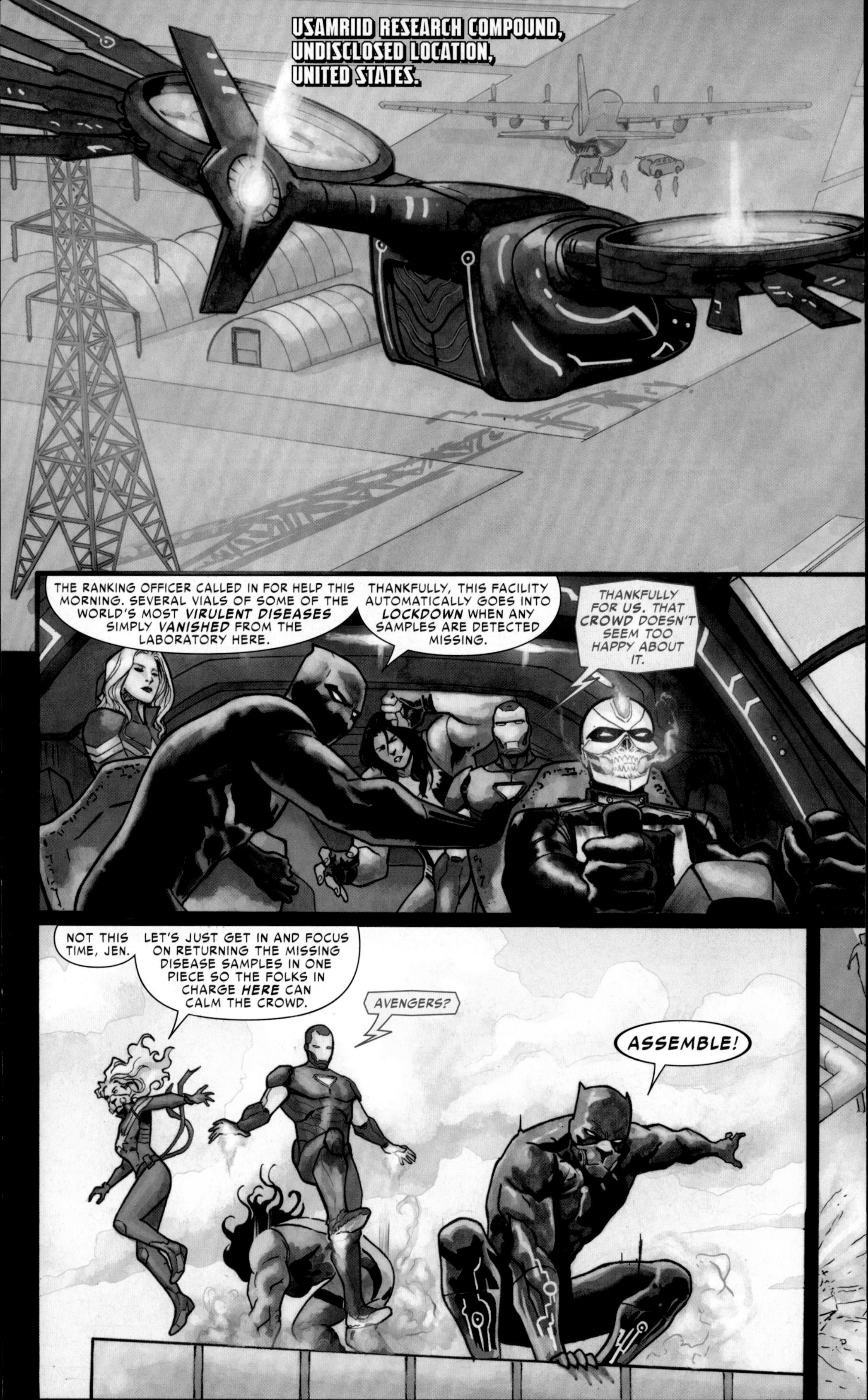
USAMRIID RESEARCH COMPOUND, UNDISCLOSED LOCATION, UNITED STATES.
THE RANKING OFFICER CALLED IN FOR HELP THIS MORNING. SEVERAL VIALS OF SOME OF THE WORLD'S MOST VIRULENT DISEASES SIMPLY VANISHED FROM THE LABORATORY HERE.
THANKFULLY, THIS FACILITY AUTOMATICALLY GOES INTO LOCKDOWN WHEN ANY SAMPLES ARE DETECTED MISSING.
THANKFULLY FOR US. THAT CROWD DOESN'T SEEM TOO HAPPY ABOUT IT.
NOT THIS TIME, JEN.
LET'S JUST GET IN AND FOCUS ON RETURNING THE MISSING DISEASE SAMPLES IN ONE PIECE SO THE FOLKS IN CHARGE HERE CAN CALM THE CROWD.
AVENGERS?
ASSEMBLE!

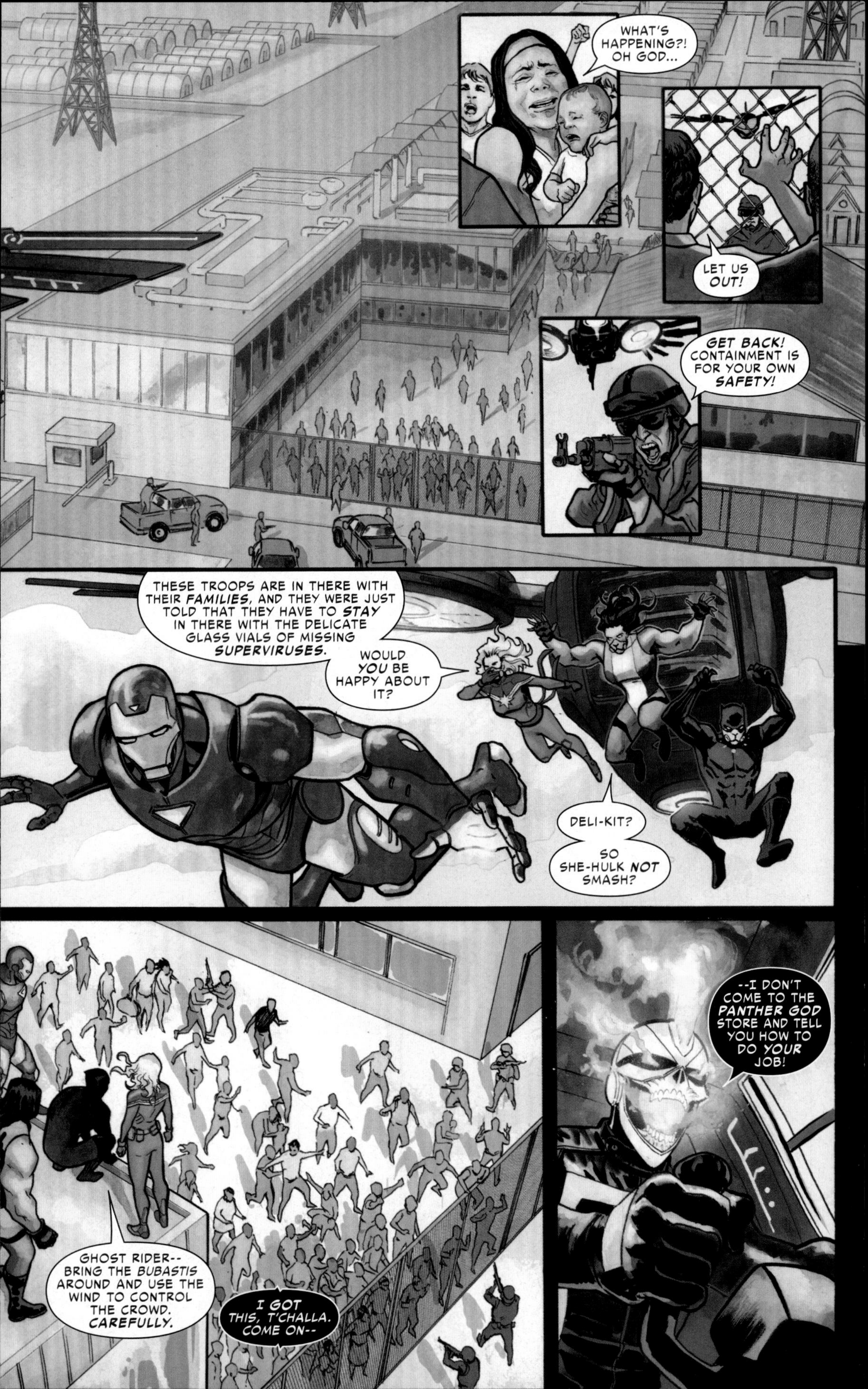
WHAT'S HAPPENING?! OH GOD...
LET US OUT!
GET BACK! CONTAINMENT IS FOR YOUR OWN SAFETY!
THESE TROOPS ARE IN THERE WITH THEIR FAMILIES, AND THEY WERE JUST TOLD THAT THEY HAVE TO STAY IN THERE WITH THE DELICATE GLASS VIALS OF MISSING SUPERVIRUSES.
WOULD YOU BE HAPPY ABOUT IT?
DELI-KIT?
SO SHE-HULK NOT SMASH?
GHOST RIDER--BRING THE BUBASTIS AROUND AND USE THE WIND TO CONTROL THE CROWD. CAREFULLY.
I GOT THIS, T'CHALLA. COME ON--
--I DON'T COME TO THE PANTHER GOD STORE AND TELL YOU HOW TO DO YOUR JOB!

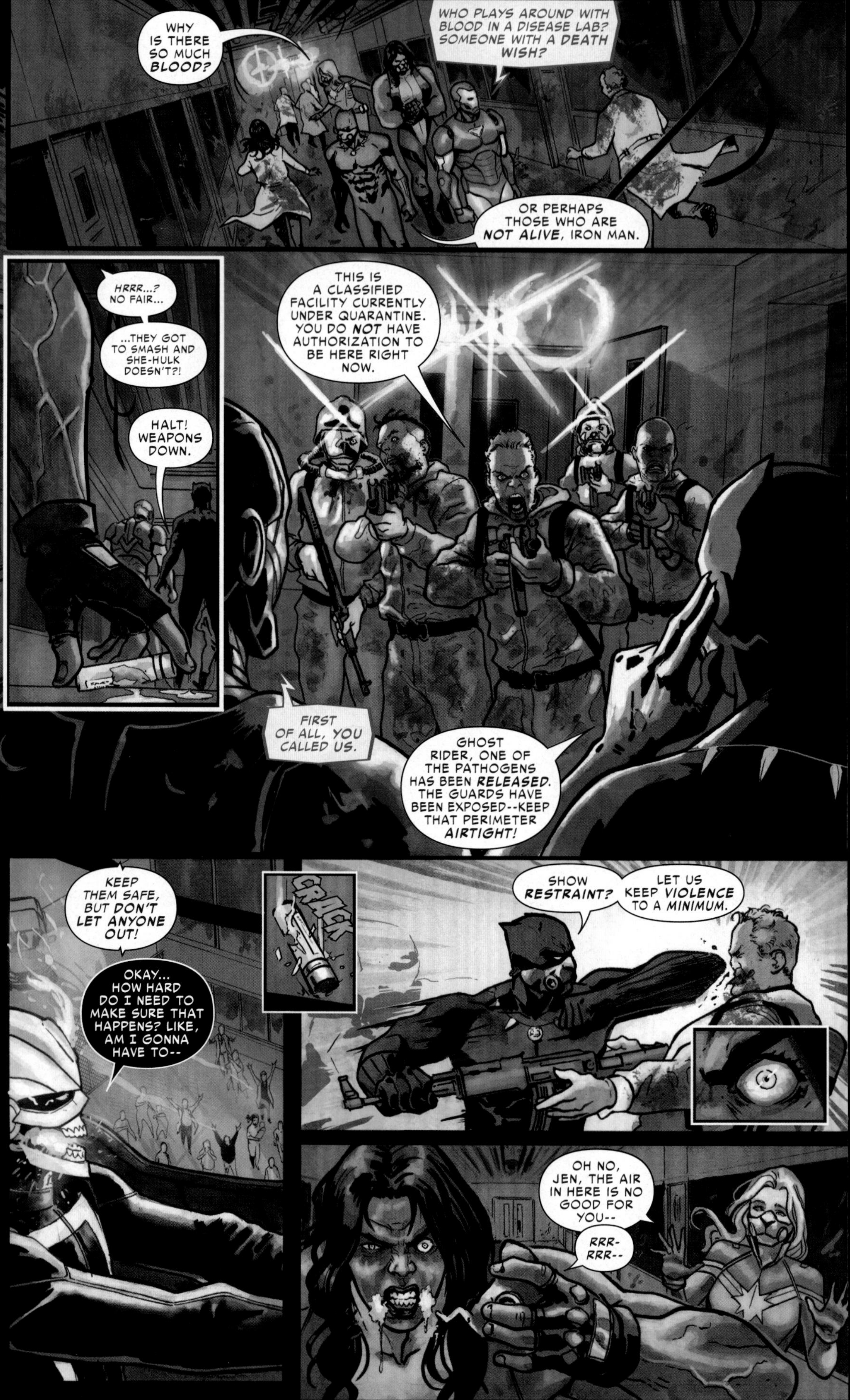
WHY IS THERE SO MUCH BLOOD?
WHO PLAYS AROUND WITH BLOOD IN A DISEASE LAB? SOMEONE WITH A DEATH WISH?
OR PERHAPS THOSE WHO ARE NOT ALIVE, IRON MAN.
HRRR...? NO FAIR...
...THEY GOT TO SMASH AND SHE-HULK DOESN'T?!
HALT! WEAPONS DOWN.
THIS IS A CLASSIFIED FACILITY CURRENTLY UNDER QUARANTINE. YOU DO NOT HAVE AUTHORIZATION TO BE HERE RIGHT NOW.
FIRST OF ALL, YOU CALLED US.
GHOST RIDER, ONE OF THE PATHOGENS HAS BEEN RELEASED. THE GUARDS HAVE BEEN EXPOSED--KEEP THAT PERIMETER AIRTIGHT!
KEEP THEM SAFE, BUT DON'T LET ANYONE OUT!
OKAY... HOW HARD DO I NEED TO MAKE SURE THAT HAPPENS? LIKE, AM I GONNA HAVE TO--
CRACK
SHOW RESTRAINT?
LET US KEEP VIOLENCE TO A MINIMUM.
OH NO, JEN, THE AIR IN HERE IS NO GOOD FOR YOU--
RRR-RRR--

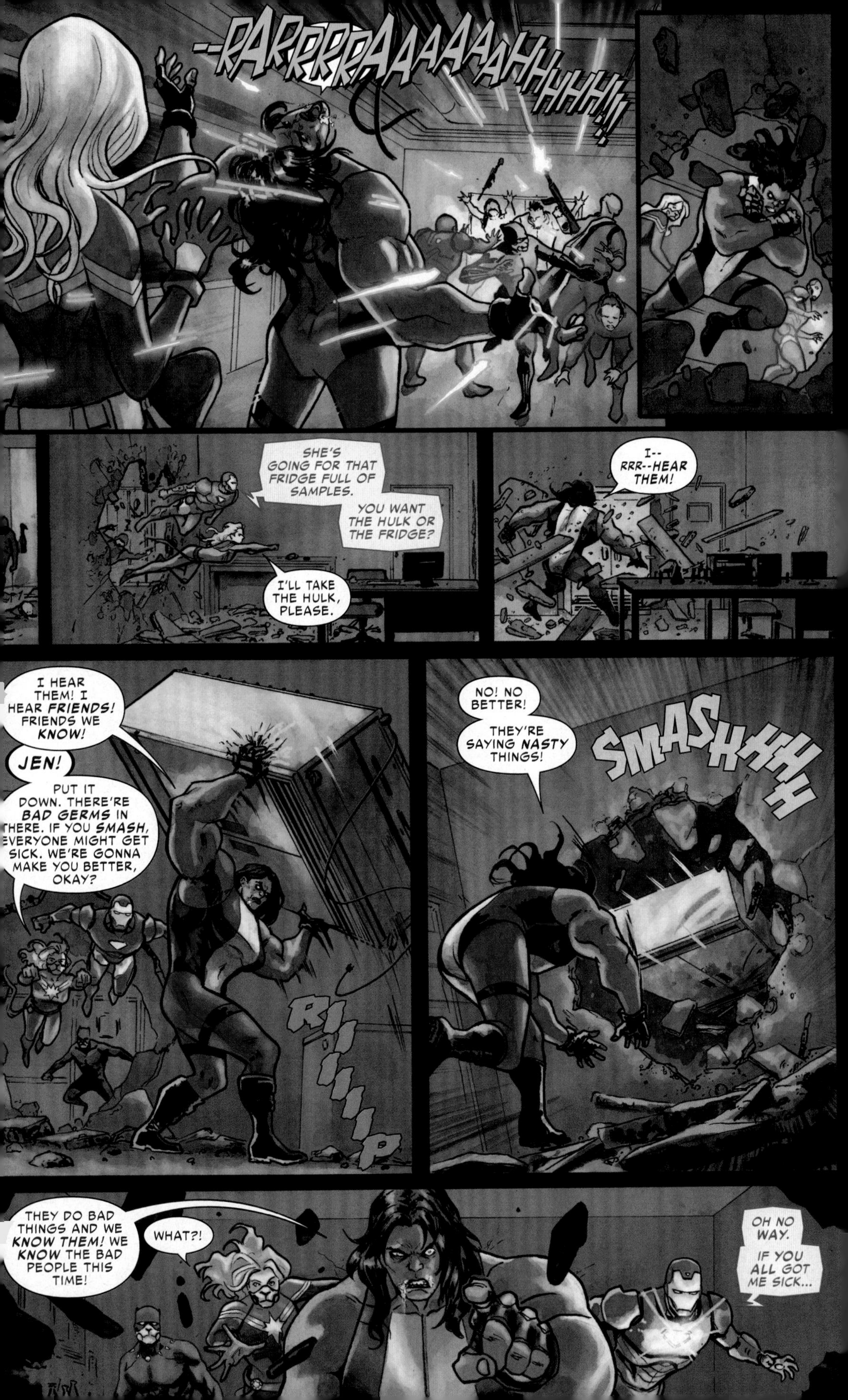
--RARRRRAAAAAAAHHHHH!!
SHE'S GOING FOR THAT FRIDGE FULL OF SAMPLES.
YOU WANT THE HULK OR THE FRIDGE?
I'LL TAKE THE HULK, PLEASE.
I-- RRR--HEAR THEM!
I HEAR THEM! I HEAR FRIENDS! FRIENDS WE KNOW!
JEN!
PUT IT DOWN. THERE'RE BAD GERMS IN THERE. IF YOU SMASH, EVERYONE MIGHT GET SICK. WE'RE GONNA MAKE YOU BETTER, OKAY?
RIIIIIIP
NO! NO BETTER!
THEY'RE SAYING NASTY THINGS!
SMASHHHH
THEY DO BAD THINGS AND WE KNOW THEM! WE KNOW THE BAD PEOPLE THIS TIME!
WHAT?!
OH NO WAY.
IF YOU ALL GOT ME SICK...

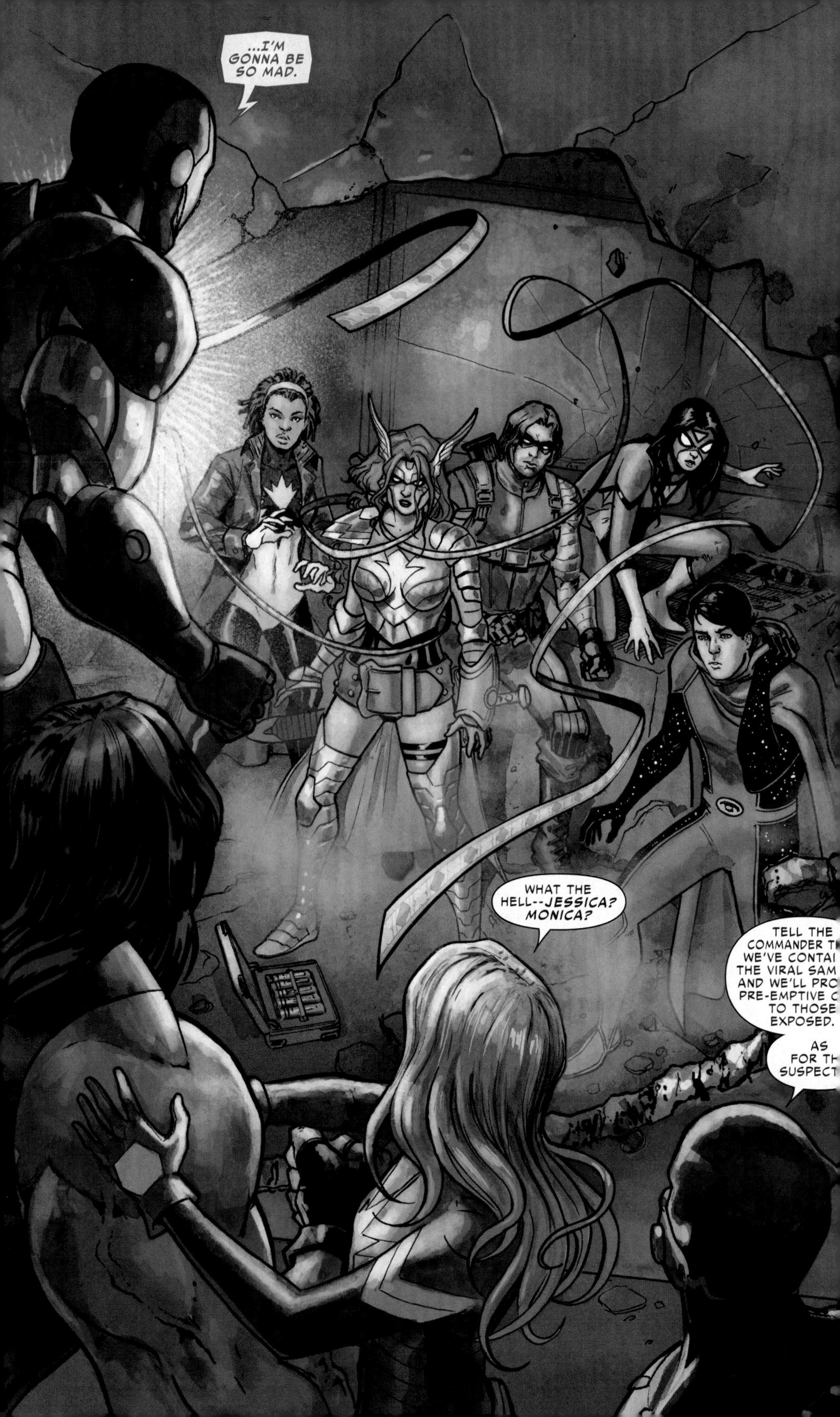
...I'M GONNA BE SO MAD.
WHAT THE HELL--*JESSICA? MONICA?*
TELL THE COMMANDER T WE'VE CONTAI THE VIRAL SAM AND WE'LL PRO PRE-EMPTIVE C TO THOSE EXPOSED.
AS FOR TH SUSPECT

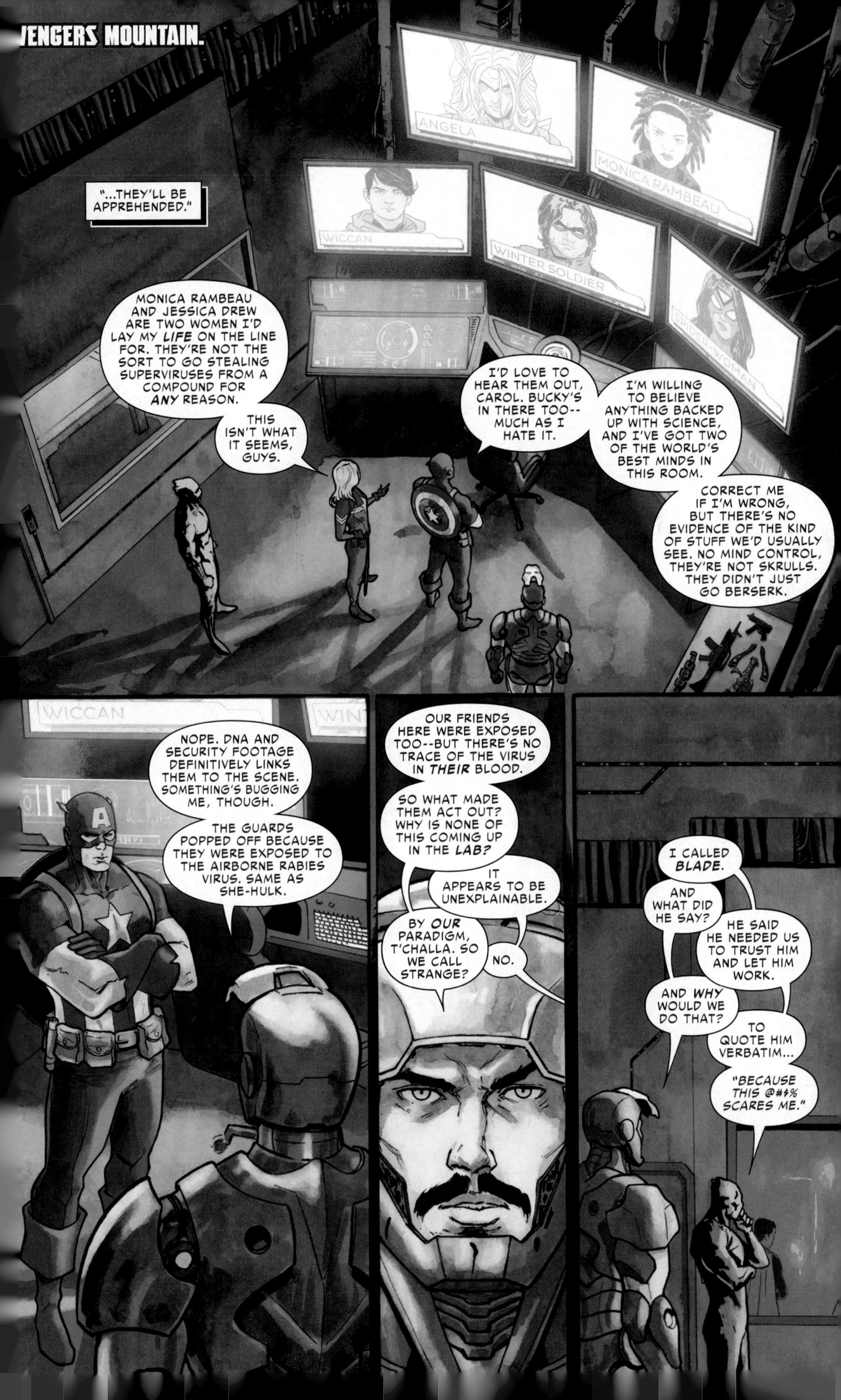

VENGERS MOUNTAIN.
"...THEY'LL BE APPREHENDED."
ANGELA
MONICA RAMBEAU
WICCAN
WINTER SOLDIER
SPIDER-WOMAN
MONICA RAMBEAU AND JESSICA DREW ARE TWO WOMEN I'D LAY MY LIFE ON THE LINE FOR. THEY'RE NOT THE SORT TO GO STEALING SUPERVIRUSES FROM A COMPOUND FOR ANY REASON.
THIS ISN'T WHAT IT SEEMS, GUYS.
I'D LOVE TO HEAR THEM OUT, CAROL. BUCKY'S IN THERE TOO--MUCH AS I HATE IT.
I'M WILLING TO BELIEVE ANYTHING BACKED UP WITH SCIENCE, AND I'VE GOT TWO OF THE WORLD'S BEST MINDS IN THIS ROOM.
CORRECT ME IF I'M WRONG, BUT THERE'S NO EVIDENCE OF THE KIND OF STUFF WE'D USUALLY SEE. NO MIND CONTROL, THEY'RE NOT SKRULLS. THEY DIDN'T JUST GO BERSERK.
WICCAN
WINT
NOPE. DNA AND SECURITY FOOTAGE DEFINITIVELY LINKS THEM TO THE SCENE. SOMETHING'S BUGGING ME, THOUGH.
THE GUARDS POPPED OFF BECAUSE THEY WERE EXPOSED TO THE AIRBORNE RABIES VIRUS. SAME AS SHE-HULK.
OUR FRIENDS HERE WERE EXPOSED TOO--BUT THERE'S NO TRACE OF THE VIRUS IN THEIR BLOOD.
SO WHAT MADE THEM ACT OUT? WHY IS NONE OF THIS COMING UP IN THE LAB?
IT APPEARS TO BE UNEXPLAINABLE.
BY OUR PARADIGM, T'CHALLA. SO WE CALL STRANGE?
NO.
I CALLED BLADE.
AND WHAT DID HE SAY?
HE SAID HE NEEDED US TO TRUST HIM AND LET HIM WORK.
AND WHY WOULD WE DO THAT?
TO QUOTE HIM VERBATIM...
"BECAUSE THIS @#$% SCARES ME."

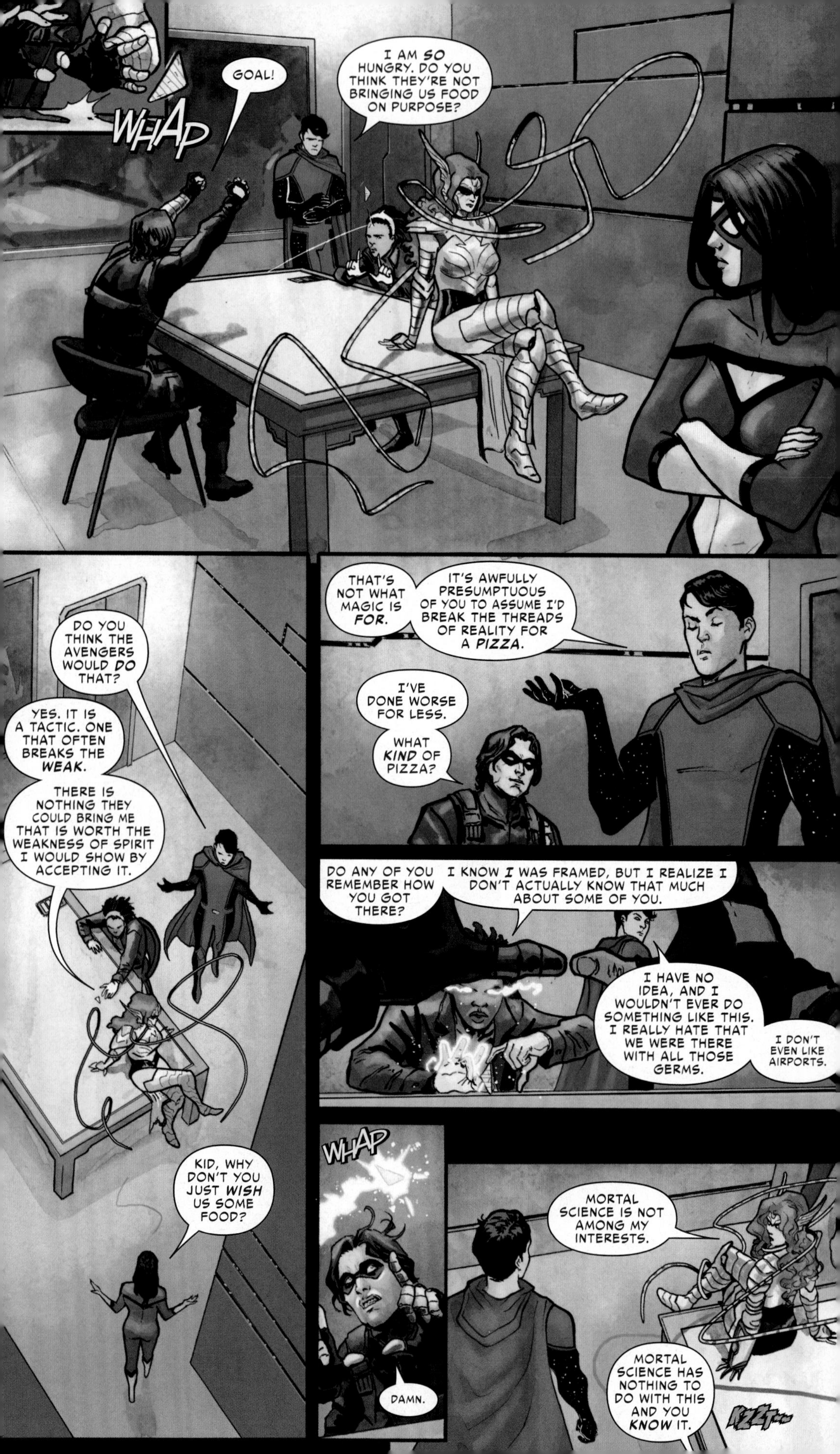

WHAP
GOAL!
I AM SO HUNGRY. DO YOU THINK THEY'RE NOT BRINGING US FOOD ON PURPOSE?
DO YOU THINK THE AVENGERS WOULD DO THAT?
YES. IT IS A TACTIC. ONE THAT OFTEN BREAKS THE WEAK.
THERE IS NOTHING THEY COULD BRING ME THAT IS WORTH THE WEAKNESS OF SPIRIT I WOULD SHOW BY ACCEPTING IT.
KID, WHY DON'T YOU JUST WISH US SOME FOOD?
THAT'S NOT WHAT MAGIC IS FOR.
IT'S AWFULLY PRESUMPTUOUS OF YOU TO ASSUME I'D BREAK THE THREADS OF REALITY FOR A PIZZA.
I'VE DONE WORSE FOR LESS.
WHAT KIND OF PIZZA?
DO ANY OF YOU REMEMBER HOW YOU GOT THERE?
I KNOW I WAS FRAMED, BUT I REALIZE I DON'T ACTUALLY KNOW THAT MUCH ABOUT SOME OF YOU.
I HAVE NO IDEA, AND I WOULDN'T EVER DO SOMETHING LIKE THIS. I REALLY HATE THAT WE WERE THERE WITH ALL THOSE GERMS.
I DON'T EVEN LIKE AIRPORTS.
WHAP
DAMN.
MORTAL SCIENCE IS NOT AMONG MY INTERESTS.
MORTAL SCIENCE HAS NOTHING TO DO WITH THIS AND YOU KNOW IT.
KZZT

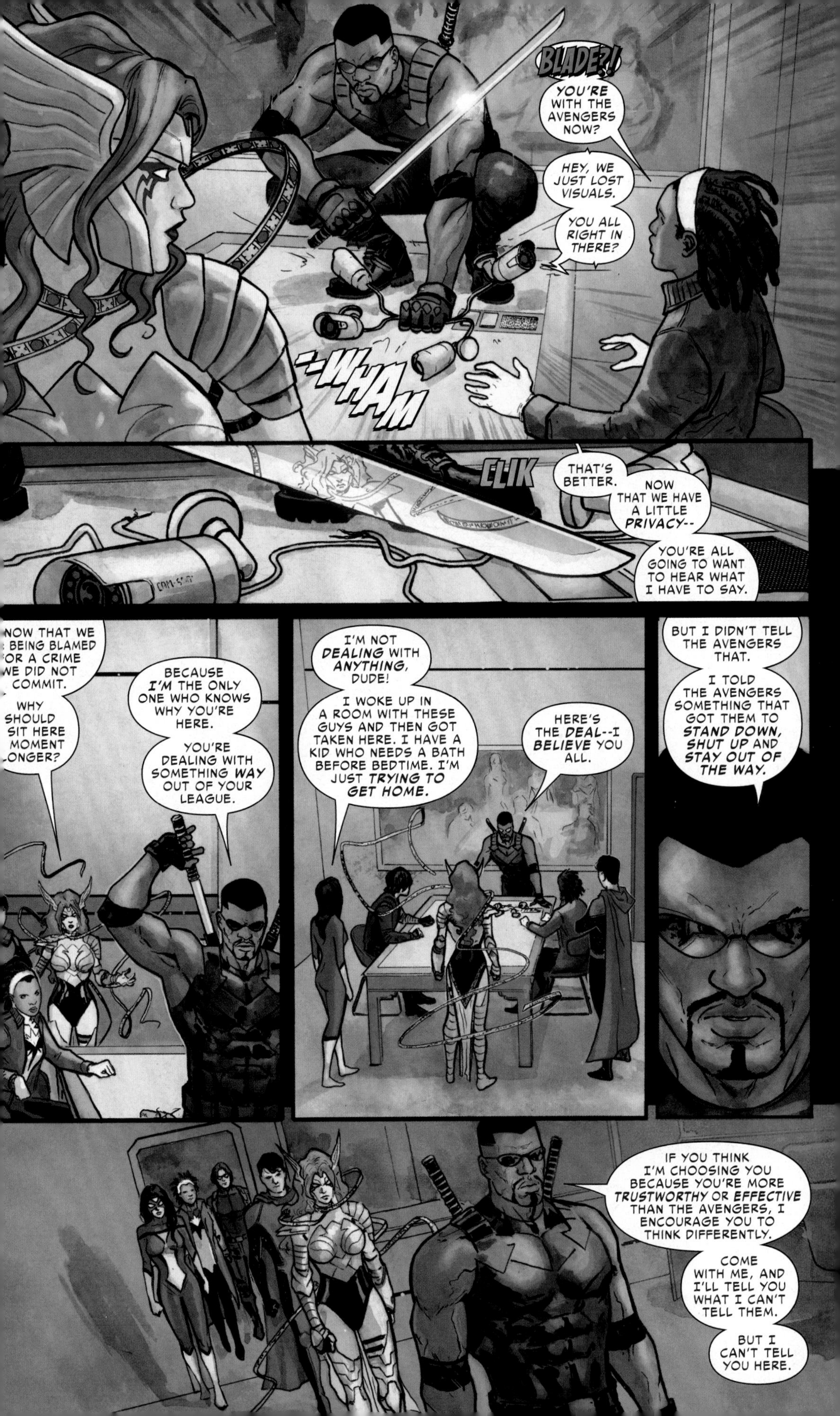
BLADE?!
YOU'RE WITH THE AVENGERS NOW?
HEY, WE JUST LOST VISUALS.
YOU ALL RIGHT IN THERE?
--WHAM
CLIK
THAT'S BETTER.
NOW THAT WE HAVE A LITTLE PRIVACY--
YOU'RE ALL GOING TO WANT TO HEAR WHAT I HAVE TO SAY.
NOW THAT WE BEING BLAMED OR A CRIME WE DID NOT COMMIT.
WHY SHOULD SIT HERE MOMENT ONGER?
BECAUSE I'M THE ONLY ONE WHO KNOWS WHY YOU'RE HERE.
YOU'RE DEALING WITH SOMETHING WAY OUT OF YOUR LEAGUE.
I'M NOT DEALING WITH ANYTHING, DUDE!
I WOKE UP IN A ROOM WITH THESE GUYS AND THEN GOT TAKEN HERE. I HAVE A KID WHO NEEDS A BATH BEFORE BEDTIME. I'M JUST TRYING TO GET HOME.
HERE'S THE DEAL--I BELIEVE YOU ALL.
BUT I DIDN'T TELL THE AVENGERS THAT.
I TOLD THE AVENGERS SOMETHING THAT GOT THEM TO STAND DOWN, SHUT UP AND STAY OUT OF THE WAY.
IF YOU THINK I'M CHOOSING YOU BECAUSE YOU'RE MORE TRUSTWORTHY OR EFFECTIVE THAN THE AVENGERS, I ENCOURAGE YOU TO THINK DIFFERENTLY.
COME WITH ME, AND I'LL TELL YOU WHAT I CAN'T TELL THEM.
BUT I CAN'T TELL YOU HERE.

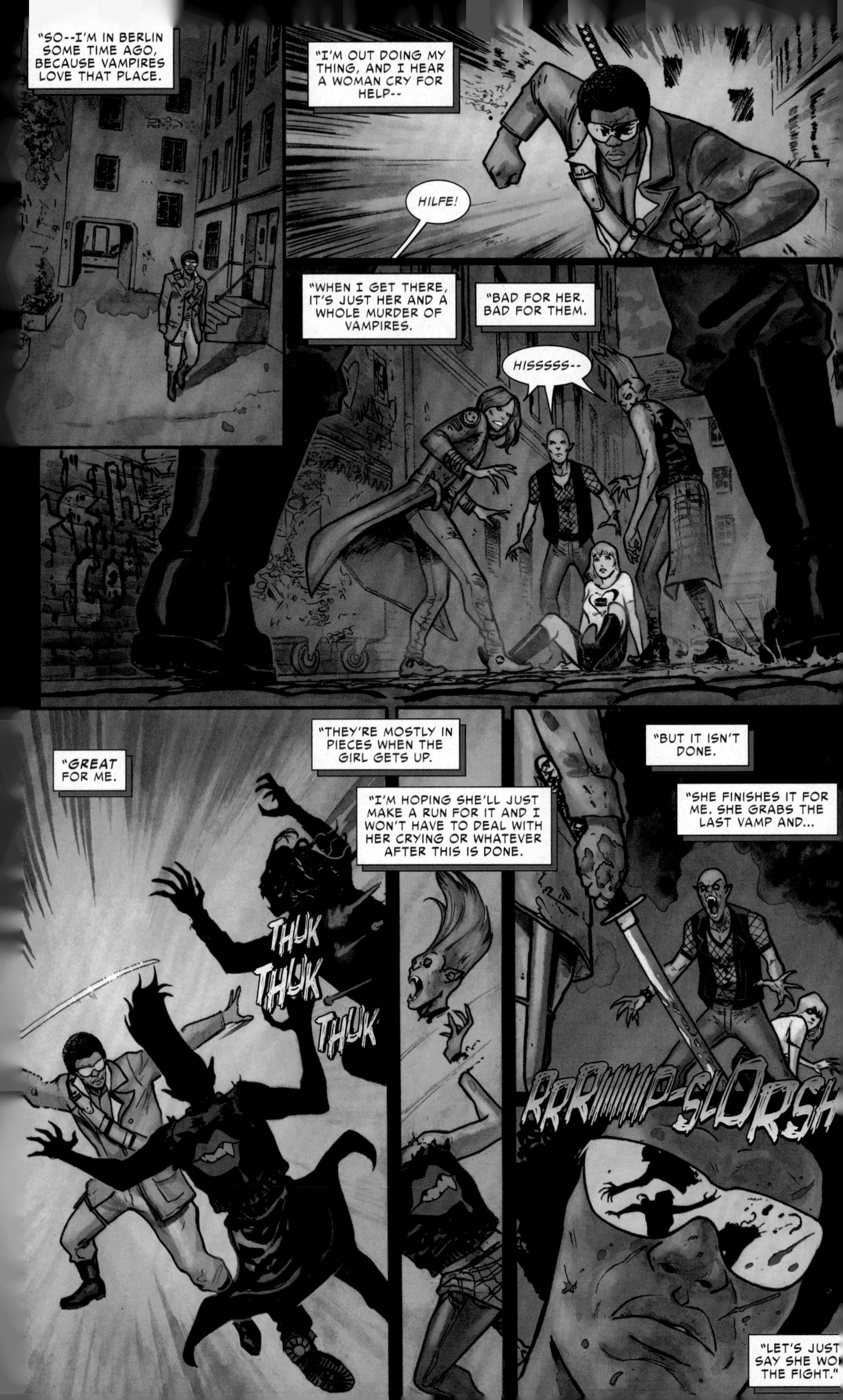
"SO--I'M IN BERLIN SOME TIME AGO, BECAUSE VAMPIRES LOVE THAT PLACE.
"I'M OUT DOING MY THING, AND I HEAR A WOMAN CRY FOR HELP--
HILFE!
"WHEN I GET THERE, IT'S JUST HER AND A WHOLE MURDER OF VAMPIRES.
"BAD FOR HER. BAD FOR THEM.
HISSSSS--
"GREAT FOR ME.
THUK
THUK
THUK
"THEY'RE MOSTLY IN PIECES WHEN THE GIRL GETS UP.
"I'M HOPING SHE'LL JUST MAKE A RUN FOR IT AND I WON'T HAVE TO DEAL WITH HER CRYING OR WHATEVER AFTER THIS IS DONE.
"BUT IT ISN'T DONE.
"SHE FINISHES IT FOR ME. SHE GRABS THE LAST VAMP AND...
RRRIIIIIP-SLORSH
"LET'S JUST SAY SHE WO THE FIGHT."

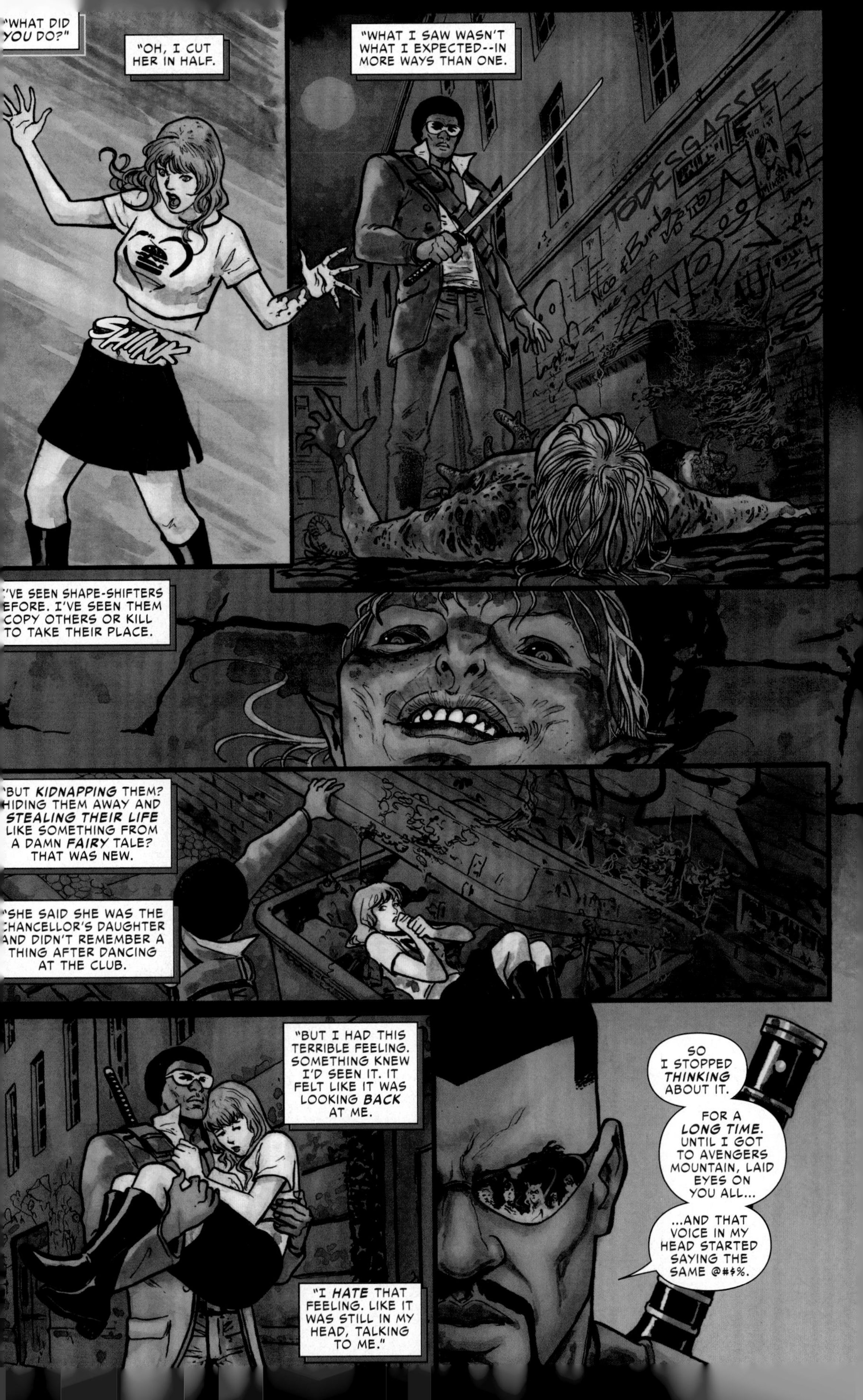
"WHAT DID YOU DO?"
"OH, I CUT HER IN HALF.
"WHAT I SAW WASN'T WHAT I EXPECTED--IN MORE WAYS THAN ONE.
SHINK
TODESGASSE
"I'VE SEEN SHAPE-SHIFTERS BEFORE. I'VE SEEN THEM COPY OTHERS OR KILL TO TAKE THEIR PLACE.
"BUT KIDNAPPING THEM? HIDING THEM AWAY AND STEALING THEIR LIFE LIKE SOMETHING FROM A DAMN FAIRY TALE? THAT WAS NEW.
"SHE SAID SHE WAS THE CHANCELLOR'S DAUGHTER AND DIDN'T REMEMBER A THING AFTER DANCING AT THE CLUB.
"BUT I HAD THIS TERRIBLE FEELING. SOMETHING KNEW I'D SEEN IT. IT FELT LIKE IT WAS LOOKING BACK AT ME.
"I HATE THAT FEELING. LIKE IT WAS STILL IN MY HEAD, TALKING TO ME."
SO I STOPPED THINKING ABOUT IT.
FOR A LONG TIME. UNTIL I GOT TO AVENGERS MOUNTAIN, LAID EYES ON YOU ALL...
...AND THAT VOICE IN MY HEAD STARTED SAYING THE SAME @#$%.

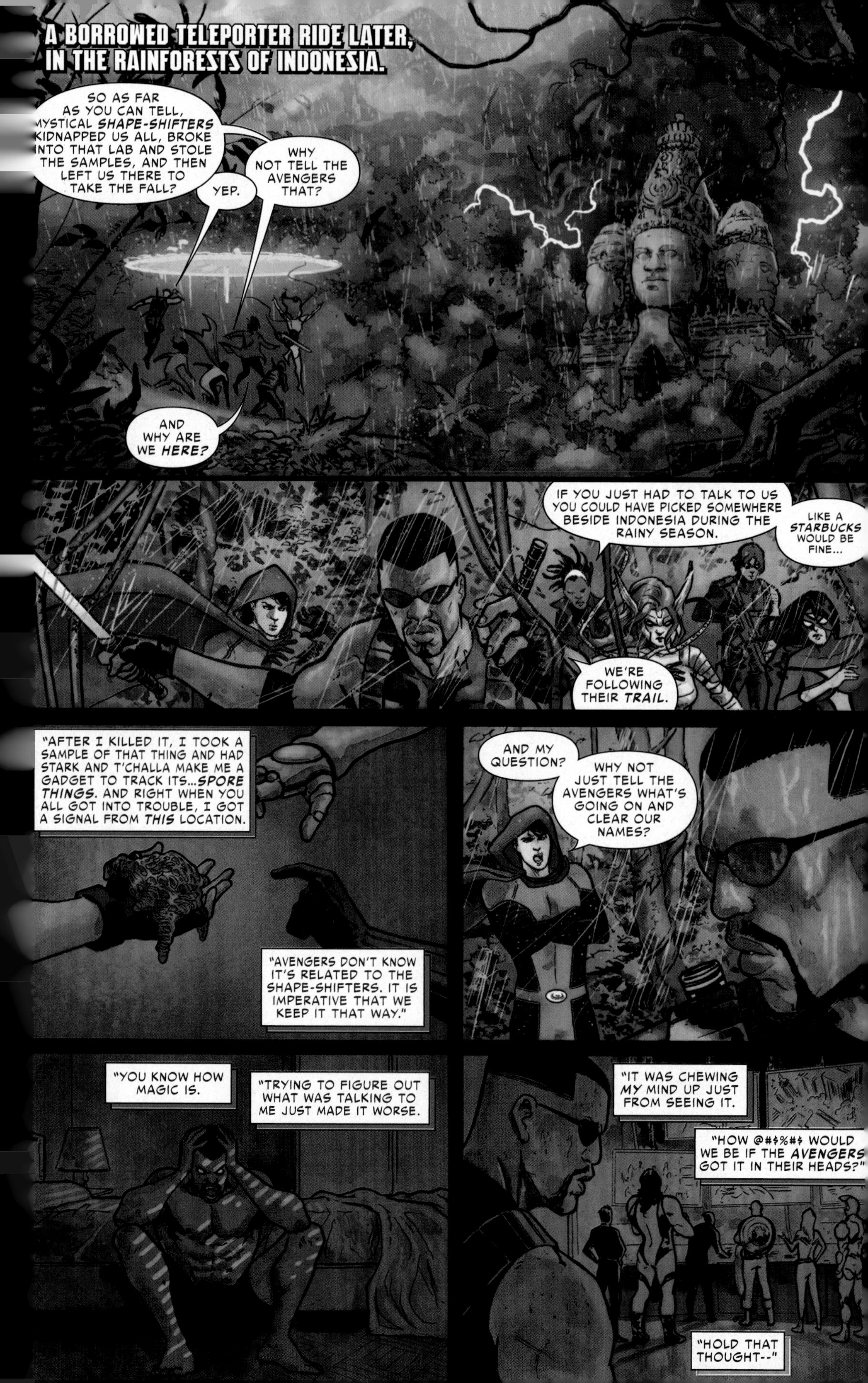
A BORROWED TELEPORTER RIDE LATER, IN THE RAINFORESTS OF INDONESIA.
SO AS FAR AS YOU CAN TELL, MYSTICAL SHAPE-SHIFTERS KIDNAPPED US ALL, BROKE INTO THAT LAB AND STOLE THE SAMPLES, AND THEN LEFT US THERE TO TAKE THE FALL?
YEP.
WHY NOT TELL THE AVENGERS THAT?
AND WHY ARE WE HERE?
IF YOU JUST HAD TO TALK TO US YOU COULD HAVE PICKED SOMEWHERE BESIDE INDONESIA DURING THE RAINY SEASON.
LIKE A STARBUCKS WOULD BE FINE...
WE'RE FOLLOWING THEIR TRAIL.
"AFTER I KILLED IT, I TOOK A SAMPLE OF THAT THING AND HAD STARK AND T'CHALLA MAKE ME A GADGET TO TRACK ITS...SPORE THINGS. AND RIGHT WHEN YOU ALL GOT INTO TROUBLE, I GOT A SIGNAL FROM THIS LOCATION.
"AVENGERS DON'T KNOW IT'S RELATED TO THE SHAPE-SHIFTERS. IT IS IMPERATIVE THAT WE KEEP IT THAT WAY."
AND MY QUESTION?
WHY NOT JUST TELL THE AVENGERS WHAT'S GOING ON AND CLEAR OUR NAMES?
"YOU KNOW HOW MAGIC IS.
"TRYING TO FIGURE OUT WHAT WAS TALKING TO ME JUST MADE IT WORSE.
"IT WAS CHEWING MY MIND UP JUST FROM SEEING IT.
"HOW @#$%#$ WOULD WE BE IF THE AVENGERS GOT IT IN THEIR HEADS?"
"HOLD THAT THOUGHT--"

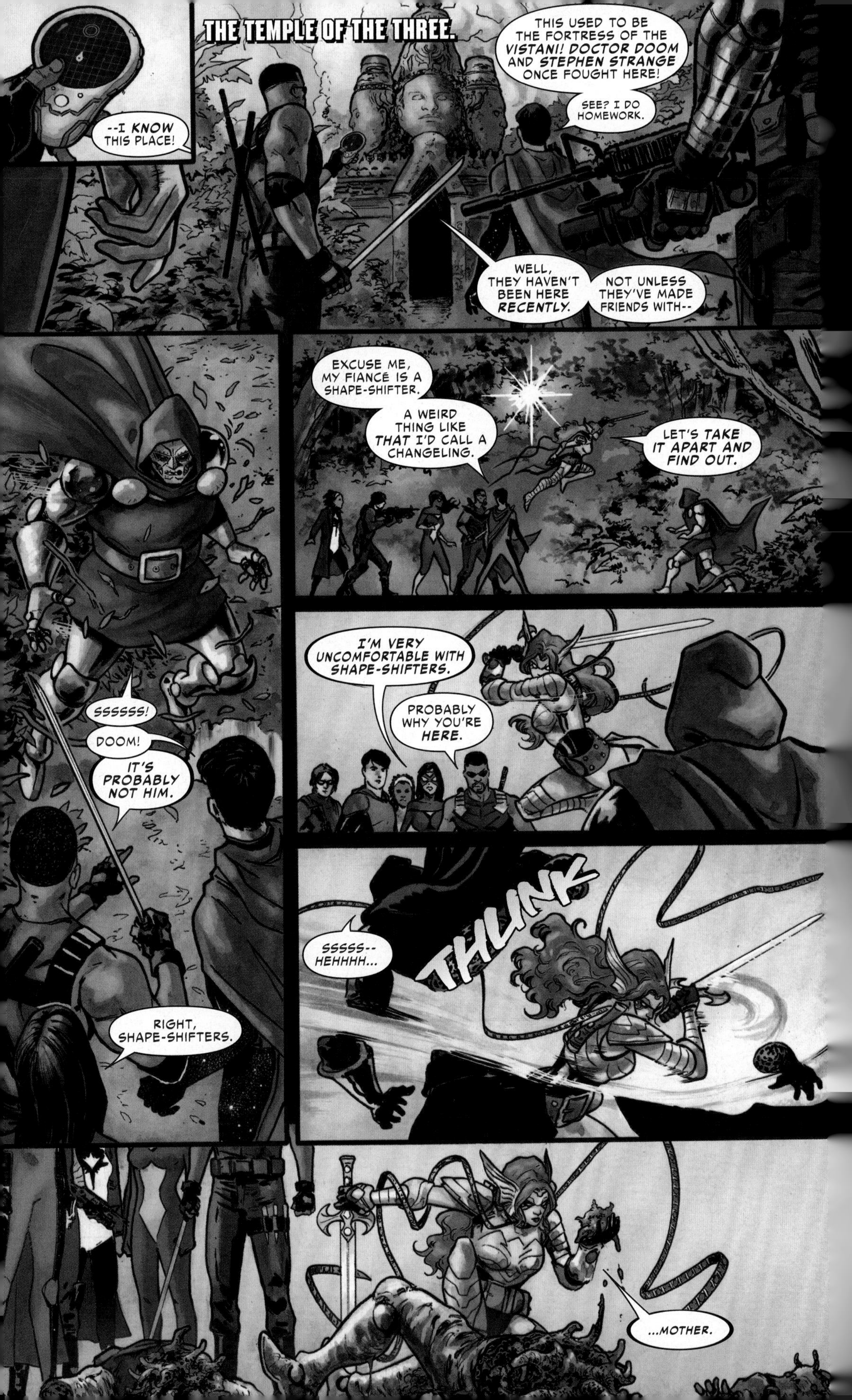
THE TEMPLE OF THE THREE.
--I KNOW THIS PLACE!
THIS USED TO BE THE FORTRESS OF THE VISTANI! DOCTOR DOOM AND STEPHEN STRANGE ONCE FOUGHT HERE!
SEE? I DO HOMEWORK.
WELL, THEY HAVEN'T BEEN HERE RECENTLY.
NOT UNLESS THEY'VE MADE FRIENDS WITH--
SSSSSS!
DOOM!
IT'S PROBABLY NOT HIM.
RIGHT, SHAPE-SHIFTERS.
EXCUSE ME, MY FIANCÉ IS A SHAPE-SHIFTER.
A WEIRD THING LIKE THAT I'D CALL A CHANGELING.
LET'S TAKE IT APART AND FIND OUT.
I'M VERY UNCOMFORTABLE WITH SHAPE-SHIFTERS.
PROBABLY WHY YOU'RE HERE.
THUNK
SSSSS-- HEHHHH...
...MOTHER.

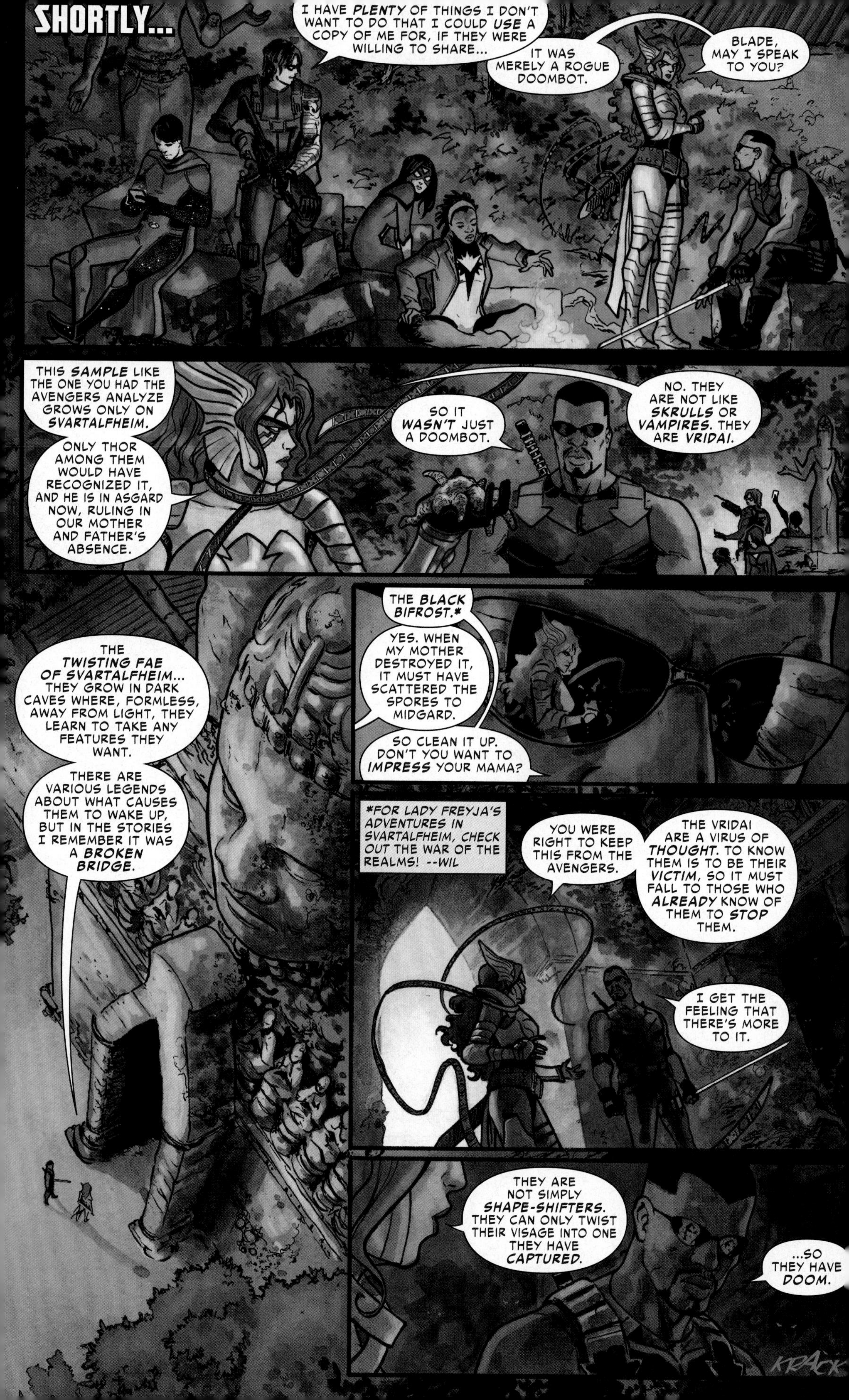
SHORTLY...
I HAVE PLENTY OF THINGS I DON'T WANT TO DO THAT I COULD USE A COPY OF ME FOR, IF THEY WERE WILLING TO SHARE...
IT WAS MERELY A ROGUE DOOMBOT.
BLADE, MAY I SPEAK TO YOU?
THIS SAMPLE LIKE THE ONE YOU HAD THE AVENGERS ANALYZE GROWS ONLY ON SVARTALFHEIM.
ONLY THOR AMONG THEM WOULD HAVE RECOGNIZED IT, AND HE IS IN ASGARD NOW, RULING IN OUR MOTHER AND FATHER'S ABSENCE.
SO IT WASN'T JUST A DOOMBOT.
NO. THEY ARE NOT LIKE SKRULLS OR VAMPIRES. THEY ARE VRIDAI.
THE TWISTING FAE OF SVARTALFHEIM... THEY GROW IN DARK CAVES WHERE, FORMLESS, AWAY FROM LIGHT, THEY LEARN TO TAKE ANY FEATURES THEY WANT.
THERE ARE VARIOUS LEGENDS ABOUT WHAT CAUSES THEM TO WAKE UP, BUT IN THE STORIES I REMEMBER IT WAS A BROKEN BRIDGE.
THE BLACK BIFROST.*
YES. WHEN MY MOTHER DESTROYED IT, IT MUST HAVE SCATTERED THE SPORES TO MIDGARD.
SO CLEAN IT UP. DON'T YOU WANT TO IMPRESS YOUR MAMA?
*FOR LADY FREYJA'S ADVENTURES IN SVARTALFHEIM, CHECK OUT THE WAR OF THE REALMS! --WIL
YOU WERE RIGHT TO KEEP THIS FROM THE AVENGERS.
THE VRIDAI ARE A VIRUS OF THOUGHT. TO KNOW THEM IS TO BE THEIR VICTIM, SO IT MUST FALL TO THOSE WHO ALREADY KNOW OF THEM TO STOP THEM.
I GET THE FEELING THAT THERE'S MORE TO IT.
THEY ARE NOT SIMPLY SHAPE-SHIFTERS. THEY CAN ONLY TWIST THEIR VISAGE INTO ONE THEY HAVE CAPTURED.
...SO THEY HAVE DOOM.
KRACK

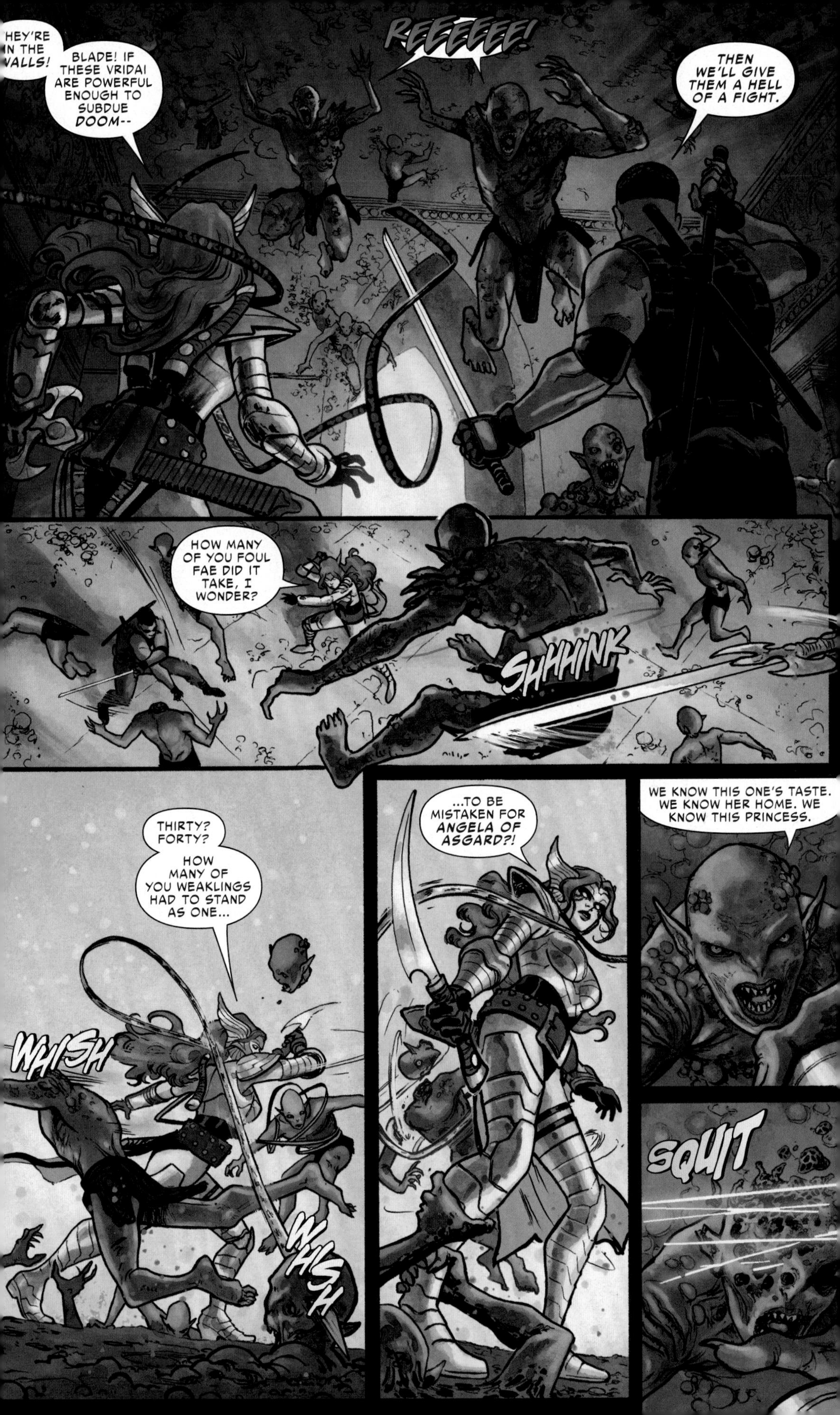

HEY'RE
N THE
VALLS!
REEEEEE!
BLADE! IF THESE VRIDAI ARE POWERFUL ENOUGH TO SUBDUE DOOM--
THEN WE'LL GIVE THEM A HELL OF A FIGHT.
HOW MANY OF YOU FOUL FAE DID IT TAKE, I WONDER?
SHHHINK
THIRTY? FORTY?
HOW MANY OF YOU WEAKLINGS HAD TO STAND AS ONE...
WHISH
WHISH
...TO BE MISTAKEN FOR ANGELA OF ASGARD?!
WE KNOW THIS ONE'S TASTE. WE KNOW HER HOME. WE KNOW THIS PRINCESS.
SQUIT

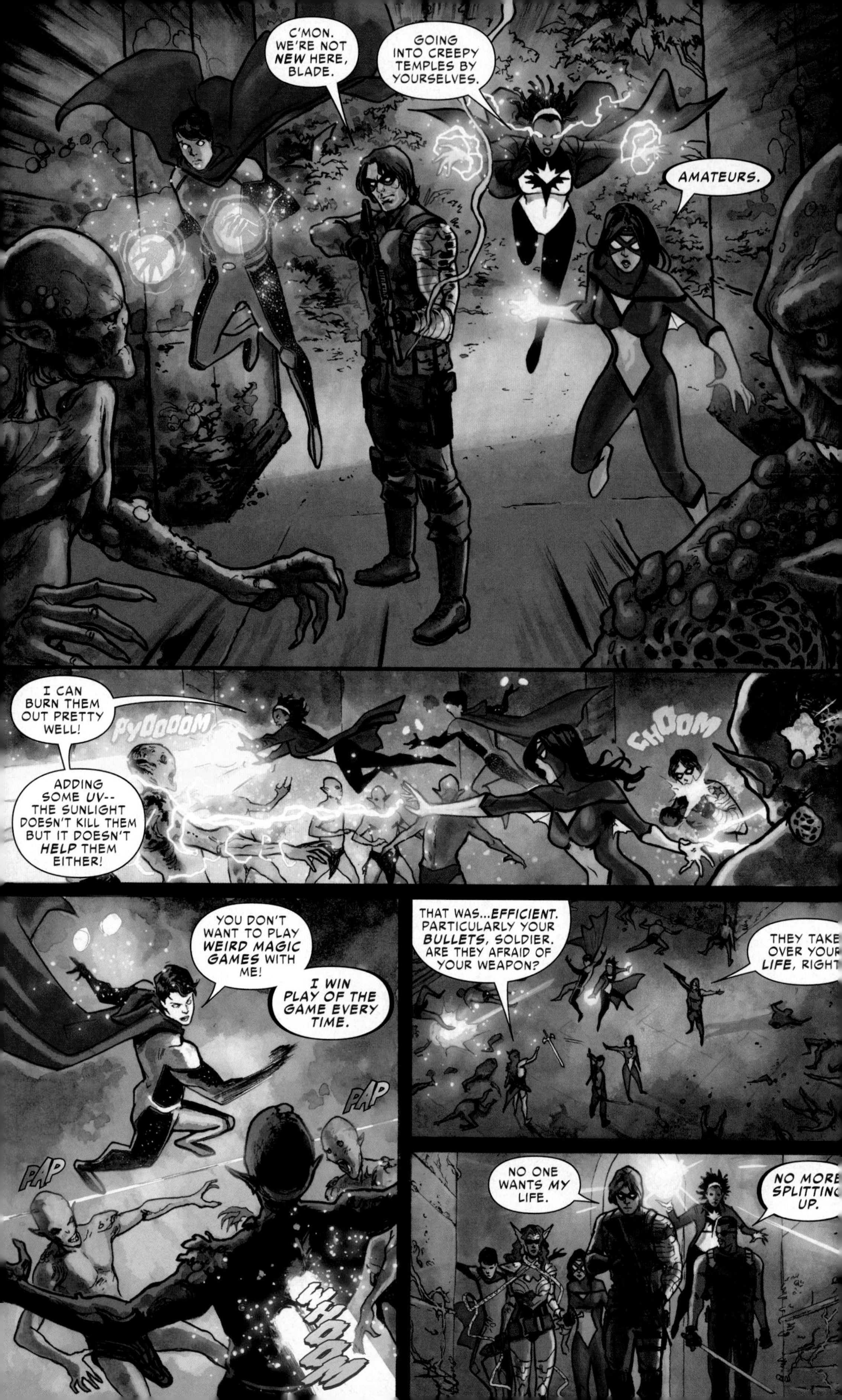
C'MON. WE'RE NOT NEW HERE, BLADE.
GOING INTO CREEPY TEMPLES BY YOURSELVES.
AMATEURS.
I CAN BURN THEM OUT PRETTY WELL!
ADDING SOME UV-- THE SUNLIGHT DOESN'T KILL THEM BUT IT DOESN'T HELP THEM EITHER!
PYOOOOM
CHOOM
YOU DON'T WANT TO PLAY WEIRD MAGIC GAMES WITH ME!
I WIN PLAY OF THE GAME EVERY TIME.
PAP
PAP
WHOOM
THAT WAS...EFFICIENT. PARTICULARLY YOUR BULLETS, SOLDIER. ARE THEY AFRAID OF YOUR WEAPON?
THEY TAKE OVER YOUR LIFE, RIGHT
NO ONE WANTS MY LIFE.
NO MORE SPLITTING UP.

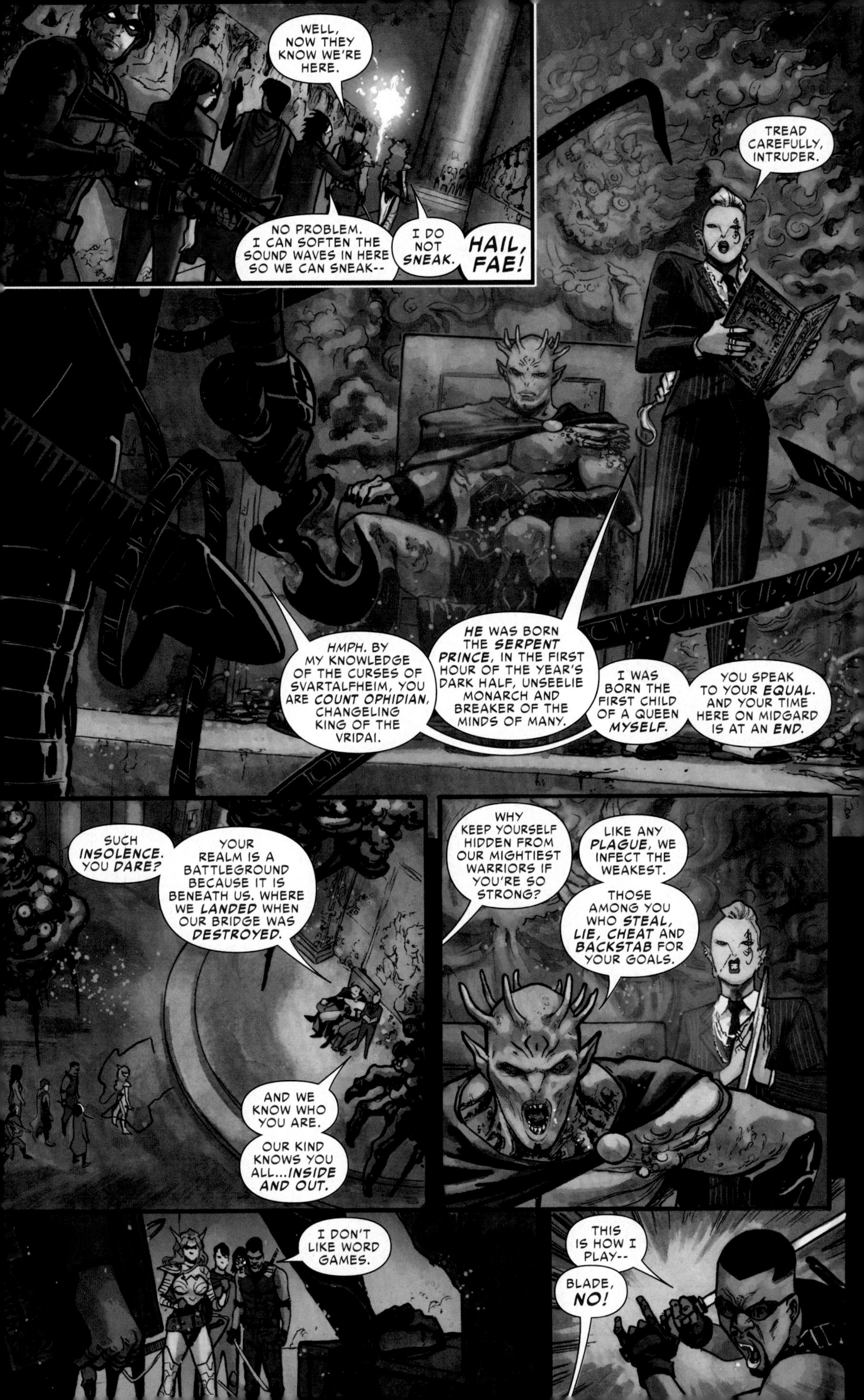
WELL, NOW THEY KNOW WE'RE HERE.
NO PROBLEM. I CAN SOFTEN THE SOUND WAVES IN HERE SO WE CAN SNEAK--
I DO NOT SNEAK.
HAIL, FAE!
TREAD CAREFULLY, INTRUDER.
HMPH. BY MY KNOWLEDGE OF THE CURSES OF SVARTALFHEIM, YOU ARE COUNT OPHIDIAN, CHANGELING KING OF THE VRIDAI.
HE WAS BORN THE SERPENT PRINCE, IN THE FIRST HOUR OF THE YEAR'S DARK HALF, UNSEELIE MONARCH AND BREAKER OF THE MINDS OF MANY.
I WAS BORN THE FIRST CHILD OF A QUEEN MYSELF.
YOU SPEAK TO YOUR EQUAL. AND YOUR TIME HERE ON MIDGARD IS AT AN END.
SUCH INSOLENCE. YOU DARE?
YOUR REALM IS A BATTLEGROUND BECAUSE IT IS BENEATH US. WHERE WE LANDED WHEN OUR BRIDGE WAS DESTROYED.
AND WE KNOW WHO YOU ARE.
OUR KIND KNOWS YOU ALL...INSIDE AND OUT.
WHY KEEP YOURSELF HIDDEN FROM OUR MIGHTIEST WARRIORS IF YOU'RE SO STRONG?
LIKE ANY PLAGUE, WE INFECT THE WEAKEST.
THOSE AMONG YOU WHO STEAL, LIE, CHEAT AND BACKSTAB FOR YOUR GOALS.
I DON'T LIKE WORD GAMES.
THIS IS HOW I PLAY--
BLADE, NO!

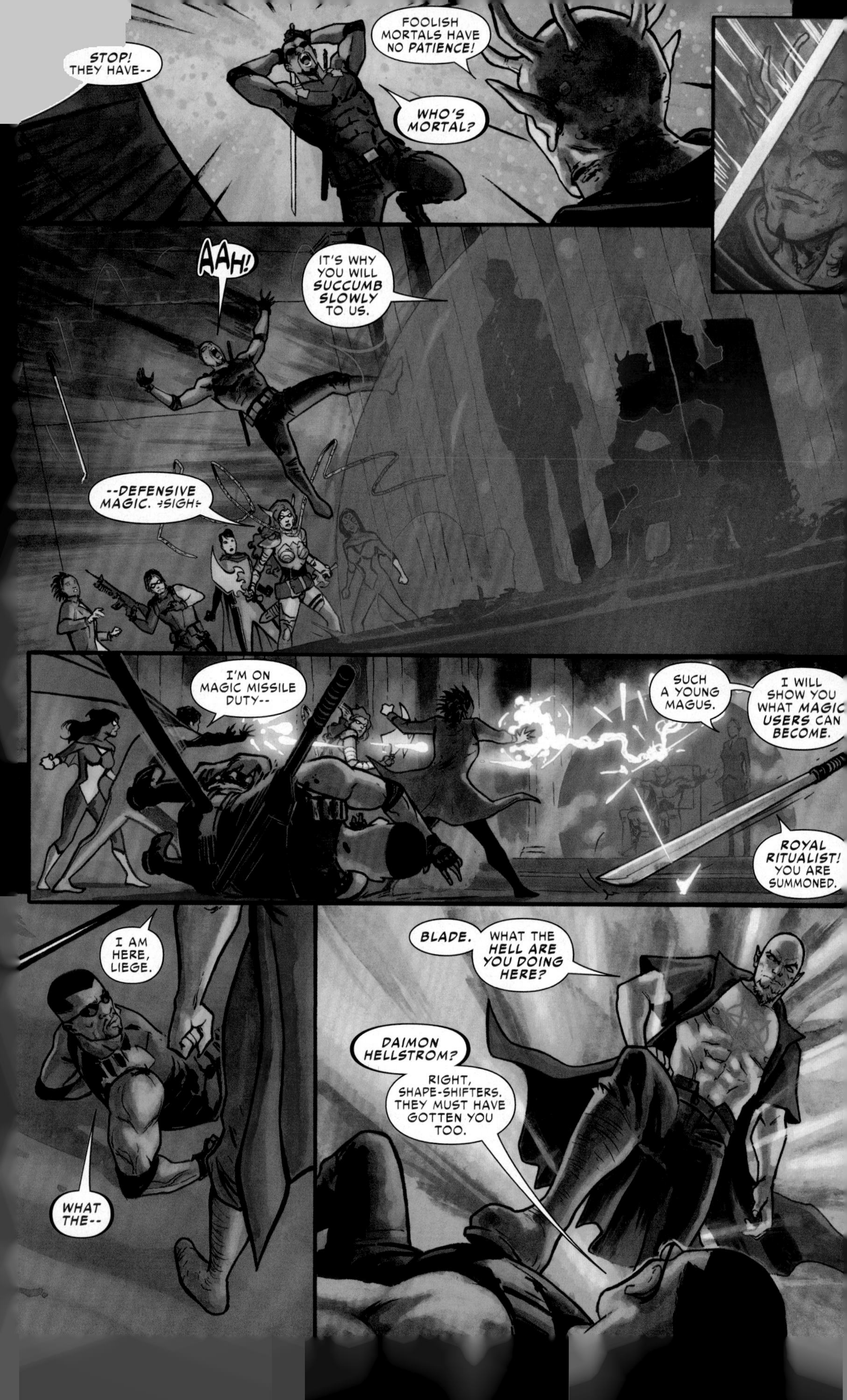
STOP! THEY HAVE--
FOOLISH MORTALS HAVE NO PATIENCE!
WHO'S MORTAL?
AAH!
IT'S WHY YOU WILL SUCCUMB SLOWLY TO US.
--DEFENSIVE MAGIC. ÷SIGH÷
I'M ON MAGIC MISSILE DUTY--
SUCH A YOUNG MAGUS.
I WILL SHOW YOU WHAT MAGIC USERS CAN BECOME.
ROYAL RITUALIST! YOU ARE SUMMONED.
I AM HERE, LIEGE.
WHAT THE--
BLADE.
WHAT THE HELL ARE YOU DOING HERE?
DAIMON HELLSTROM?
RIGHT, SHAPE-SHIFTERS. THEY MUST HAVE GOTTEN YOU TOO.

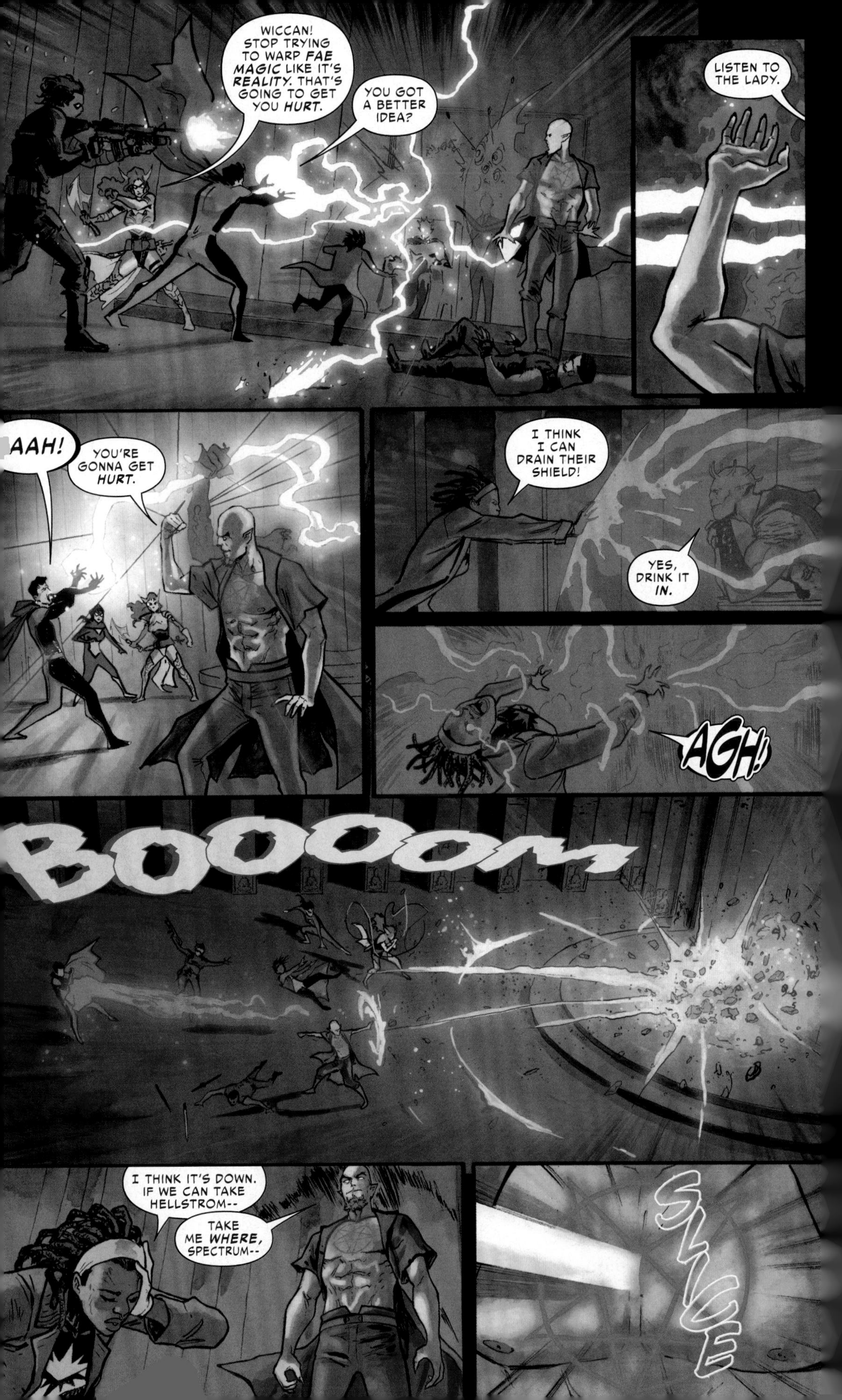
WICCAN! STOP TRYING TO WARP FAE MAGIC LIKE IT'S REALITY. THAT'S GOING TO GET YOU HURT.
YOU GOT A BETTER IDEA?
LISTEN TO THE LADY.
AAH!
YOU'RE GONNA GET HURT.
I THINK I CAN DRAIN THEIR SHIELD!
YES, DRINK IT IN.
AGH!
BOOOOOM
I THINK IT'S DOWN. IF WE CAN TAKE HELLSTROM--
TAKE ME WHERE, SPECTRUM--
SLICE

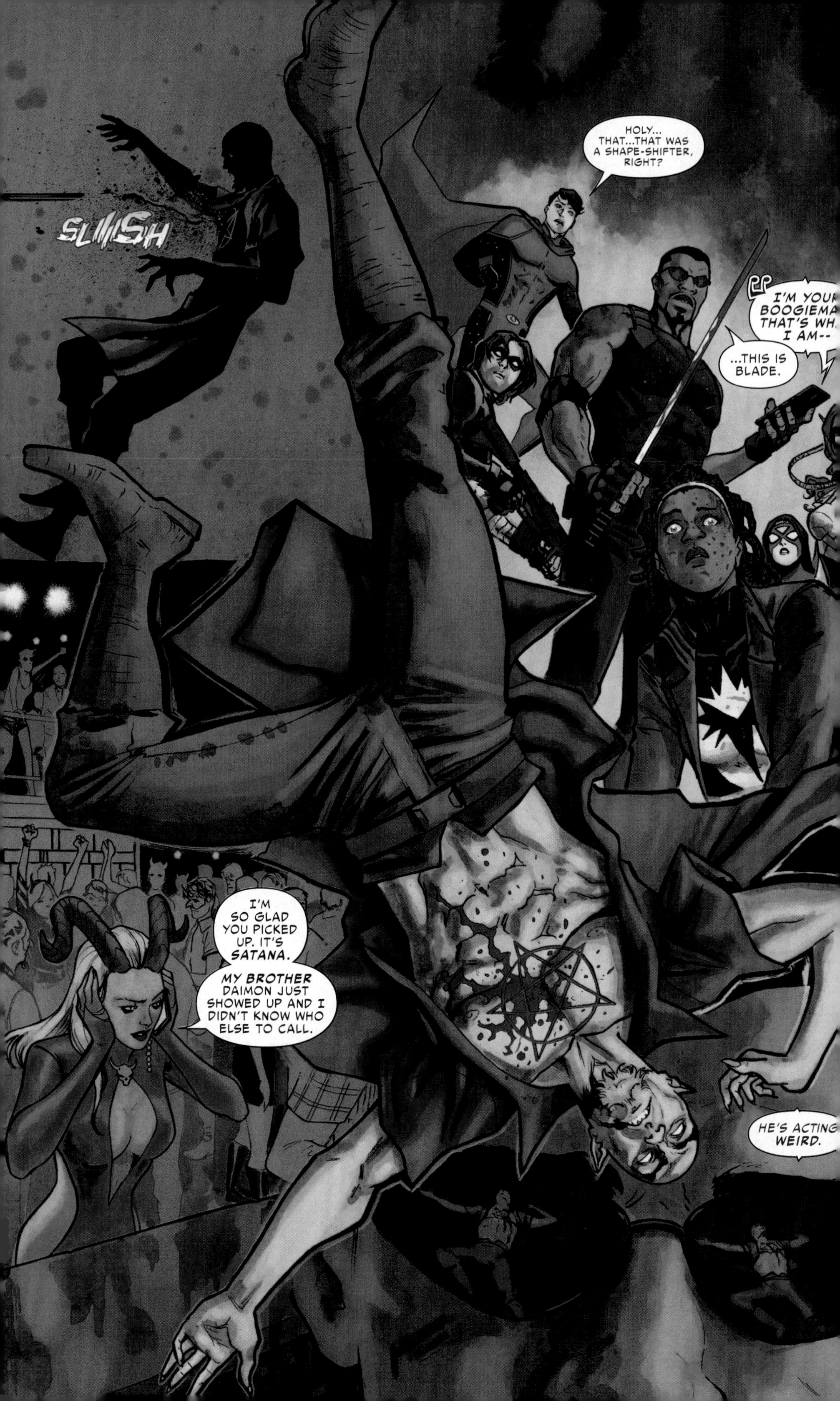
SLIIISH
HOLY... THAT...THAT WAS A SHAPE-SHIFTER, RIGHT?
I'M YOUR BOOGIEMA THAT'S WH I AM--
...THIS IS BLADE.
I'M SO GLAD YOU PICKED UP. IT'S SATANA.
MY BROTHER DAIMON JUST SHOWED UP AND I DIDN'T KNOW WHO ELSE TO CALL.
HE'S ACTING WEIRD.

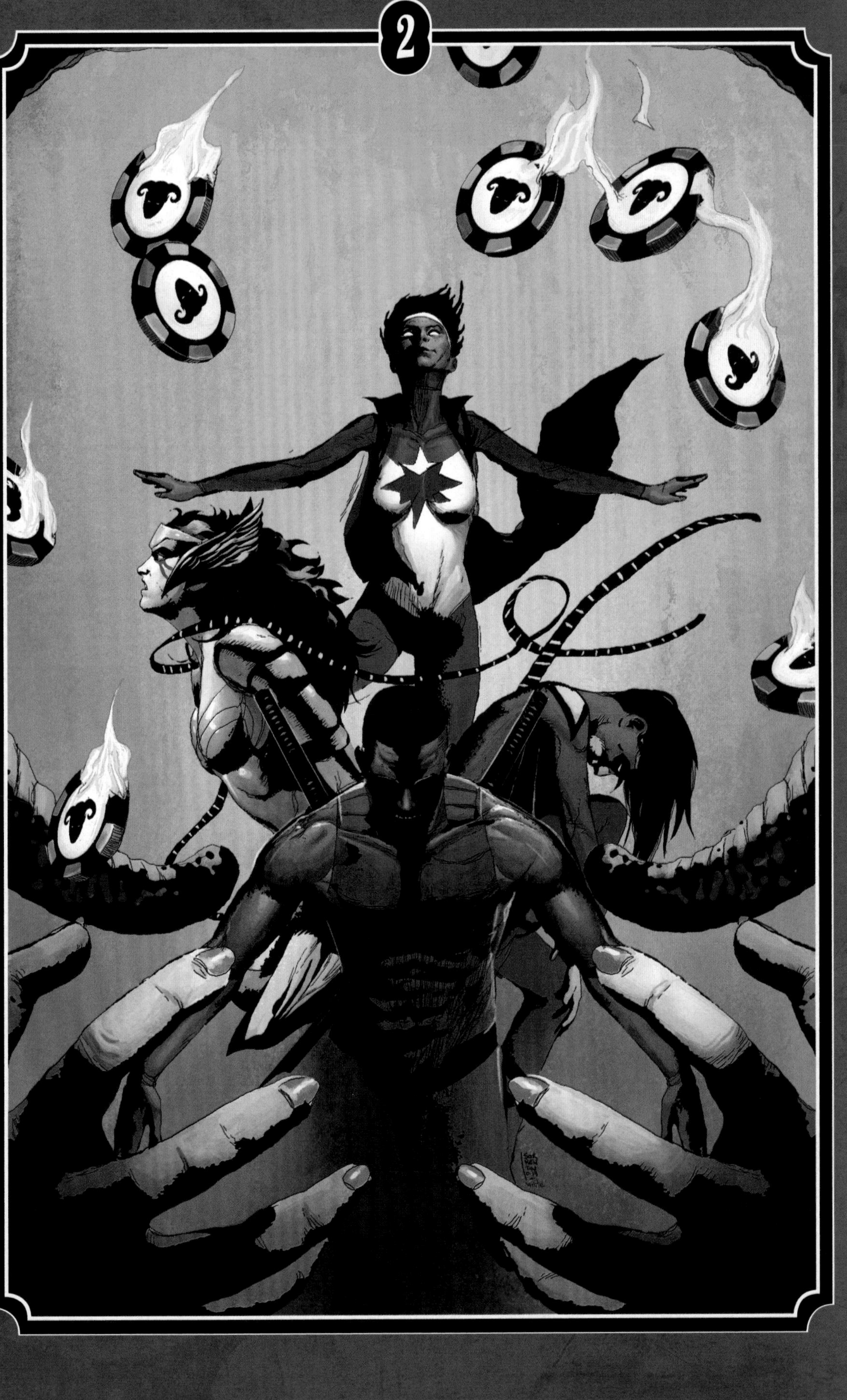
2

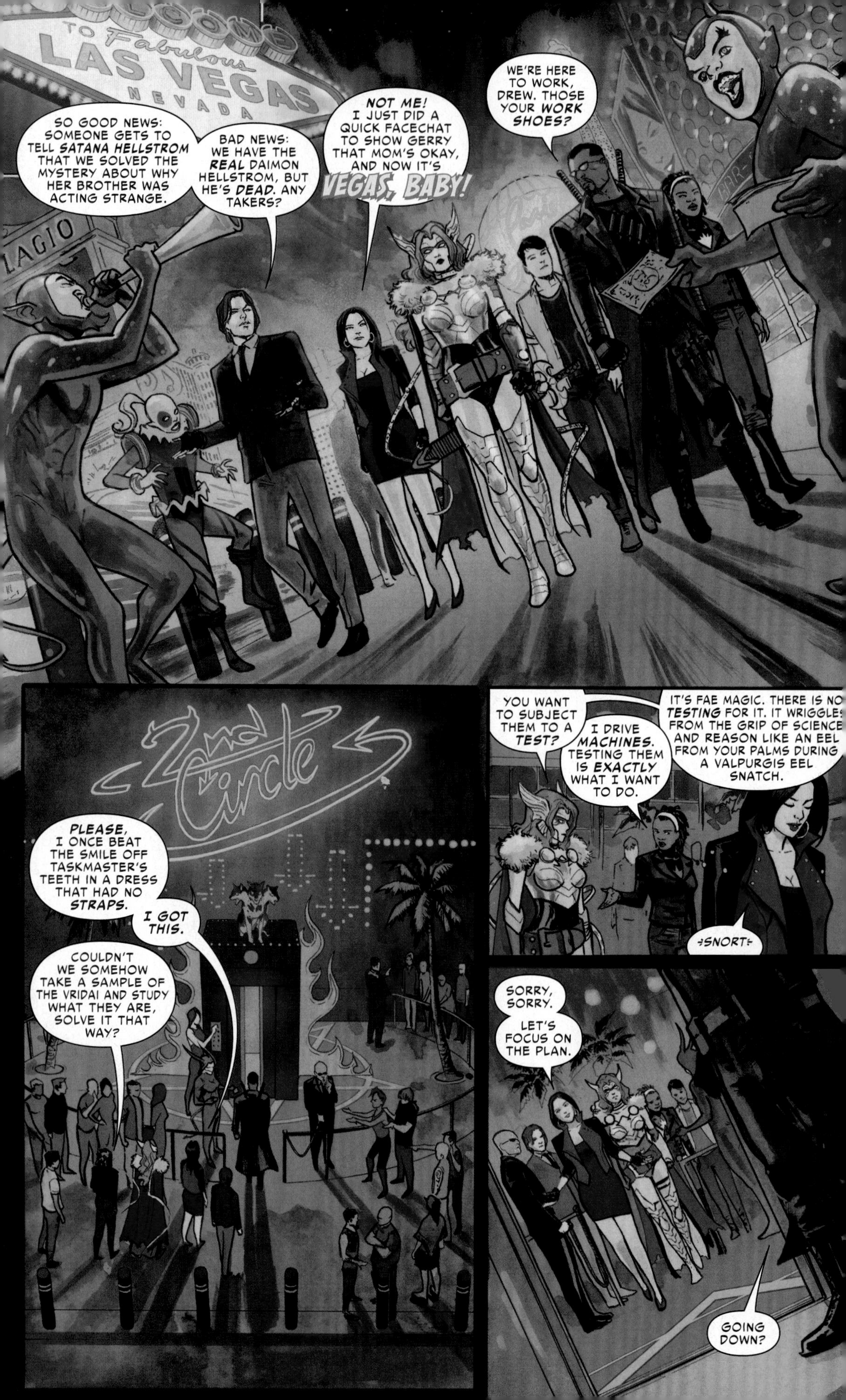
WELCOME TO Fabulous LAS VEGAS NEVADA
SO GOOD NEWS: SOMEONE GETS TO TELL SATANA HELLSTROM THAT WE SOLVED THE MYSTERY ABOUT WHY HER BROTHER WAS ACTING STRANGE.
BAD NEWS: WE HAVE THE REAL DAIMON HELLSTROM, BUT HE'S DEAD. ANY TAKERS?
NOT ME! I JUST DID A QUICK FACECHAT TO SHOW GERRY THAT MOM'S OKAY, AND NOW IT'S VEGAS, BABY!
WE'RE HERE TO WORK, DREW. THOSE YOUR WORK SHOES?
LAGIO
2nd Circle
PLEASE, I ONCE BEAT THE SMILE OFF TASKMASTER'S TEETH IN A DRESS THAT HAD NO STRAPS.
I GOT THIS.
COULDN'T WE SOMEHOW TAKE A SAMPLE OF THE VRIDAI AND STUDY WHAT THEY ARE, SOLVE IT THAT WAY?
YOU WANT TO SUBJECT THEM TO A TEST?
I DRIVE MACHINES. TESTING THEM IS EXACTLY WHAT I WANT TO DO.
IT'S FAE MAGIC. THERE IS NO TESTING FOR IT. IT WRIGGLES FROM THE GRIP OF SCIENCE AND REASON LIKE AN EEL FROM YOUR PALMS DURING A VALPURGIS EEL SNATCH.
SNORT
SORRY, SORRY.
LET'S FOCUS ON THE PLAN.
GOING DOWN?

DING

LASCIATE OGNE SPERANZA VOI CH'INTRATE

∞ ...-IX-VIII-VII-VI- -V- -IV- -III- -II- -I- 0

SO, WE ACCIDENTALLY KILLED DAIMON HELLSTROM.

I DON'T DO ACCIDENTS. I KILLED SOMETHING THAT *LOOKED* LIKE DAIMON HELLSTROM.

JUST HAPPENED TO ACTUALLY *BE* HIM.

SATANA WILL FIX IT, IF SHE HASN'T BEEN CORRUPTED BY THE VRIDAI AS WELL. PLACE LIKE VEGAS, IT'S EASY TO MAKE FRIENDS *REAL QUICK.*

KEEP CLOSE WATCH.

SHOULD THE VRIDAI ESCAPE THIS DESERT, IT WOULD SPELL DOOM FOR OUR AVENGER FRIENDS...

...AND FROM THERE, THE WORLD.

HEY, SPEAKING OF DOOM, ANGELA...

THAT WAS A MERE VRIDAI.

RIGHT, WHICH MEANS THEY HAVE THE *REAL* DOOM... SOMEWHERE.

DING

YEAH, YEAH...

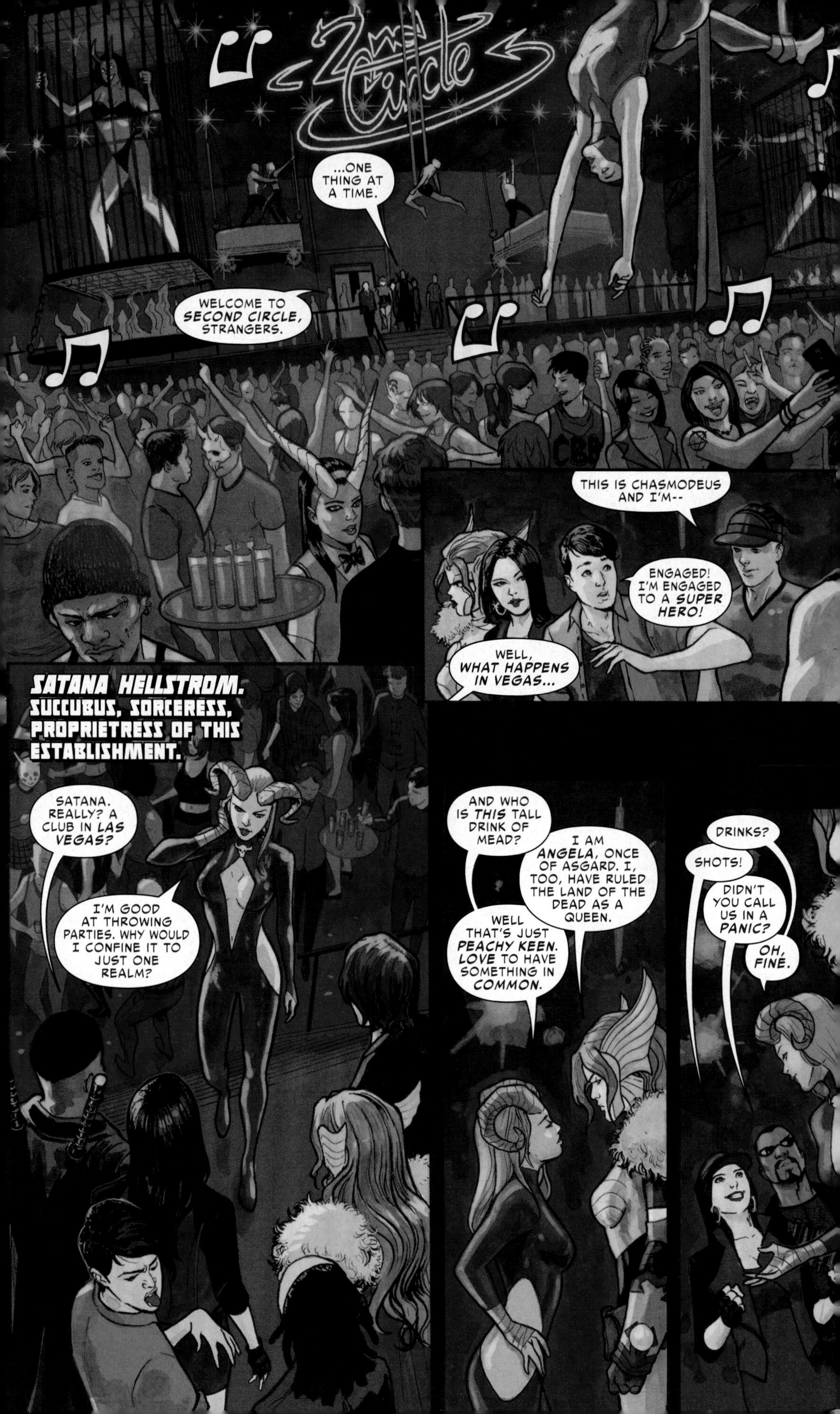
2nd Circle
...ONE THING AT A TIME.
WELCOME TO SECOND CIRCLE, STRANGERS.
THIS IS CHASMODEUS AND I'M--
ENGAGED! I'M ENGAGED TO A SUPER HERO!
WELL, WHAT HAPPENS IN VEGAS...
SATANA HELLSTROM. SUCCUBUS, SORCERESS, PROPRIETRESS OF THIS ESTABLISHMENT.
SATANA. REALLY? A CLUB IN LAS VEGAS?
I'M GOOD AT THROWING PARTIES. WHY WOULD I CONFINE IT TO JUST ONE REALM?
AND WHO IS THIS TALL DRINK OF MEAD?
I AM ANGELA, ONCE OF ASGARD. I, TOO, HAVE RULED THE LAND OF THE DEAD AS A QUEEN.
WELL THAT'S JUST PEACHY KEEN. LOVE TO HAVE SOMETHING IN COMMON.
DRINKS?
SHOTS!
DIDN'T YOU CALL US IN A PANIC?
OH, FINE.

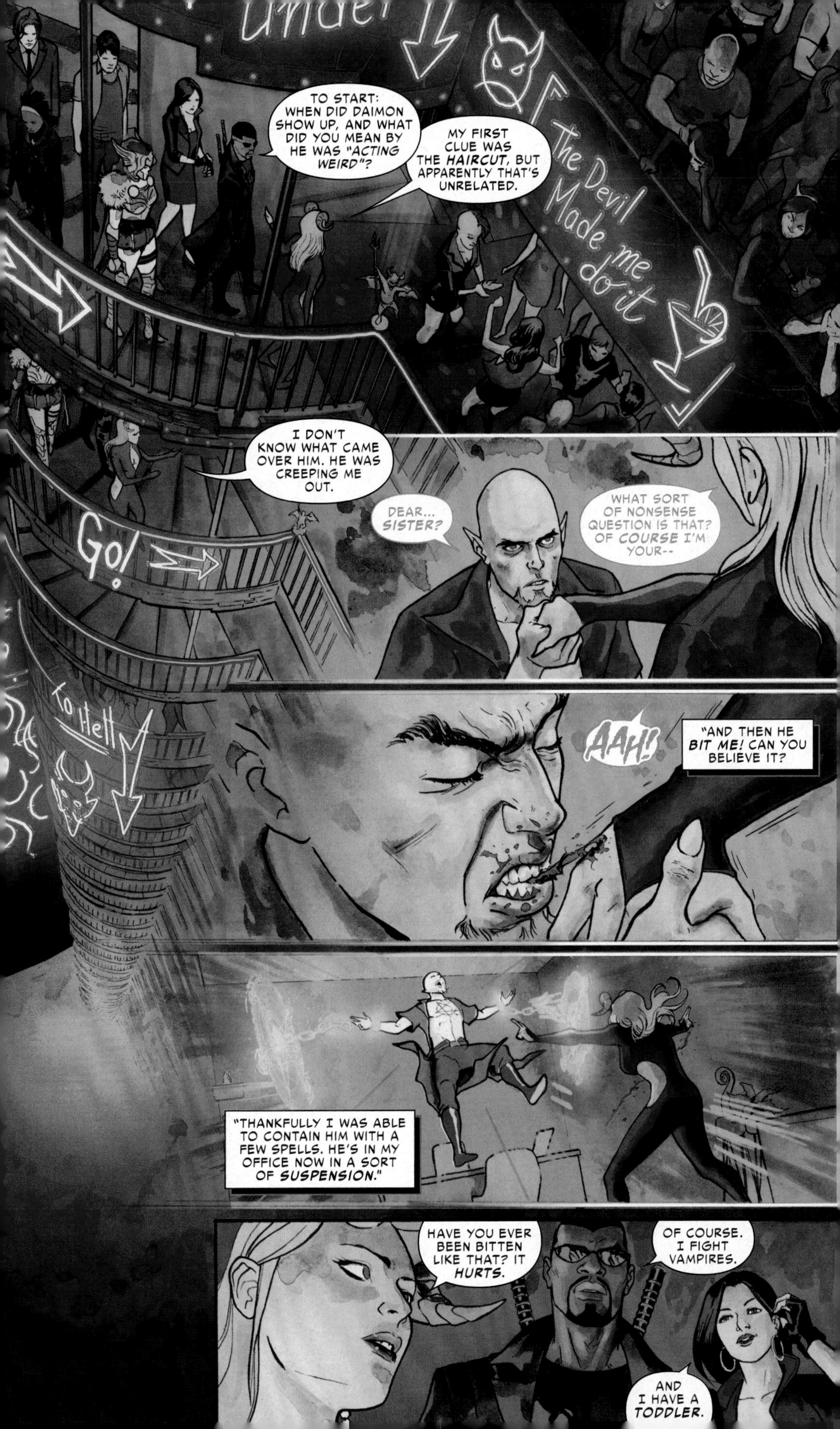
Under
TO START: WHEN DID DAIMON SHOW UP, AND WHAT DID YOU MEAN BY HE WAS "ACTING WEIRD"?
MY FIRST CLUE WAS THE HAIRCUT, BUT APPARENTLY THAT'S UNRELATED.
The Devil Made me do it
I DON'T KNOW WHAT CAME OVER HIM. HE WAS CREEPING ME OUT.
Go!
DEAR... SISTER?
WHAT SORT OF NONSENSE QUESTION IS THAT? OF COURSE I'M YOUR--
To Hell
AAH!
"AND THEN HE BIT ME! CAN YOU BELIEVE IT?
"THANKFULLY I WAS ABLE TO CONTAIN HIM WITH A FEW SPELLS. HE'S IN MY OFFICE NOW IN A SORT OF SUSPENSION."
HAVE YOU EVER BEEN BITTEN LIKE THAT? IT HURTS.
OF COURSE. I FIGHT VAMPIRES.
AND I HAVE A TODDLER.

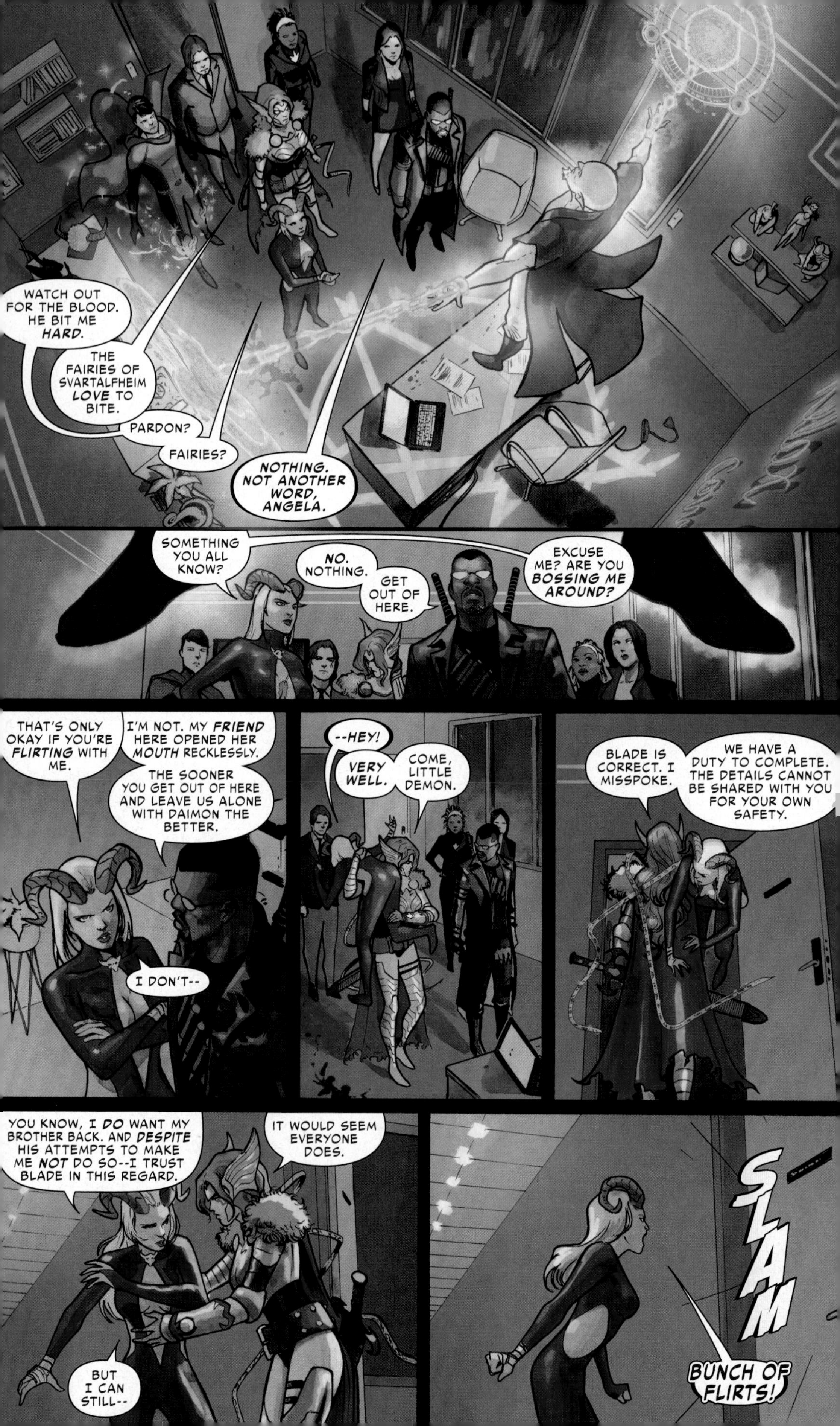
WATCH OUT FOR THE BLOOD. HE BIT ME HARD.
THE FAIRIES OF SVARTALFHEIM LOVE TO BITE.
PARDON?
FAIRIES?
NOTHING. NOT ANOTHER WORD, ANGELA.
SOMETHING YOU ALL KNOW?
NO. NOTHING.
GET OUT OF HERE.
EXCUSE ME? ARE YOU BOSSING ME AROUND?
THAT'S ONLY OKAY IF YOU'RE FLIRTING WITH ME.
I'M NOT. MY FRIEND HERE OPENED HER MOUTH RECKLESSLY.
THE SOONER YOU GET OUT OF HERE AND LEAVE US ALONE WITH DAIMON THE BETTER.
I DON'T--
--HEY!
VERY WELL.
COME, LITTLE DEMON.
BLADE IS CORRECT. I MISSPOKE.
WE HAVE A DUTY TO COMPLETE. THE DETAILS CANNOT BE SHARED WITH YOU FOR YOUR OWN SAFETY.
YOU KNOW, I DO WANT MY BROTHER BACK. AND DESPITE HIS ATTEMPTS TO MAKE ME NOT DO SO--I TRUST BLADE IN THIS REGARD.
IT WOULD SEEM EVERYONE DOES.
BUT I CAN STILL--
SLAM
BUNCH OF FLIRTS!

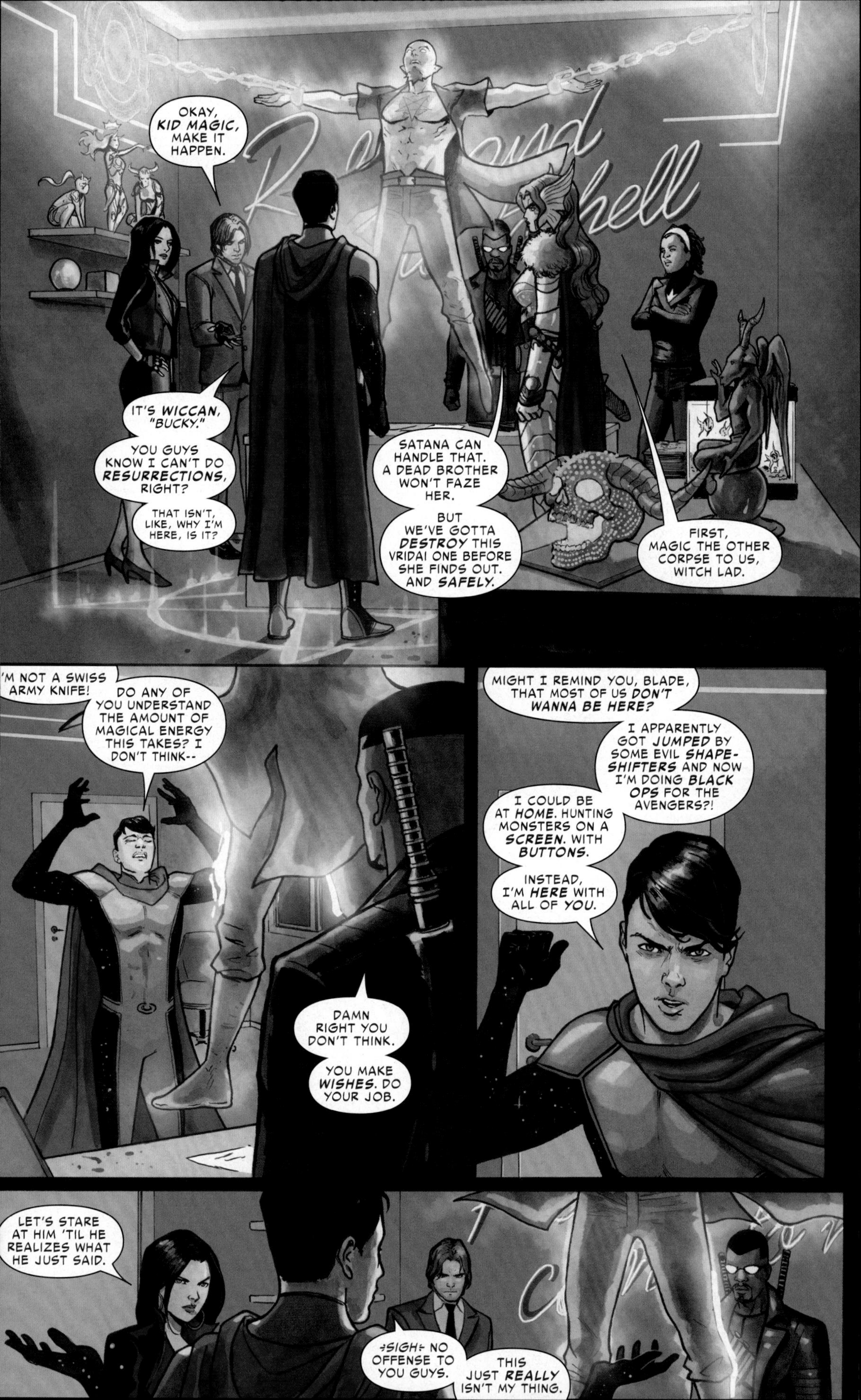
OKAY, KID MAGIC, MAKE IT HAPPEN.
IT'S WICCAN, "BUCKY."
YOU GUYS KNOW I CAN'T DO RESURRECTIONS, RIGHT?
THAT ISN'T, LIKE, WHY I'M HERE, IS IT?
SATANA CAN HANDLE THAT. A DEAD BROTHER WON'T FAZE HER.
BUT WE'VE GOTTA DESTROY THIS VRIDAI ONE BEFORE SHE FINDS OUT. AND SAFELY.
FIRST, MAGIC THE OTHER CORPSE TO US, WITCH LAD.
'M NOT A SWISS ARMY KNIFE!
DO ANY OF YOU UNDERSTAND THE AMOUNT OF MAGICAL ENERGY THIS TAKES? I DON'T THINK--
DAMN RIGHT YOU DON'T THINK.
YOU MAKE WISHES. DO YOUR JOB.
MIGHT I REMIND YOU, BLADE, THAT MOST OF US DON'T WANNA BE HERE?
I APPARENTLY GOT JUMPED BY SOME EVIL SHAPE-SHIFTERS AND NOW I'M DOING BLACK OPS FOR THE AVENGERS?!
I COULD BE AT HOME. HUNTING MONSTERS ON A SCREEN. WITH BUTTONS.
INSTEAD, I'M HERE WITH ALL OF YOU.
LET'S STARE AT HIM 'TIL HE REALIZES WHAT HE JUST SAID.
⸗SIGH⸗ NO OFFENSE TO YOU GUYS.
THIS JUST REALLY ISN'T MY THING.

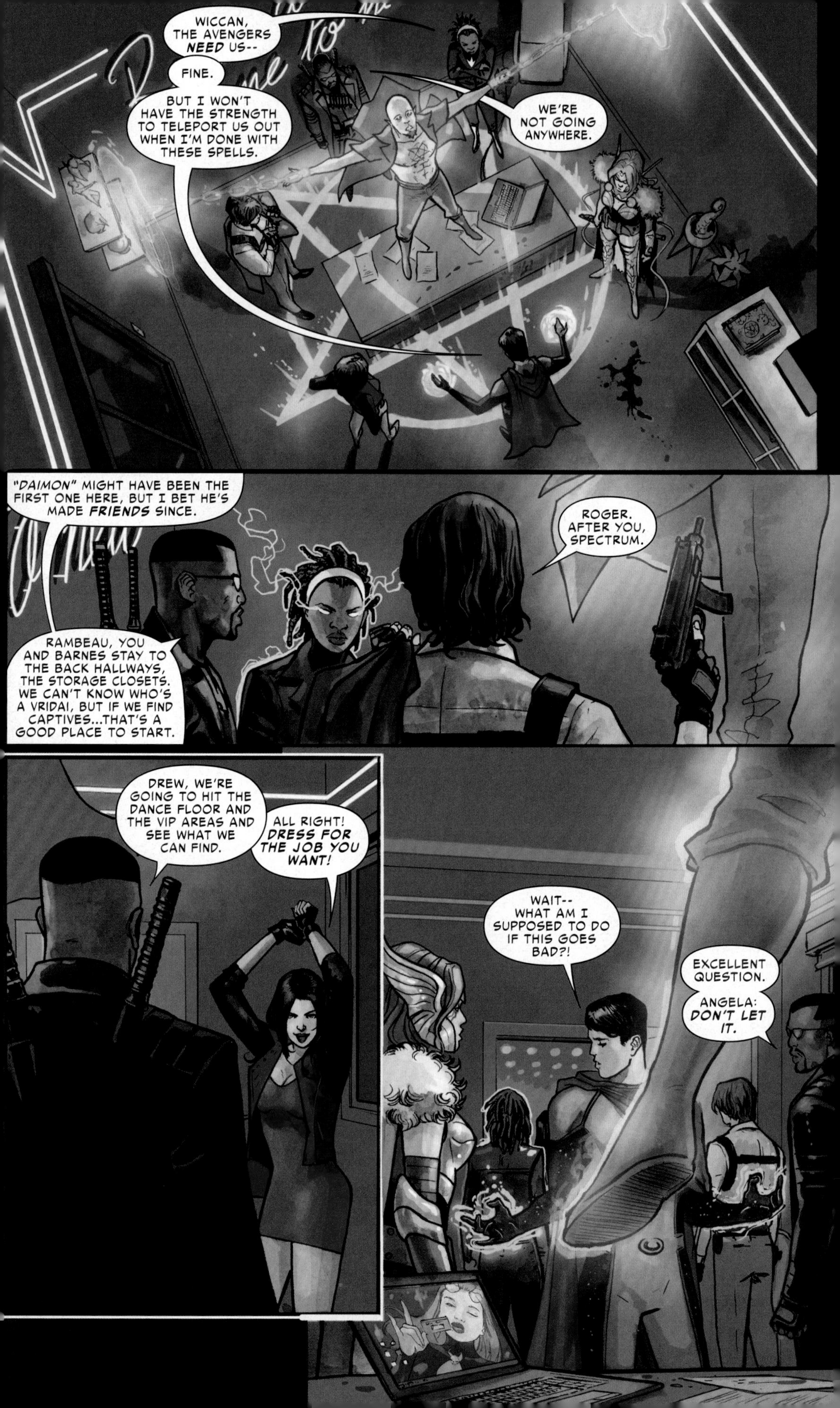
WICCAN, THE AVENGERS NEED US--
FINE.
BUT I WON'T HAVE THE STRENGTH TO TELEPORT US OUT WHEN I'M DONE WITH THESE SPELLS.
WE'RE NOT GOING ANYWHERE.
"DAIMON" MIGHT HAVE BEEN THE FIRST ONE HERE, BUT I BET HE'S MADE FRIENDS SINCE.
RAMBEAU, YOU AND BARNES STAY TO THE BACK HALLWAYS, THE STORAGE CLOSETS. WE CAN'T KNOW WHO'S A VRIDAI, BUT IF WE FIND CAPTIVES...THAT'S A GOOD PLACE TO START.
ROGER. AFTER YOU, SPECTRUM.
DREW, WE'RE GOING TO HIT THE DANCE FLOOR AND THE VIP AREAS AND SEE WHAT WE CAN FIND.
ALL RIGHT! DRESS FOR THE JOB YOU WANT!
WAIT-- WHAT AM I SUPPOSED TO DO IF THIS GOES BAD?!
EXCELLENT QUESTION.
ANGELA: DON'T LET IT.

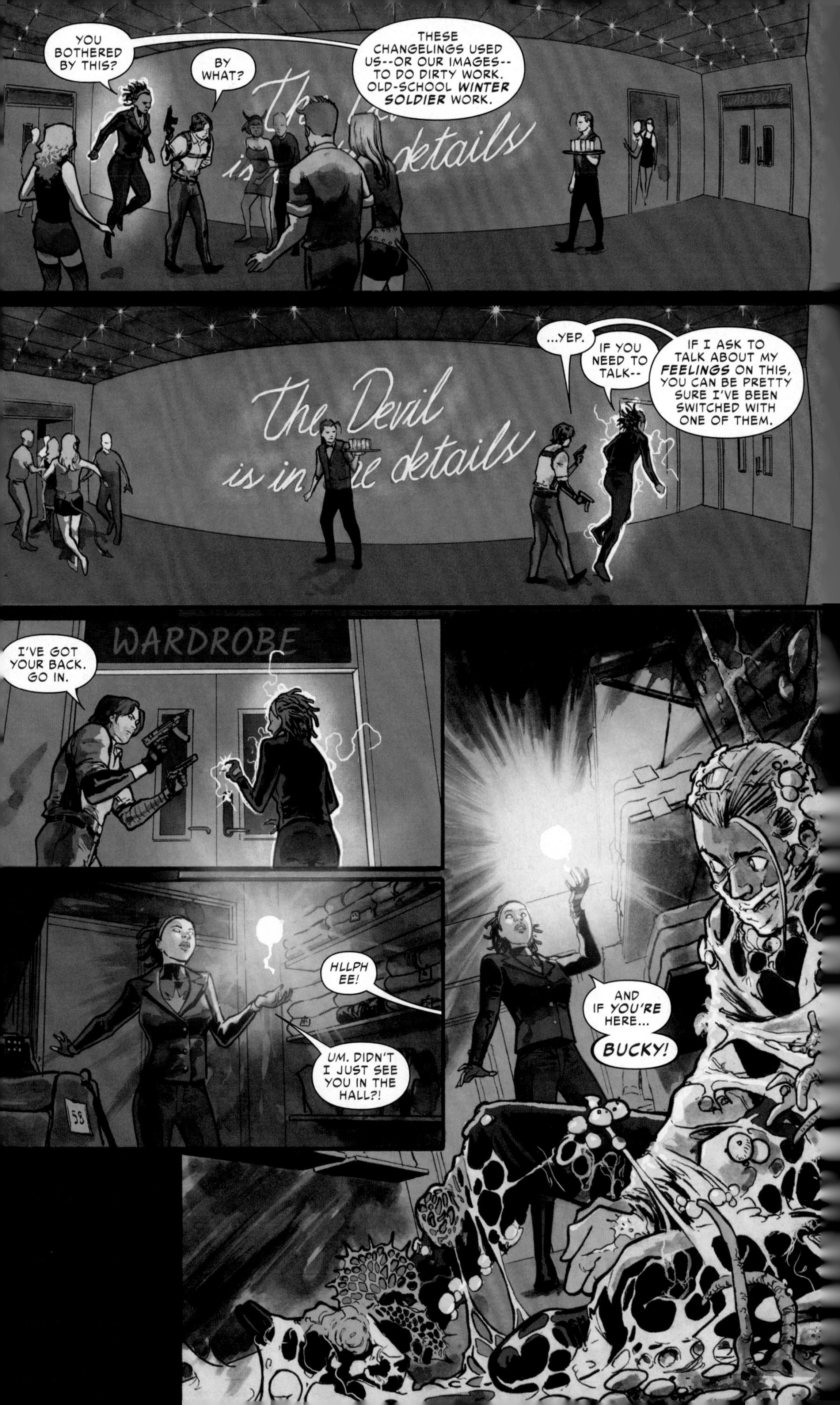
YOU BOTHERED BY THIS?
BY WHAT?
THESE CHANGELINGS USED US--OR OUR IMAGES--TO DO DIRTY WORK. OLD-SCHOOL WINTER SOLDIER WORK.
...YEP.
IF YOU NEED TO TALK--
IF I ASK TO TALK ABOUT MY FEELINGS ON THIS, YOU CAN BE PRETTY SURE I'VE BEEN SWITCHED WITH ONE OF THEM.
the Devil is in the details
WARDROBE
I'VE GOT YOUR BACK. GO IN.
HLLPH EE!
UM. DIDN'T I JUST SEE YOU IN THE HALL?!
AND IF YOU'RE HERE...
BUCKY!

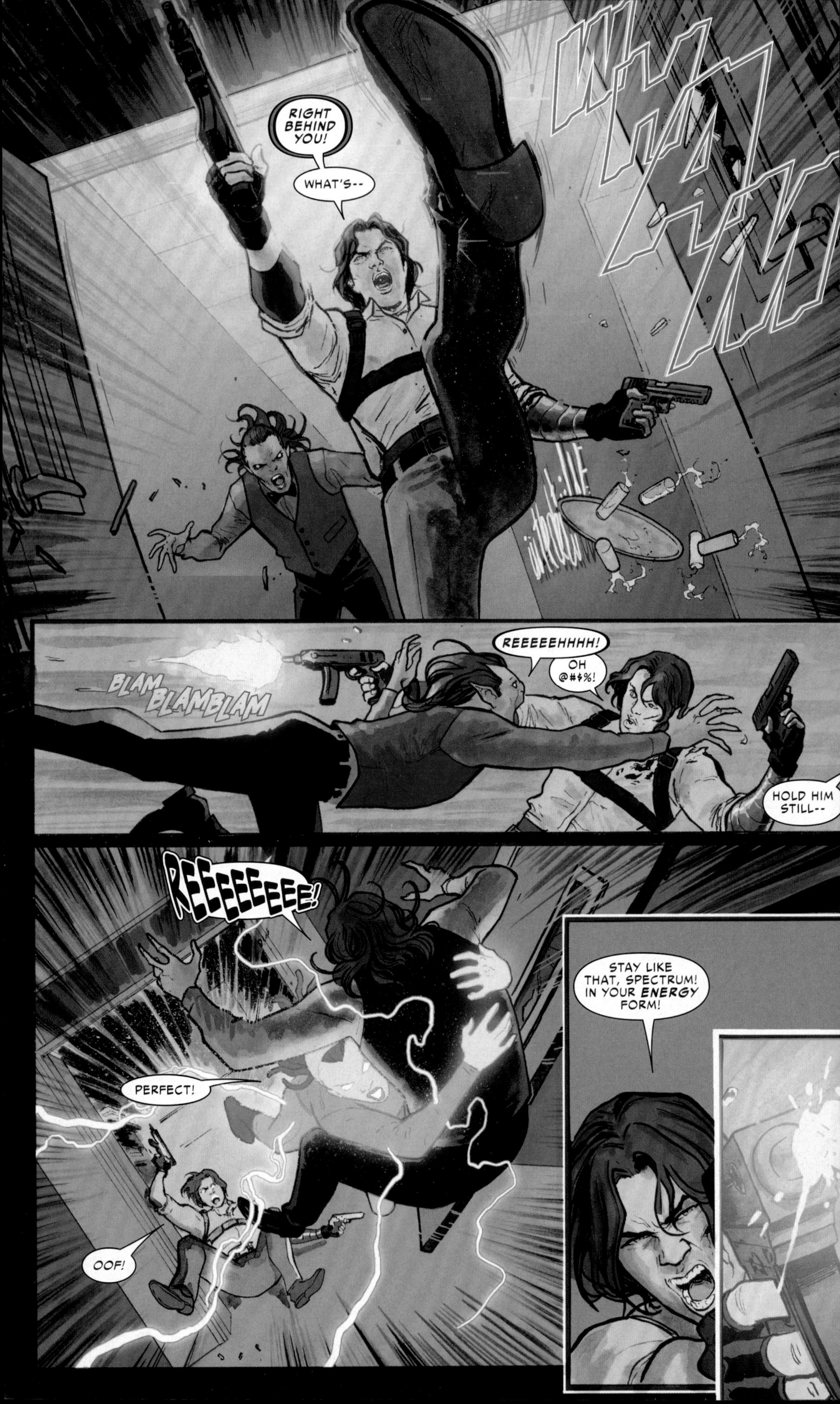
RIGHT BEHIND YOU!
WHAT'S--
REEEEEHHHH!
OH @#$%!
BLAM BLAMBLAM
HOLD HIM STILL--
REEEEEEEE!
PERFECT!
OOF!
STAY LIKE THAT, SPECTRUM! IN YOUR ENERGY FORM!

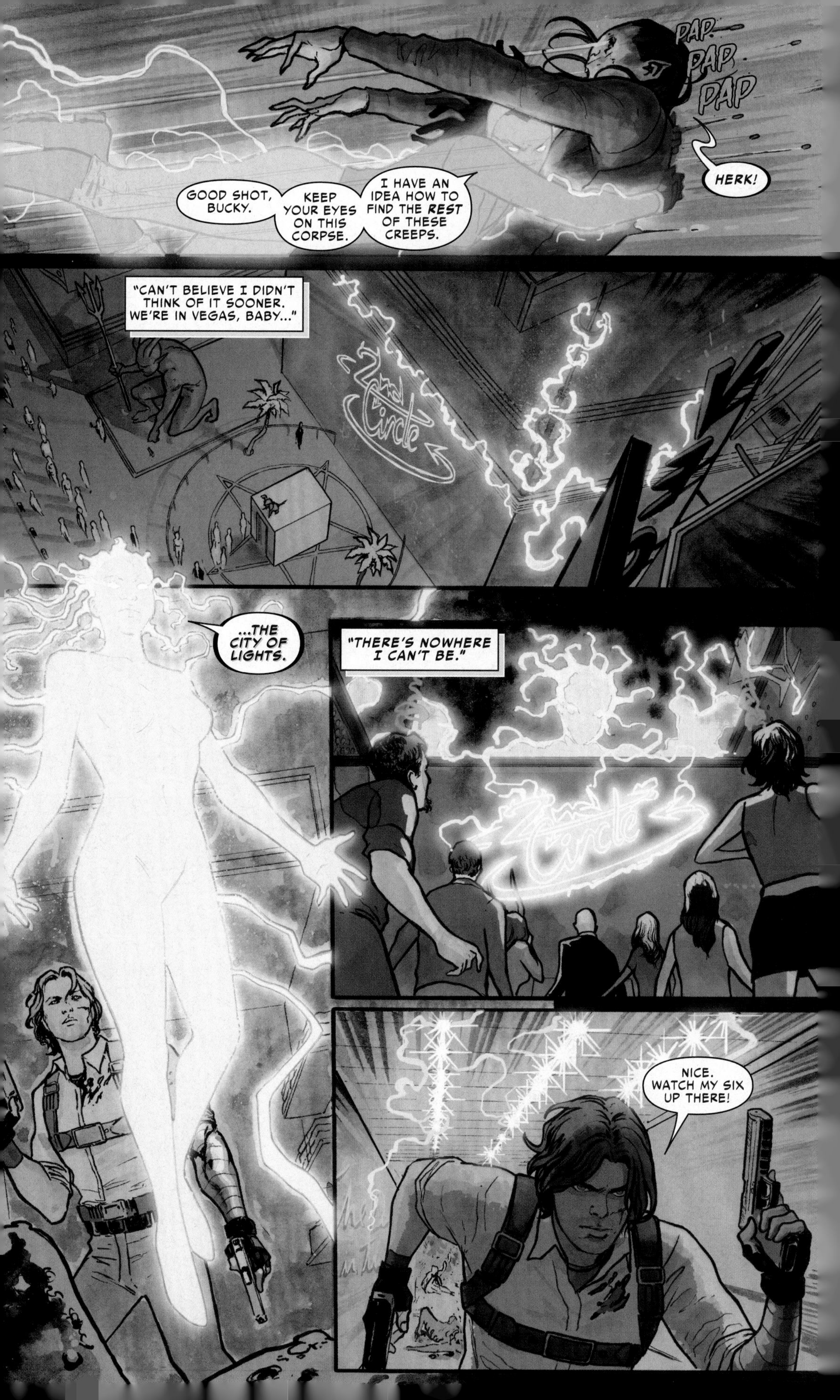
PAP PAP PAP
HERK!
GOOD SHOT, BUCKY.
KEEP YOUR EYES ON THIS CORPSE.
I HAVE AN IDEA HOW TO FIND THE REST OF THESE CREEPS.
"CAN'T BELIEVE I DIDN'T THINK OF IT SOONER. WE'RE IN VEGAS, BABY..."
2nd Circle
...THE CITY OF LIGHTS.
"THERE'S NOWHERE I CAN'T BE."
2nd Circle
NICE. WATCH MY SIX UP THERE!

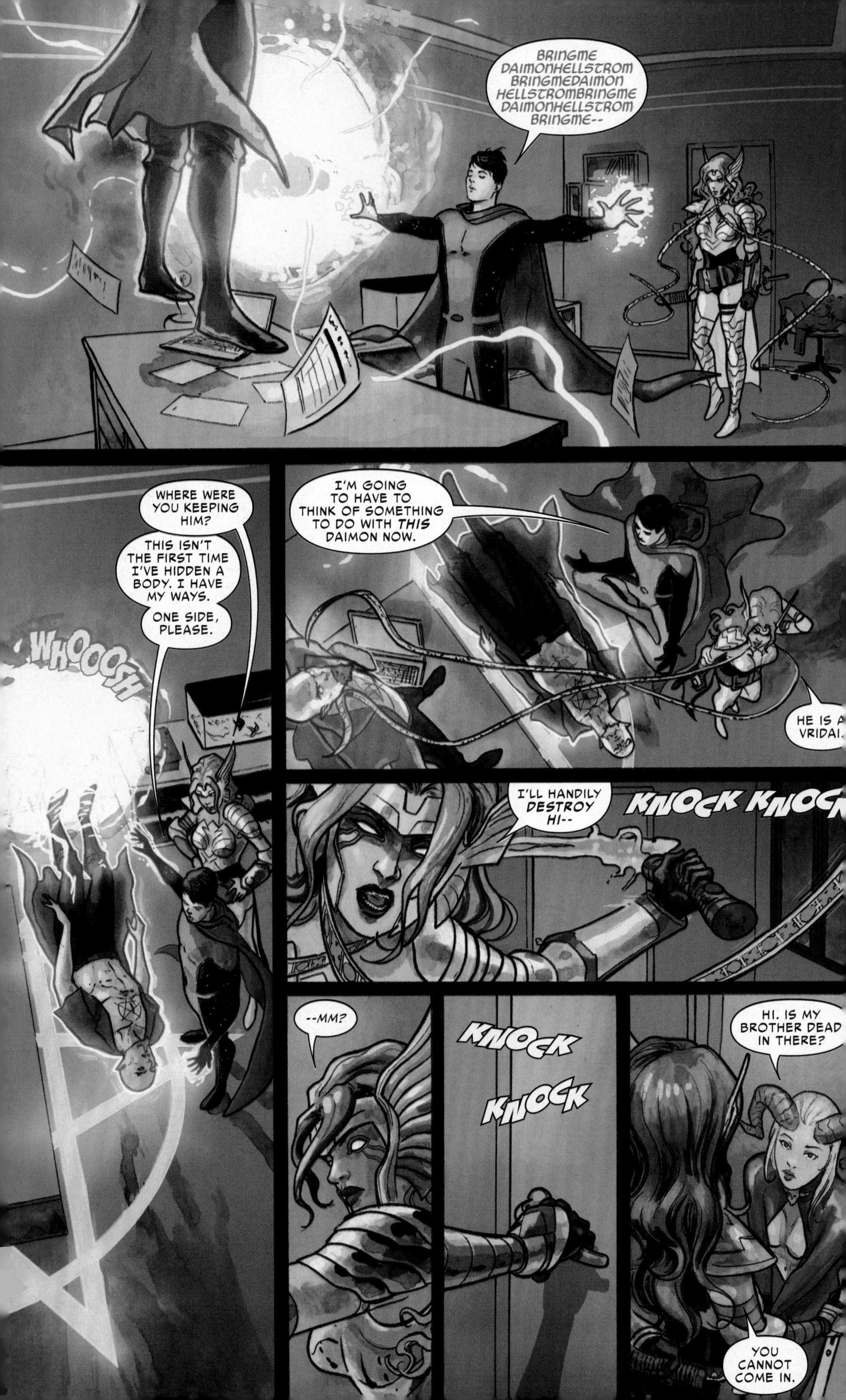
BRINGME DAIMONHELLSTROM BRINGMEDAIMON HELLSTROMBRINGME DAIMONHELLSTROM BRINGME--
WHERE WERE YOU KEEPING HIM?
THIS ISN'T THE FIRST TIME I'VE HIDDEN A BODY. I HAVE MY WAYS.
ONE SIDE, PLEASE.
WHOOOSH
I'M GOING TO HAVE TO THINK OF SOMETHING TO DO WITH THIS DAIMON NOW.
HE IS A VRIDAI.
I'LL HANDILY DESTROY HI--
KNOCK KNOCK
--MM?
KNOCK
KNOCK
HI. IS MY BROTHER DEAD IN THERE?
YOU CANNOT COME IN.

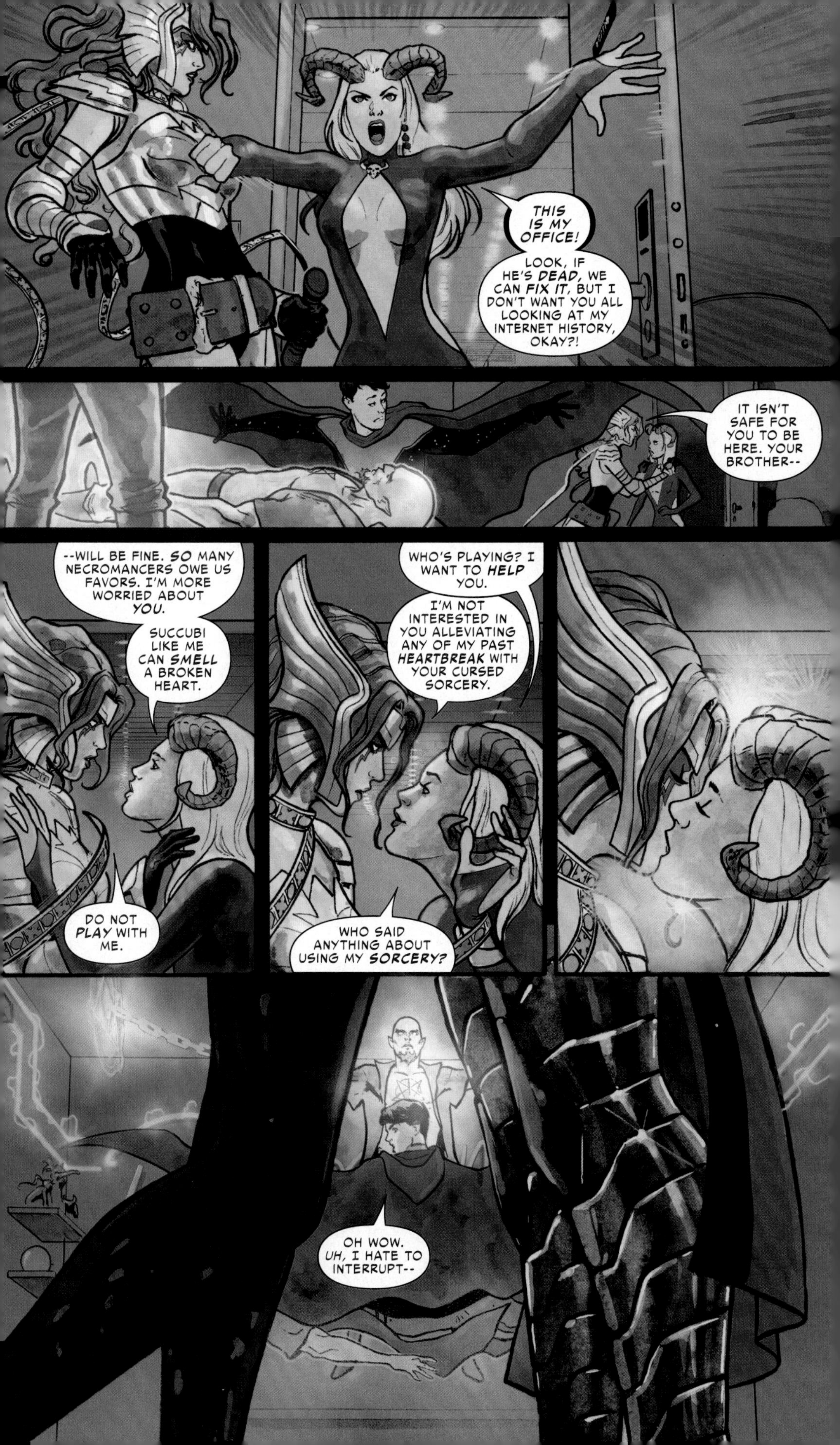
THIS IS MY OFFICE!
LOOK, IF HE'S DEAD, WE CAN FIX IT, BUT I DON'T WANT YOU ALL LOOKING AT MY INTERNET HISTORY, OKAY?!
IT ISN'T SAFE FOR YOU TO BE HERE. YOUR BROTHER--
--WILL BE FINE. SO MANY NECROMANCERS OWE US FAVORS. I'M MORE WORRIED ABOUT YOU.
SUCCUBI LIKE ME CAN SMELL A BROKEN HEART.
DO NOT PLAY WITH ME.
WHO'S PLAYING? I WANT TO HELP YOU.
I'M NOT INTERESTED IN YOU ALLEVIATING ANY OF MY PAST HEARTBREAK WITH YOUR CURSED SORCERY.
WHO SAID ANYTHING ABOUT USING MY SORCERY?
OH WOW. UH, I HATE TO INTERRUPT--

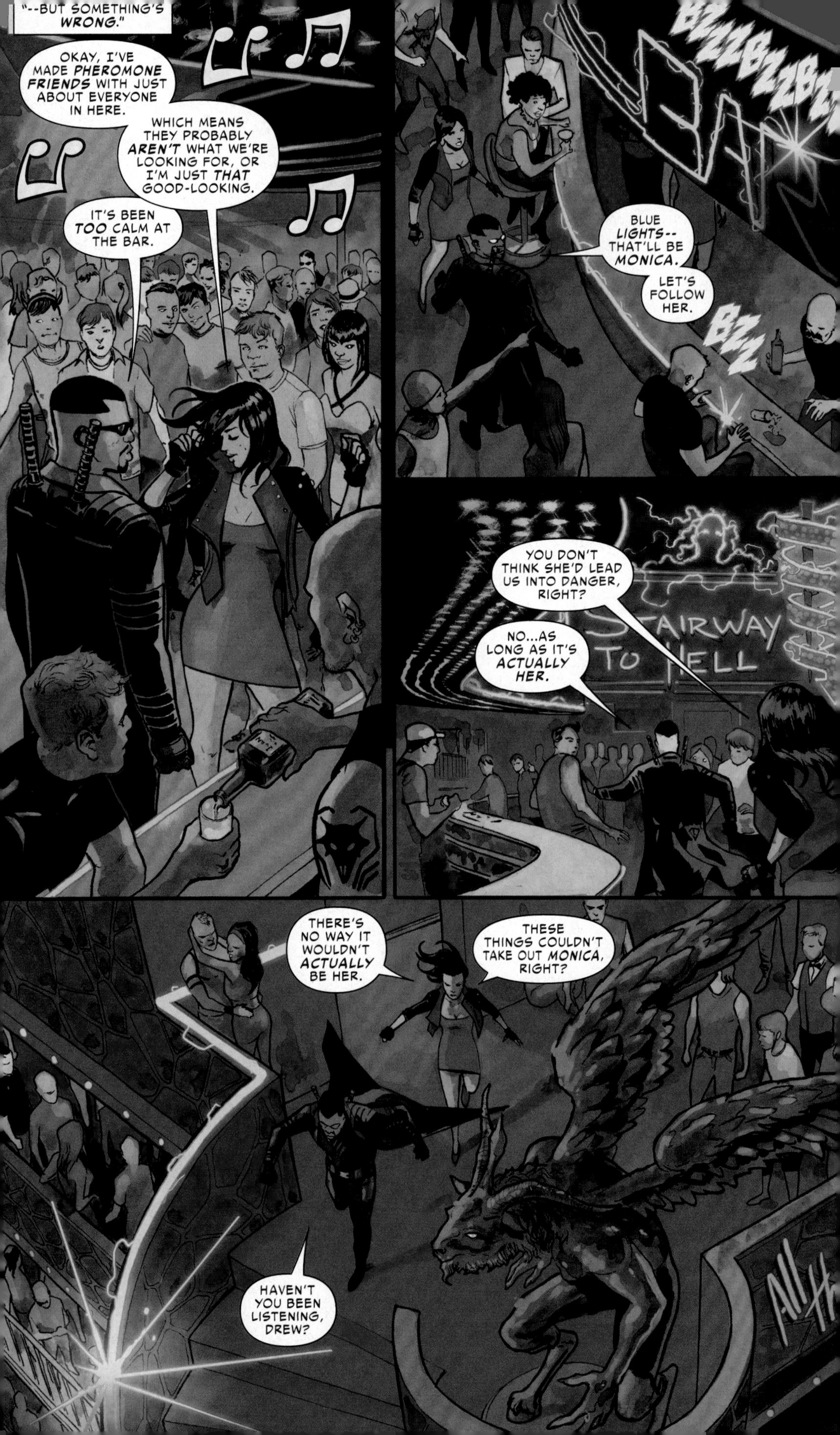
"--BUT SOMETHING'S WRONG."
OKAY, I'VE MADE PHEROMONE FRIENDS WITH JUST ABOUT EVERYONE IN HERE.
WHICH MEANS THEY PROBABLY AREN'T WHAT WE'RE LOOKING FOR, OR I'M JUST THAT GOOD-LOOKING.
IT'S BEEN TOO CALM AT THE BAR.
BLUE LIGHTS-- THAT'LL BE MONICA.
LET'S FOLLOW HER.
BZZ
YOU DON'T THINK SHE'D LEAD US INTO DANGER, RIGHT?
STAIRWAY
NO...AS LONG AS IT'S ACTUALLY HER.
THERE'S NO WAY IT WOULDN'T ACTUALLY BE HER.
THESE THINGS COULDN'T TAKE OUT MONICA, RIGHT?
HAVEN'T YOU BEEN LISTENING, DREW?

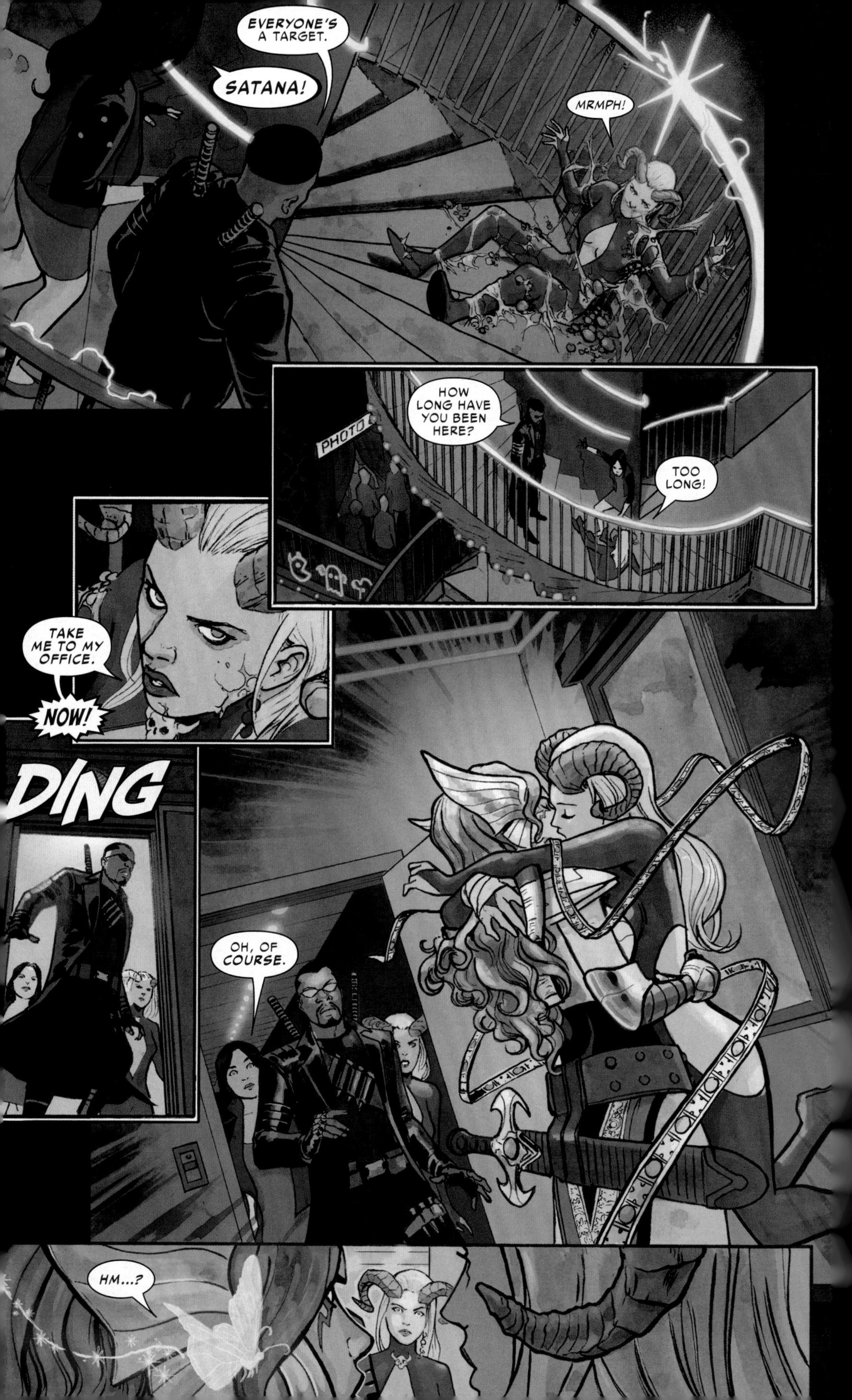
EVERYONE'S A TARGET.
SATANA!
MRMPH!
HOW LONG HAVE YOU BEEN HERE?
TOO LONG!
PHOTO
TAKE ME TO MY OFFICE.
NOW!
DING
OH, OF COURSE.
HM...?

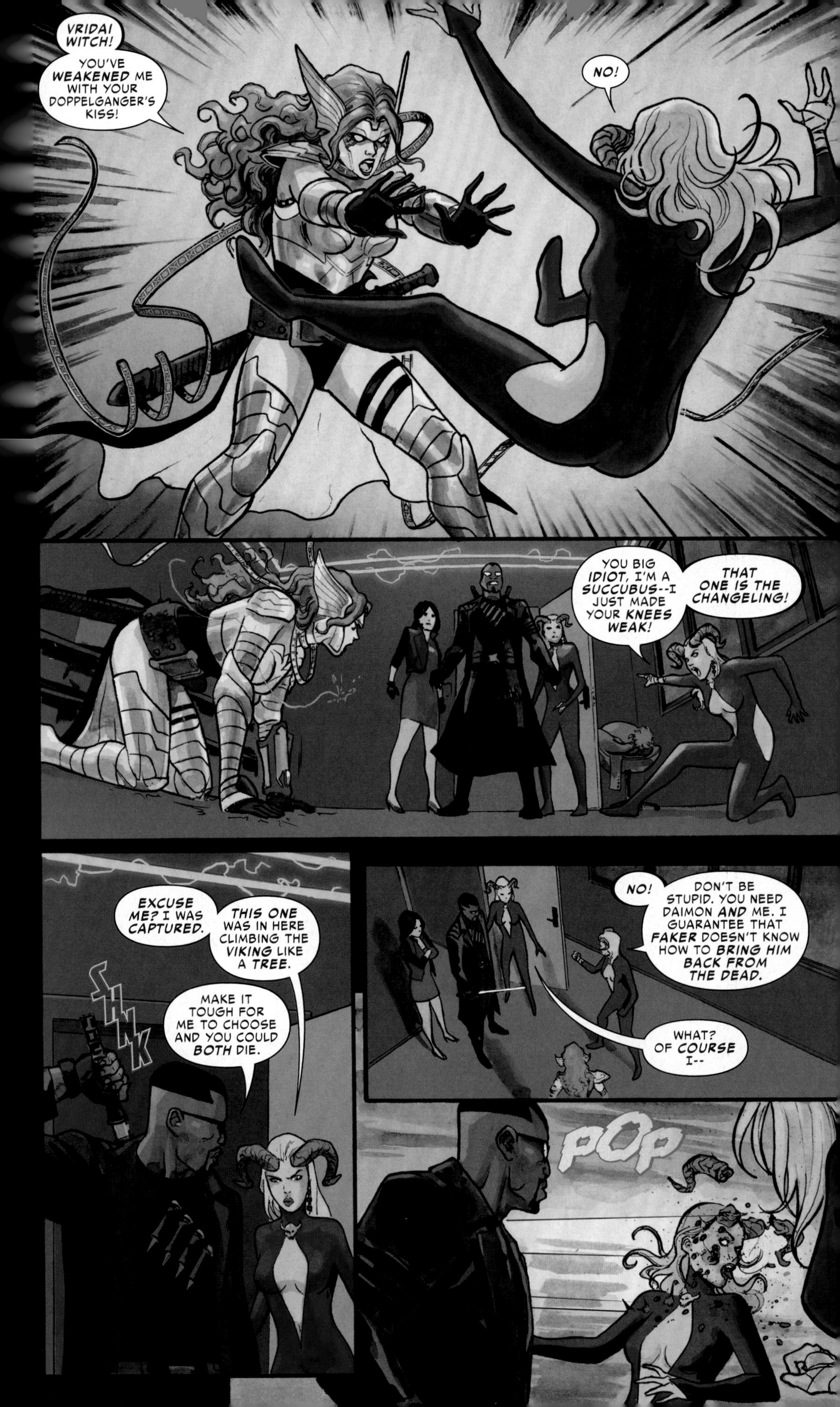

VRIDAI WITCH!
YOU'VE WEAKENED ME WITH YOUR DOPPELGANGER'S KISS!
NO!
YOU BIG IDIOT, I'M A SUCCUBUS--I JUST MADE YOUR KNEES WEAK!
THAT ONE IS THE CHANGELING!
EXCUSE ME? I WAS CAPTURED.
THIS ONE WAS IN HERE CLIMBING THE VIKING LIKE A TREE.
SHNNK
MAKE IT TOUGH FOR ME TO CHOOSE AND YOU COULD BOTH DIE.
NO!
DON'T BE STUPID. YOU NEED DAIMON AND ME. I GUARANTEE THAT FAKER DOESN'T KNOW HOW TO BRING HIM BACK FROM THE DEAD.
WHAT? OF COURSE I--
pOp

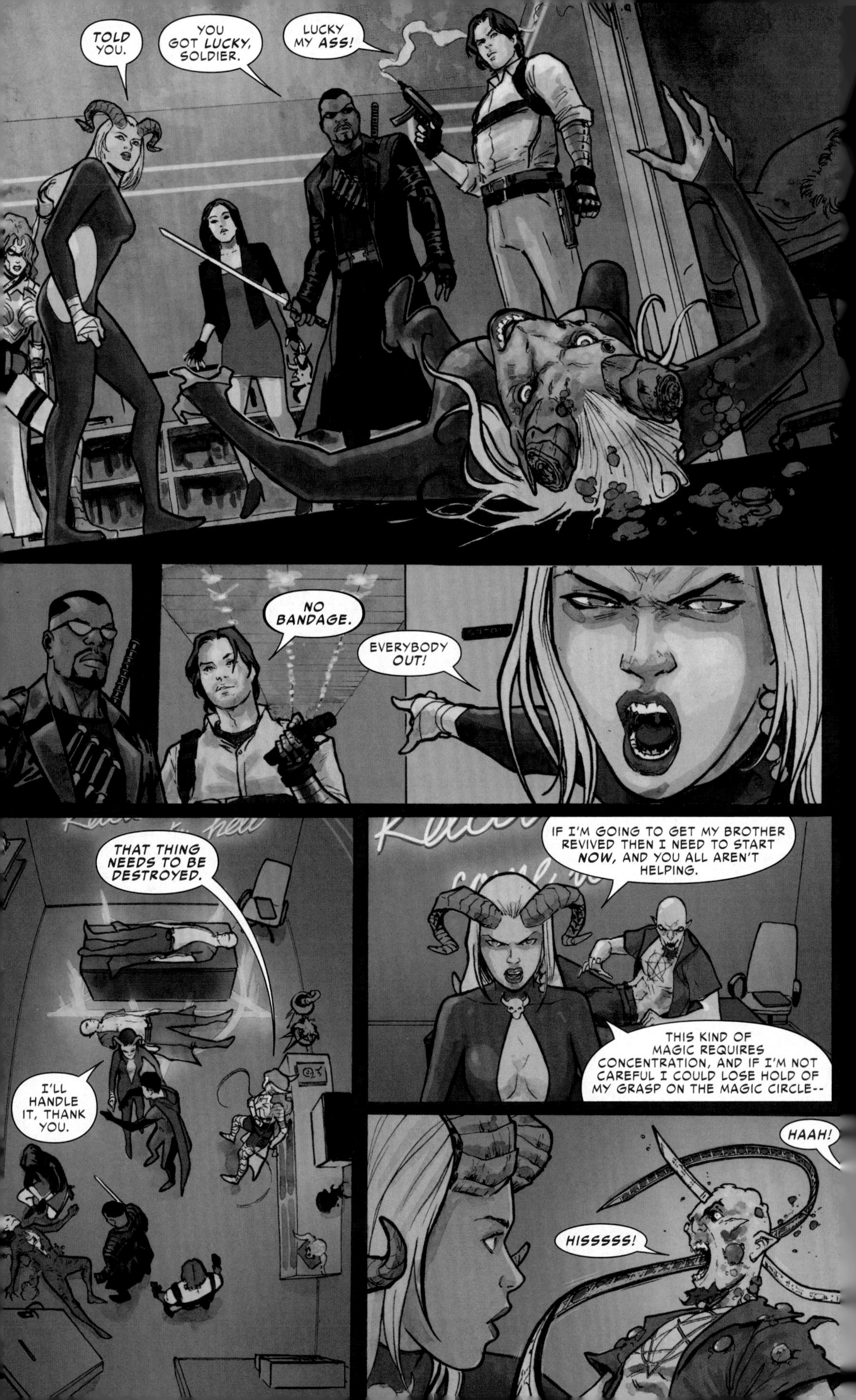

TOLD YOU.
YOU GOT LUCKY, SOLDIER.
LUCKY MY ASS!
NO BANDAGE.
EVERYBODY OUT!
THAT THING NEEDS TO BE DESTROYED.
I'LL HANDLE IT, THANK YOU.
IF I'M GOING TO GET MY BROTHER REVIVED THEN I NEED TO START NOW, AND YOU ALL AREN'T HELPING.
THIS KIND OF MAGIC REQUIRES CONCENTRATION, AND IF I'M NOT CAREFUL I COULD LOSE HOLD OF MY GRASP ON THE MAGIC CIRCLE--
HAAH!
HISSSSS!

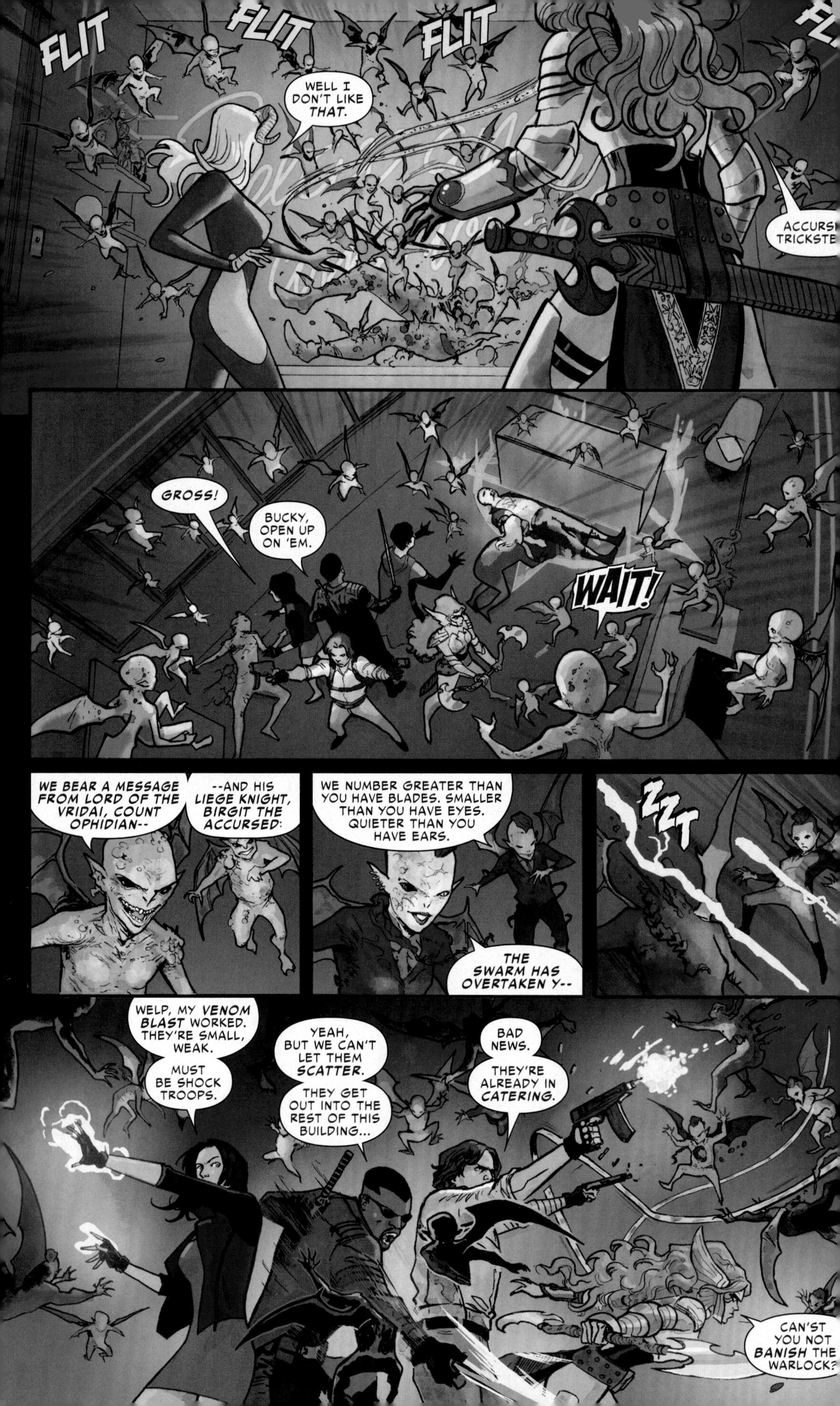
FLIT
FLIT
FLIT
FL
WELL I DON'T LIKE THAT.
ACCURS TRICKSTE
GROSS!
BUCKY, OPEN UP ON 'EM.
WAIT!
WE BEAR A MESSAGE FROM LORD OF THE VRIDAI, COUNT OPHIDIAN--
--AND HIS LIEGE KNIGHT, BIRGIT THE ACCURSED:
WE NUMBER GREATER THAN YOU HAVE BLADES. SMALLER THAN YOU HAVE EYES. QUIETER THAN YOU HAVE EARS.
THE SWARM HAS OVERTAKEN Y--
ZZT
WELP, MY VENOM BLAST WORKED. THEY'RE SMALL, WEAK.
MUST BE SHOCK TROOPS.
YEAH, BUT WE CAN'T LET THEM SCATTER.
THEY GET OUT INTO THE REST OF THIS BUILDING...
BAD NEWS.
THEY'RE ALREADY IN CATERING.
CAN'ST YOU NOT BANISH THE WARLOCK?

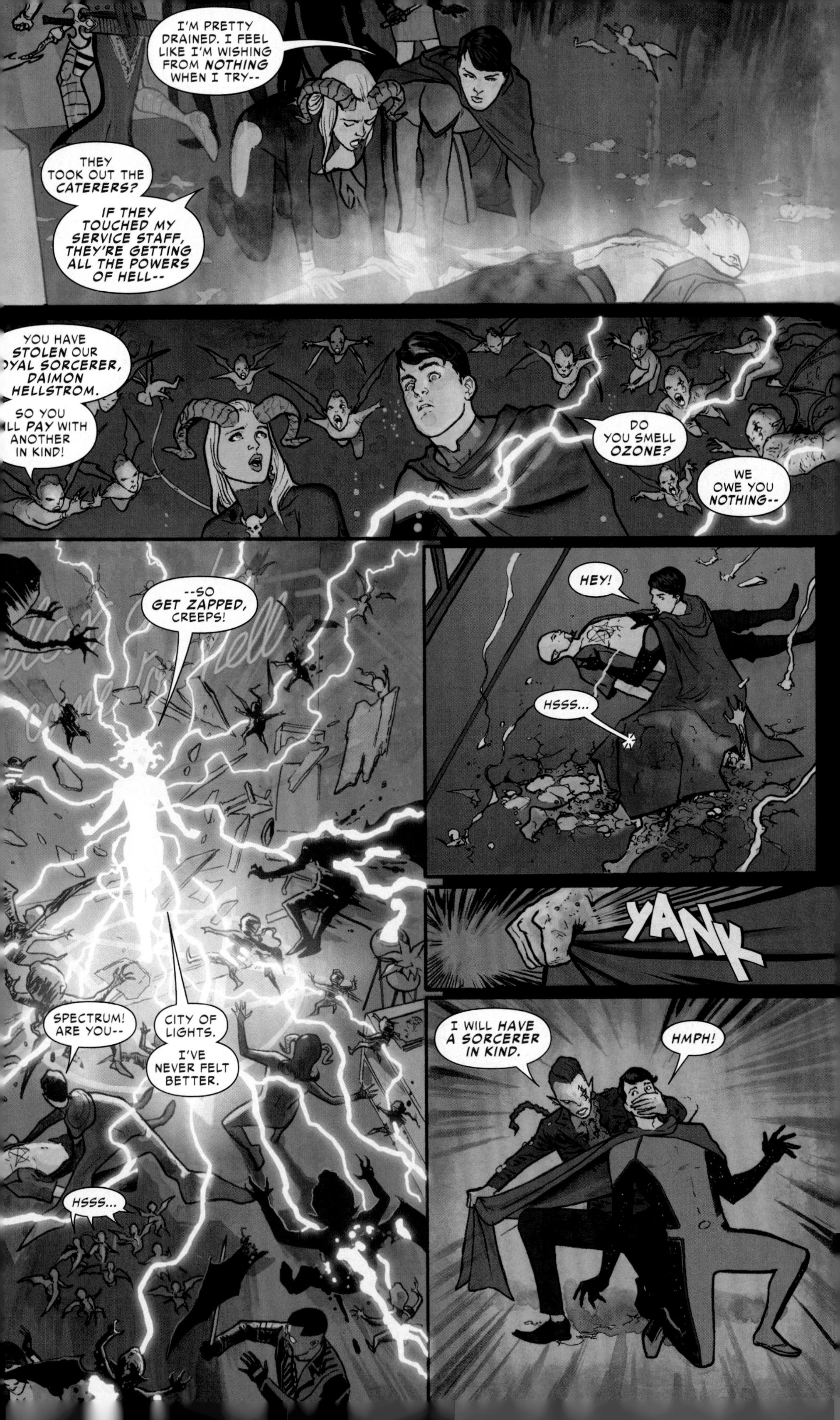

I'M PRETTY DRAINED. I FEEL LIKE I'M WISHING FROM NOTHING WHEN I TRY--
THEY TOOK OUT THE CATERERS?
IF THEY TOUCHED MY SERVICE STAFF, THEY'RE GETTING ALL THE POWERS OF HELL--
YOU HAVE STOLEN OUR OYAL SORCERER, DAIMON HELLSTROM.
SO YOU LL PAY WITH ANOTHER IN KIND!
DO YOU SMELL OZONE?
WE OWE YOU NOTHING--
--SO GET ZAPPED, CREEPS!
SPECTRUM! ARE YOU--
CITY OF LIGHTS.
I'VE NEVER FELT BETTER.
HSSS...
HEY!
HSSS...
YANK
I WILL HAVE A SORCERER IN KIND.
HMPH!

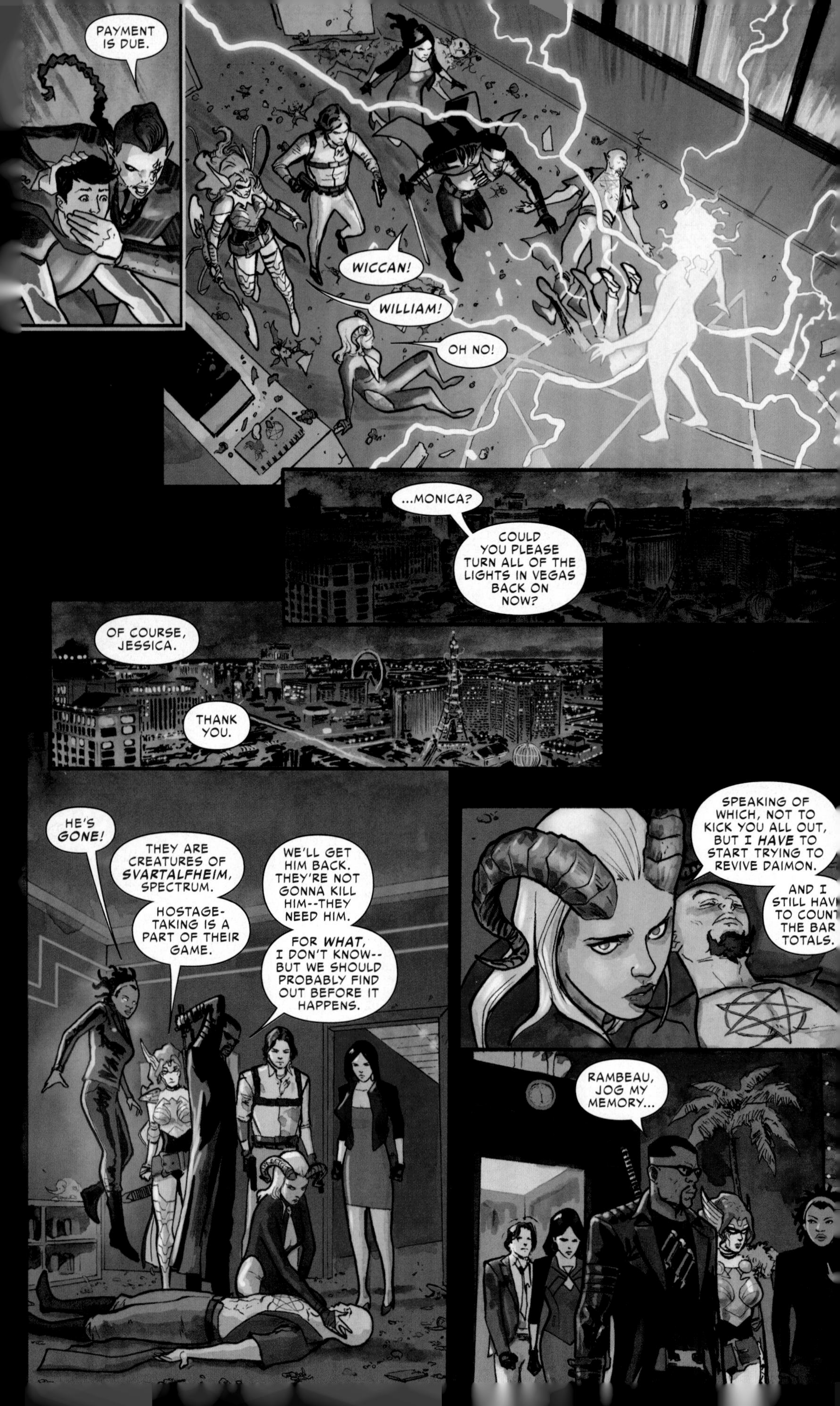

PAYMENT IS DUE.
WICCAN!
WILLIAM!
OH NO!
...MONICA?
COULD YOU PLEASE TURN ALL OF THE LIGHTS IN VEGAS BACK ON NOW?
OF COURSE, JESSICA.
THANK YOU.
HE'S GONE!
THEY ARE CREATURES OF SVARTALFHEIM, SPECTRUM.
HOSTAGE-TAKING IS A PART OF THEIR GAME.
WE'LL GET HIM BACK. THEY'RE NOT GONNA KILL HIM--THEY NEED HIM.
FOR WHAT, I DON'T KNOW--BUT WE SHOULD PROBABLY FIND OUT BEFORE IT HAPPENS.
SPEAKING OF WHICH, NOT TO KICK YOU ALL OUT, BUT I HAVE TO START TRYING TO REVIVE DAIMON.
AND I STILL HAV TO COUNT THE BAR TOTALS.
RAMBEAU, JOG MY MEMORY...

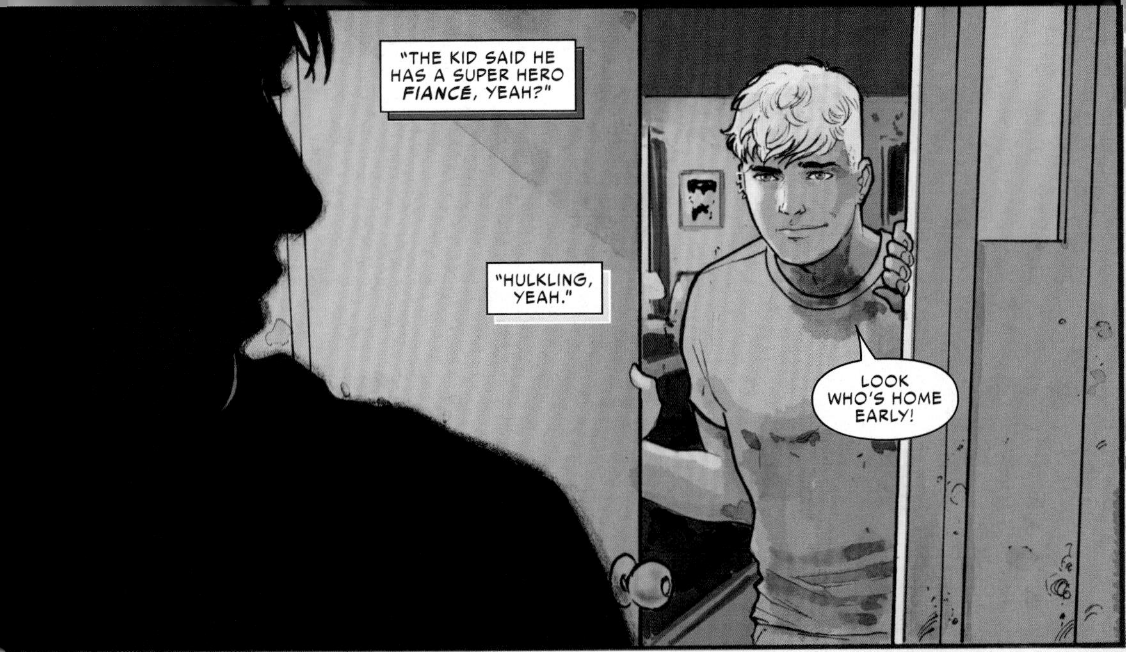
"THE KID SAID HE HAS A SUPER HERO *FIANCÉ*, YEAH?"
"HULKLING, YEAH."
LOOK WHO'S HOME EARLY!

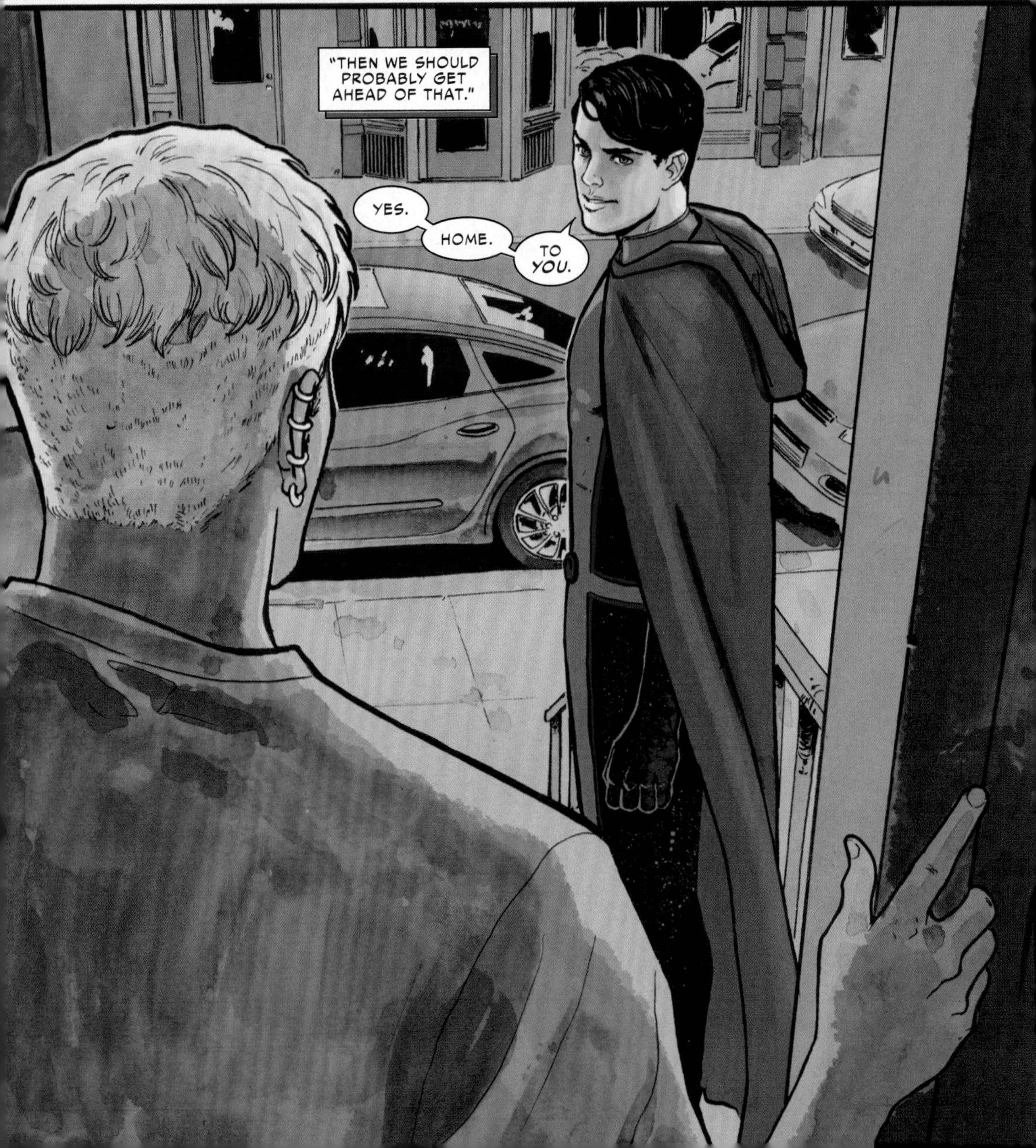
"THEN WE SHOULD PROBABLY GET AHEAD OF THAT."
YES.
HOME.
TO *YOU*.

3

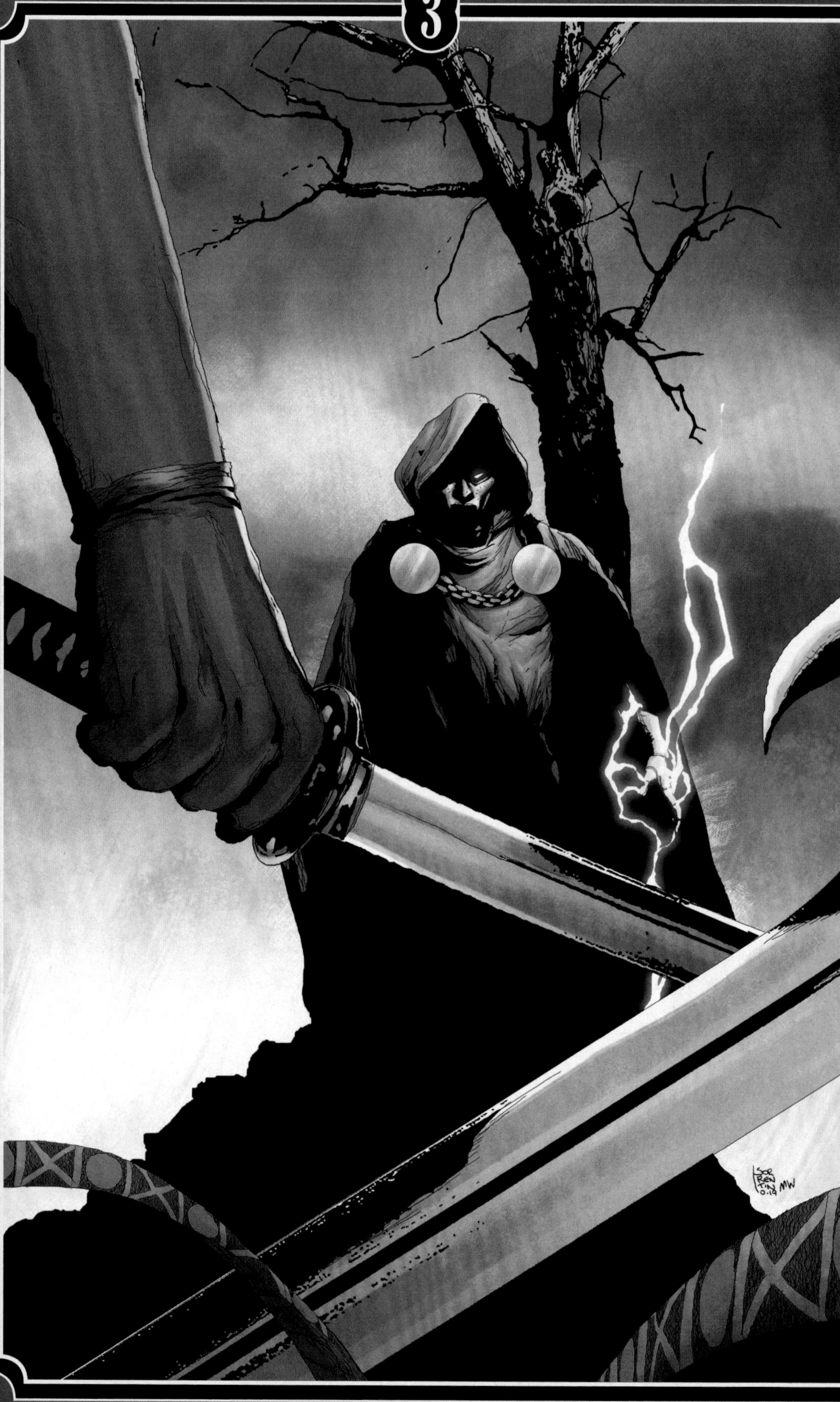

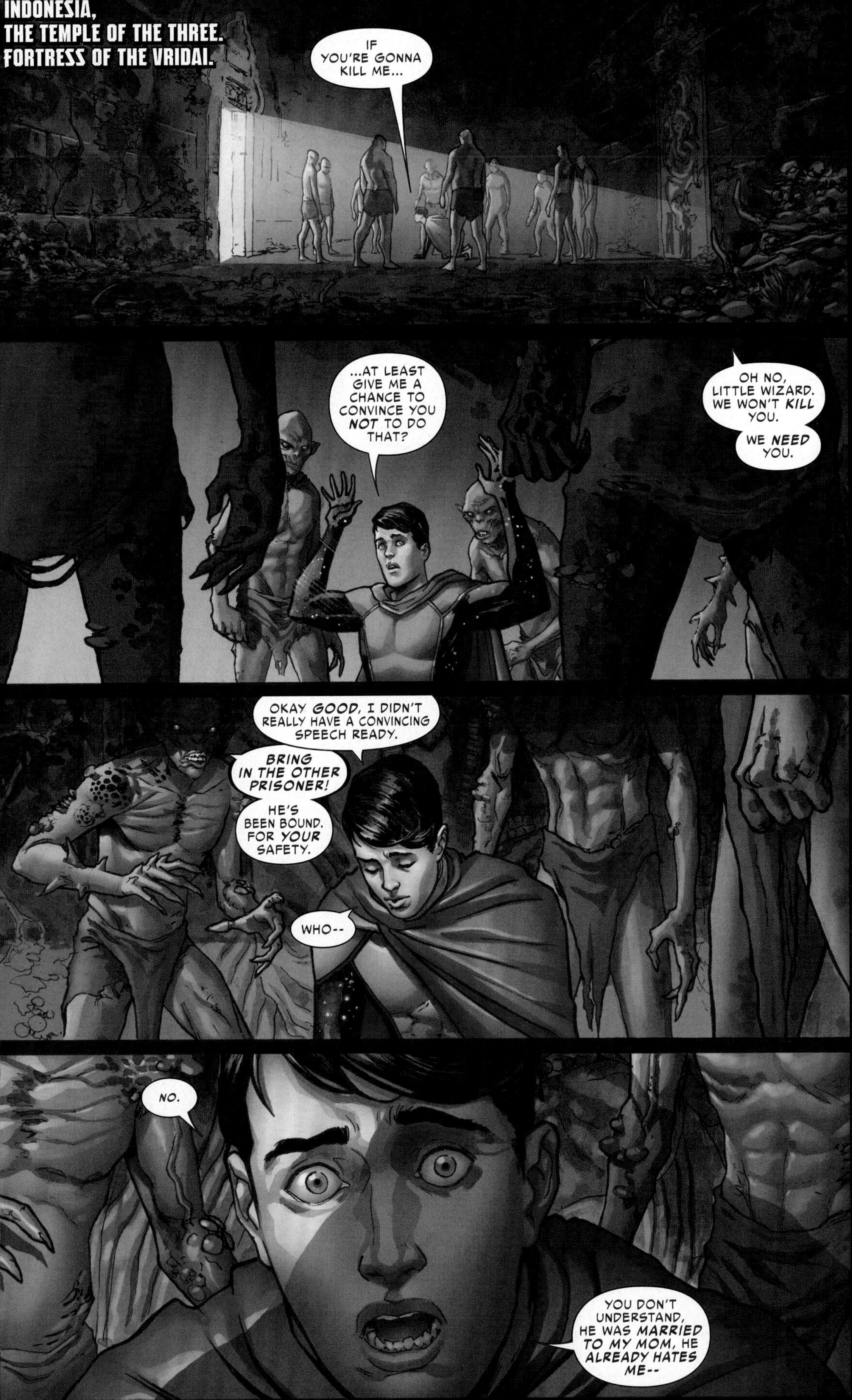
INDONESIA,
THE TEMPLE OF THE THREE.
FORTRESS OF THE VRIDAI.
IF YOU'RE GONNA KILL ME...
...AT LEAST GIVE ME A CHANCE TO CONVINCE YOU NOT TO DO THAT?
OH NO, LITTLE WIZARD. WE WON'T KILL YOU.
WE NEED YOU.
OKAY GOOD, I DIDN'T REALLY HAVE A CONVINCING SPEECH READY.
BRING IN THE OTHER PRISONER!
HE'S BEEN BOUND. FOR YOUR SAFETY.
WHO--
NO.
YOU DON'T UNDERSTAND, HE WAS MARRIED TO MY MOM, HE ALREADY HATES ME--

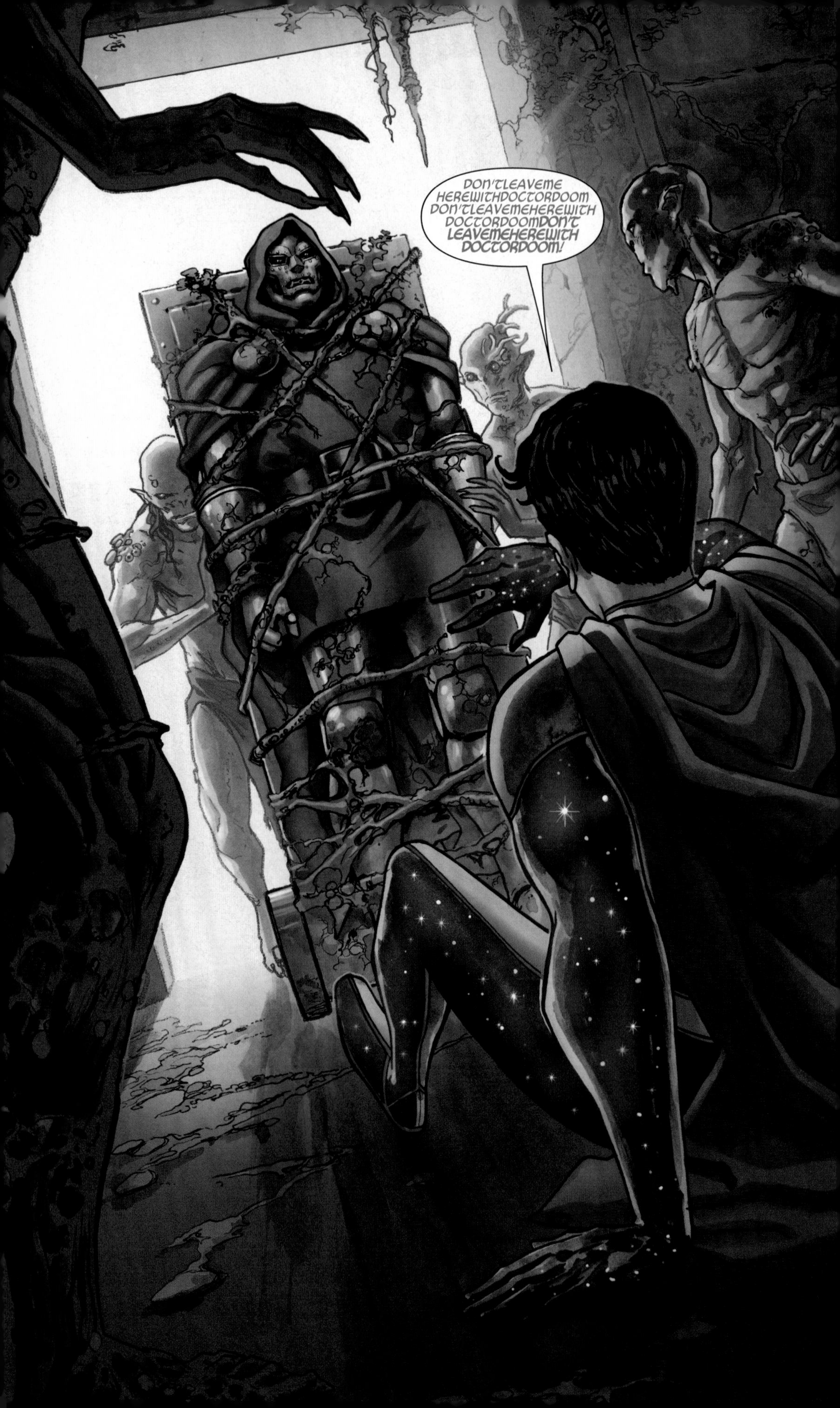
DON'TLEAVEME HEREWITHDOCTORDOOM DON'TLEAVEMEHEREWITH DOCTORDOOMDON'T LEAVEMEHEREWITH DOCTORDOOM!

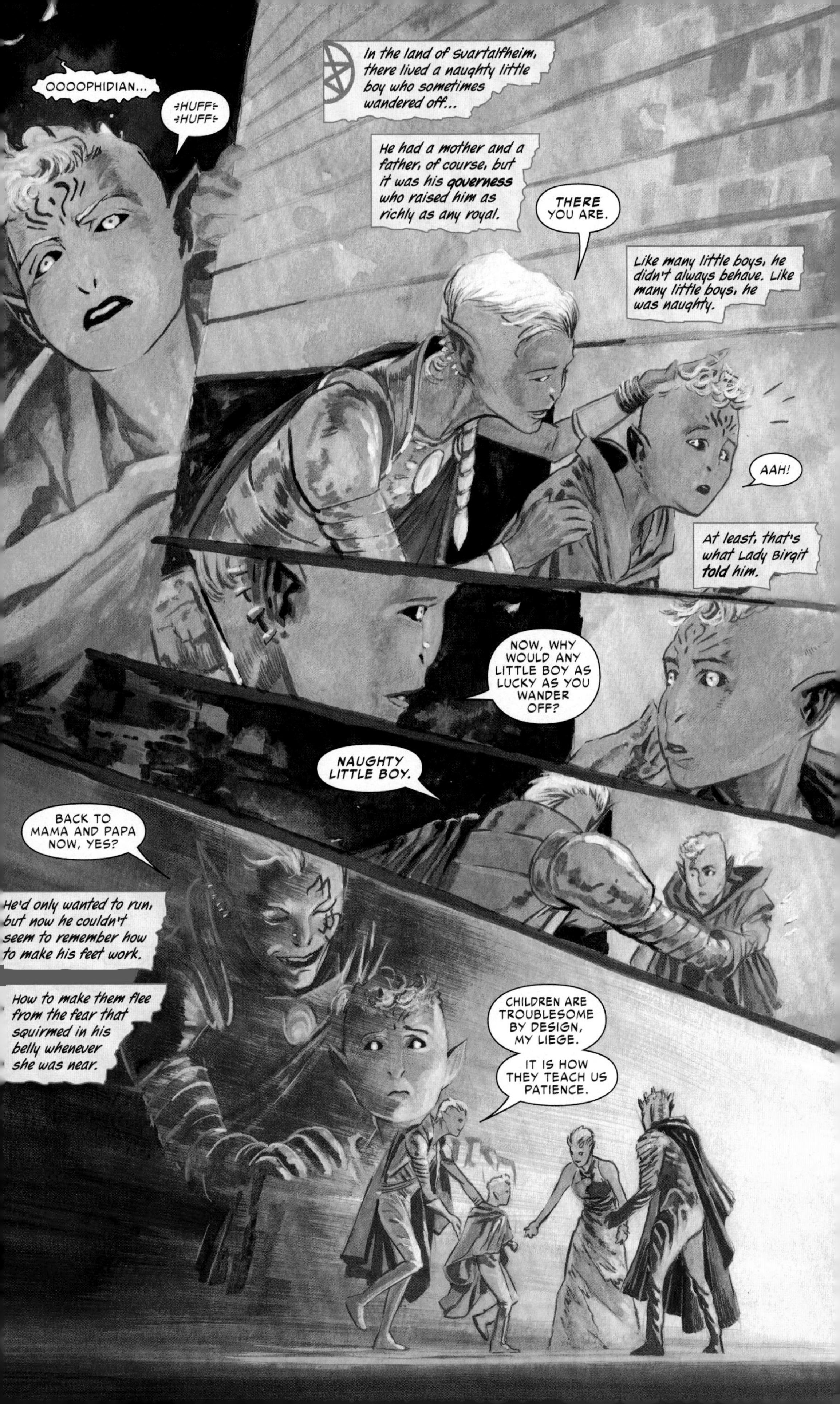
OOOOPHIDIAN...
HUFF HUFF
In the land of Svartalfheim, there lived a naughty little boy who sometimes wandered off...
He had a mother and a father, of course, but it was his governess who raised him as richly as any royal.
THERE YOU ARE.
Like many little boys, he didn't always behave. Like many little boys, he was naughty.
AAH!
At least, that's what Lady Birgit told him.
NOW, WHY WOULD ANY LITTLE BOY AS LUCKY AS YOU WANDER OFF?
NAUGHTY LITTLE BOY.
BACK TO MAMA AND PAPA NOW, YES?
He'd only wanted to run, but now he couldn't seem to remember how to make his feet work.
How to make them flee from the fear that squirmed in his belly whenever she was near.
CHILDREN ARE TROUBLESOME BY DESIGN, MY LIEGE.
IT IS HOW THEY TEACH US PATIENCE.

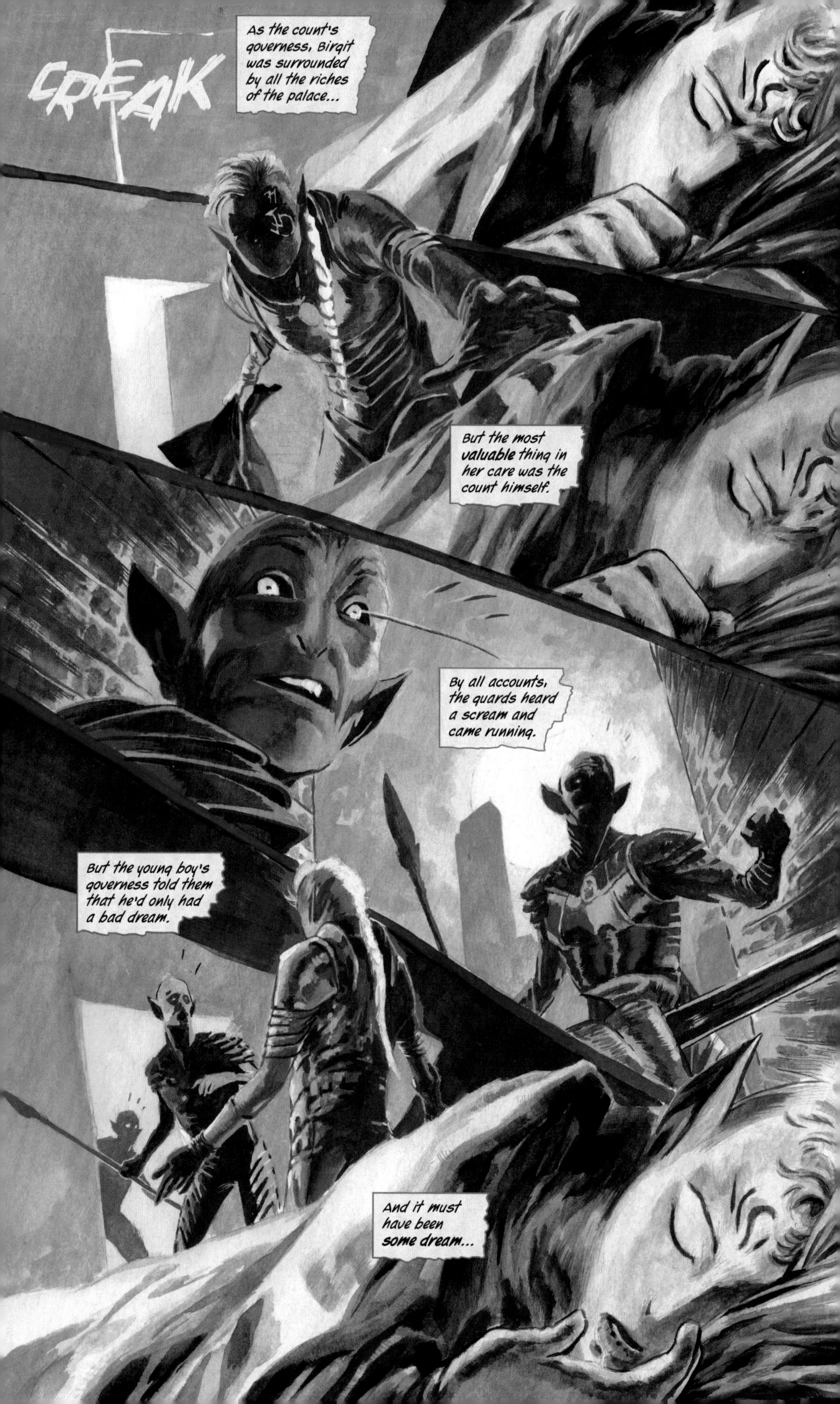
CREAK
As the count's governess, Birgit was surrounded by all the riches of the palace...
But the most valuable thing in her care was the count himself.
By all accounts, the guards heard a scream and came running.
But the young boy's governess told them that he'd only had a bad dream.
And it must have been some dream...

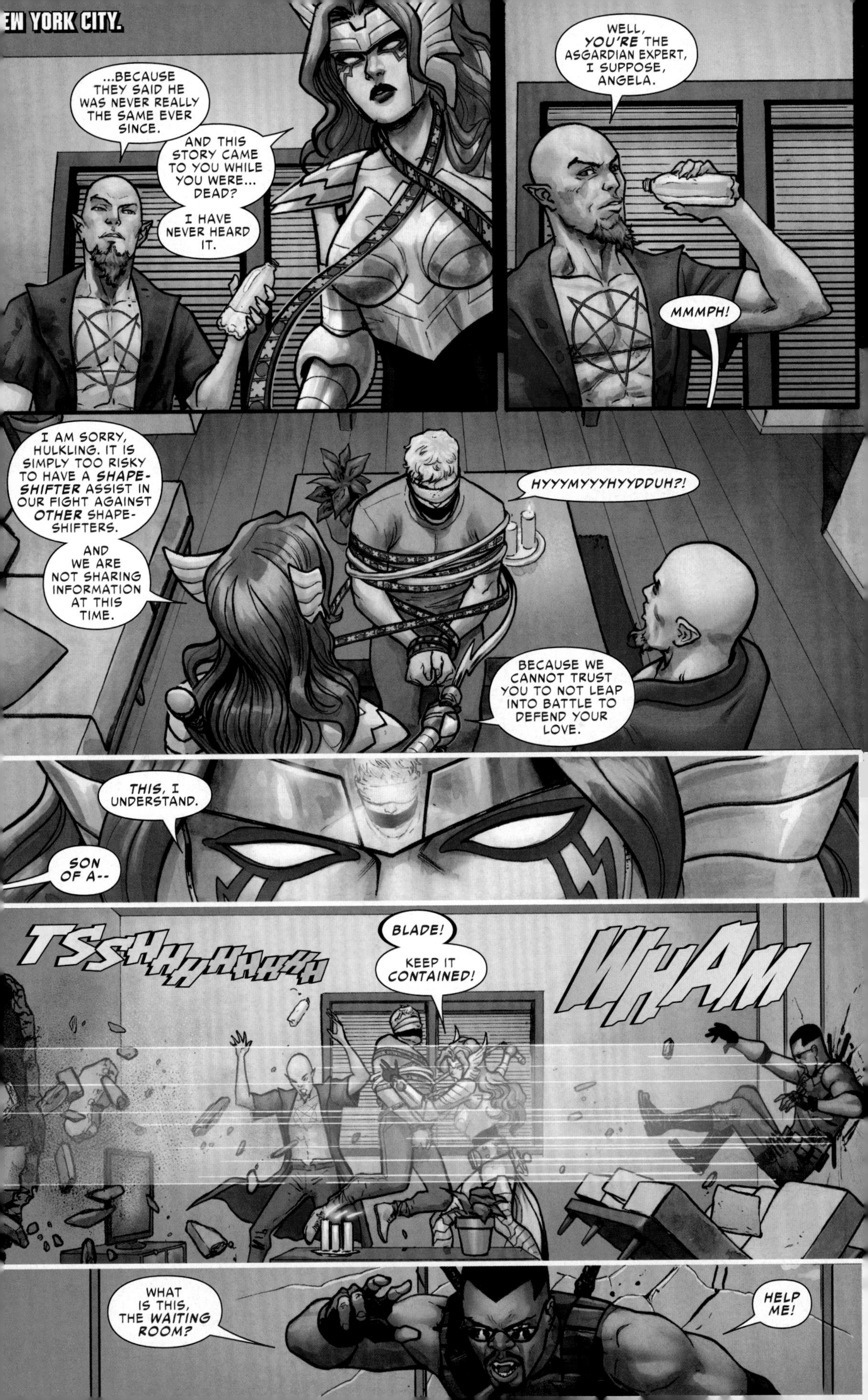

EW YORK CITY.
...BECAUSE THEY SAID HE WAS NEVER REALLY THE SAME EVER SINCE.
AND THIS STORY CAME TO YOU WHILE YOU WERE... DEAD?
I HAVE NEVER HEARD IT.
WELL, YOU'RE THE ASGARDIAN EXPERT, I SUPPOSE, ANGELA.
MMMPH!
I AM SORRY, HULKLING. IT IS SIMPLY TOO RISKY TO HAVE A SHAPE-SHIFTER ASSIST IN OUR FIGHT AGAINST OTHER SHAPE-SHIFTERS.
AND WE ARE NOT SHARING INFORMATION AT THIS TIME.
HYYYMYYYHYYDDUH?!
BECAUSE WE CANNOT TRUST YOU TO NOT LEAP INTO BATTLE TO DEFEND YOUR LOVE.
THIS, I UNDERSTAND.
SON OF A--
TSSHHHHHHHH
BLADE!
KEEP IT CONTAINED!
WHAM
WHAT IS THIS, THE WAITING ROOM?
HELP ME!

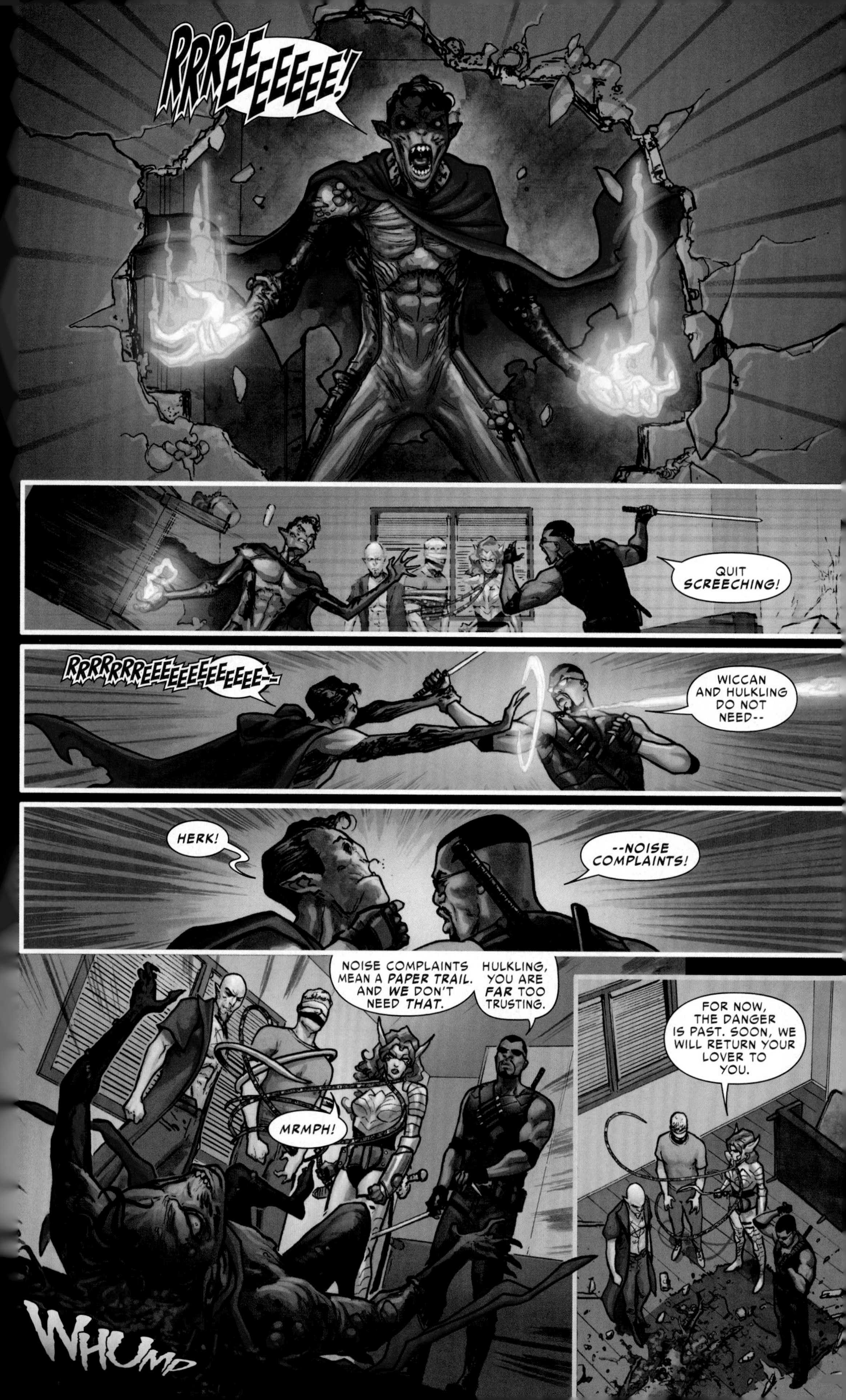
RRREEEEEEE!
QUIT SCREECHING!
RRRRRRREEEEEEEEEEEEE--
WICCAN AND HULKLING DO NOT NEED--
HERK!
--NOISE COMPLAINTS!
NOISE COMPLAINTS MEAN A PAPER TRAIL. AND WE DON'T NEED THAT.
HULKLING, YOU ARE FAR TOO TRUSTING.
MRMPH!
WHUMP
FOR NOW, THE DANGER IS PAST. SOON, WE WILL RETURN YOUR LOVER TO YOU.

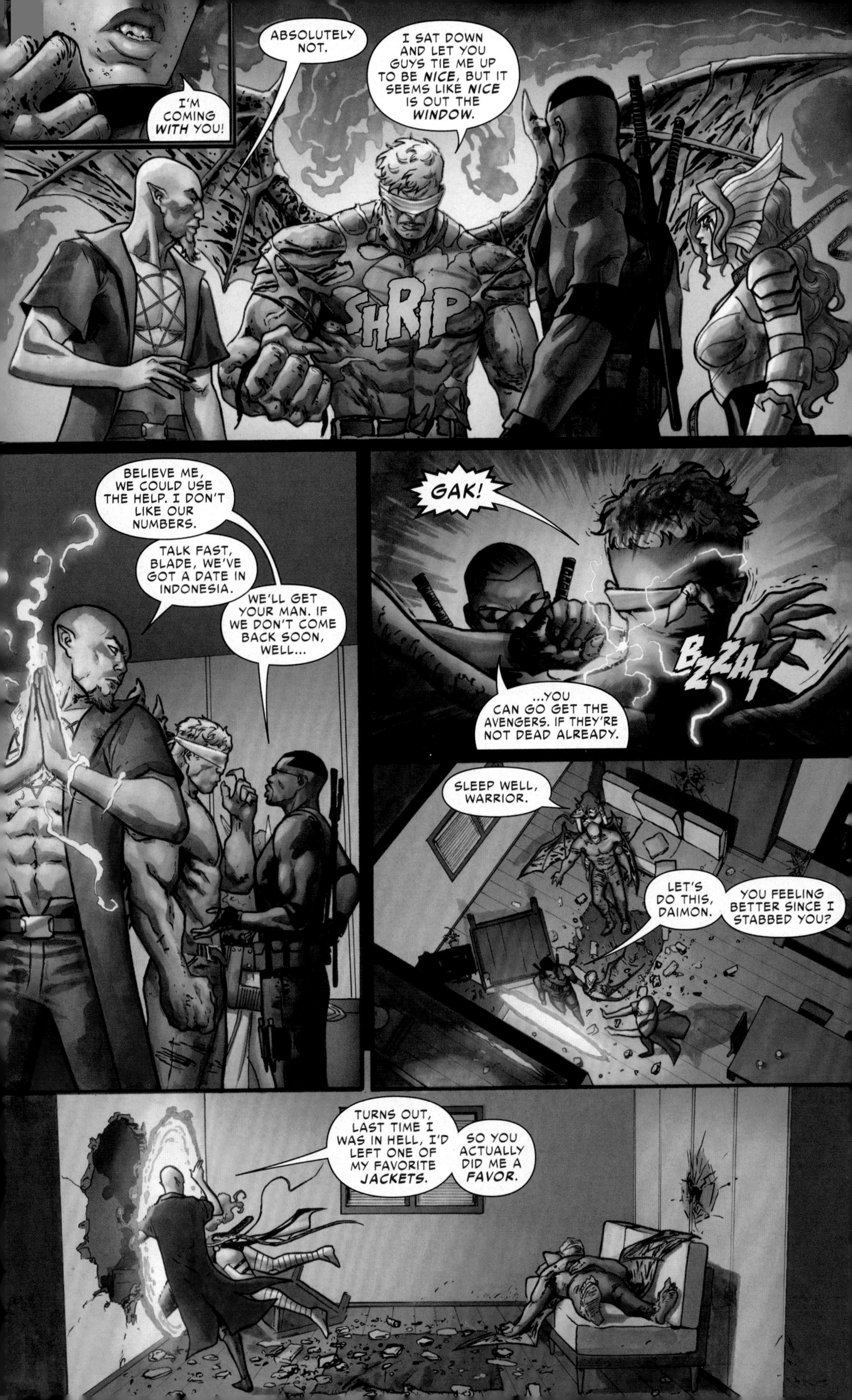
I'M COMING WITH YOU!
ABSOLUTELY NOT.
I SAT DOWN AND LET YOU GUYS TIE ME UP TO BE NICE, BUT IT SEEMS LIKE NICE IS OUT THE WINDOW.
SHRIP
BELIEVE ME, WE COULD USE THE HELP. I DON'T LIKE OUR NUMBERS.
TALK FAST, BLADE, WE'VE GOT A DATE IN INDONESIA.
WE'LL GET YOUR MAN. IF WE DON'T COME BACK SOON, WELL...
GAK!
BZZZAT
...YOU CAN GO GET THE AVENGERS. IF THEY'RE NOT DEAD ALREADY.
SLEEP WELL, WARRIOR.
LET'S DO THIS, DAIMON.
YOU FEELING BETTER SINCE I STABBED YOU?
TURNS OUT, LAST TIME I WAS IN HELL, I'D LEFT ONE OF MY FAVORITE JACKETS.
SO YOU ACTUALLY DID ME A FAVOR.

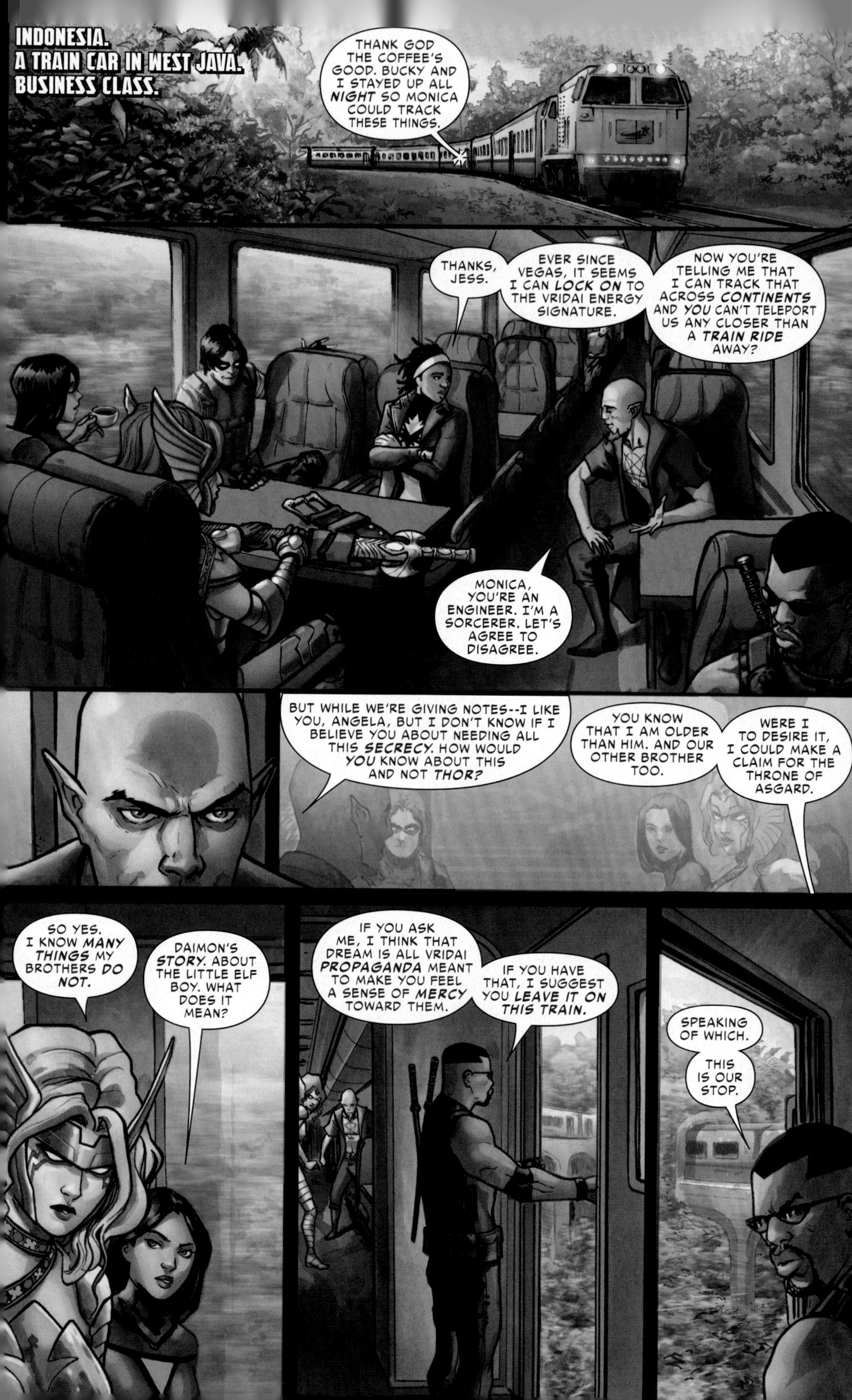
INDONESIA. A TRAIN CAR IN WEST JAVA. BUSINESS CLASS.
THANK GOD THE COFFEE'S GOOD. BUCKY AND I STAYED UP ALL NIGHT SO MONICA COULD TRACK THESE THINGS.
THANKS, JESS.
EVER SINCE VEGAS, IT SEEMS I CAN LOCK ON TO THE VRIDAI ENERGY SIGNATURE.
NOW YOU'RE TELLING ME THAT I CAN TRACK THAT ACROSS CONTINENTS AND YOU CAN'T TELEPORT US ANY CLOSER THAN A TRAIN RIDE AWAY?
MONICA, YOU'RE AN ENGINEER. I'M A SORCERER. LET'S AGREE TO DISAGREE.
BUT WHILE WE'RE GIVING NOTES--I LIKE YOU, ANGELA, BUT I DON'T KNOW IF I BELIEVE YOU ABOUT NEEDING ALL THIS SECRECY. HOW WOULD YOU KNOW ABOUT THIS AND NOT THOR?
YOU KNOW THAT I AM OLDER THAN HIM. AND OUR OTHER BROTHER TOO.
WERE I TO DESIRE IT, I COULD MAKE A CLAIM FOR THE THRONE OF ASGARD.
SO YES. I KNOW MANY THINGS MY BROTHERS DO NOT.
DAIMON'S STORY. ABOUT THE LITTLE ELF BOY. WHAT DOES IT MEAN?
IF YOU ASK ME, I THINK THAT DREAM IS ALL VRIDAI PROPAGANDA MEANT TO MAKE YOU FEEL A SENSE OF MERCY TOWARD THEM.
IF YOU HAVE THAT, I SUGGEST YOU LEAVE IT ON THIS TRAIN.
SPEAKING OF WHICH.
THIS IS OUR STOP.

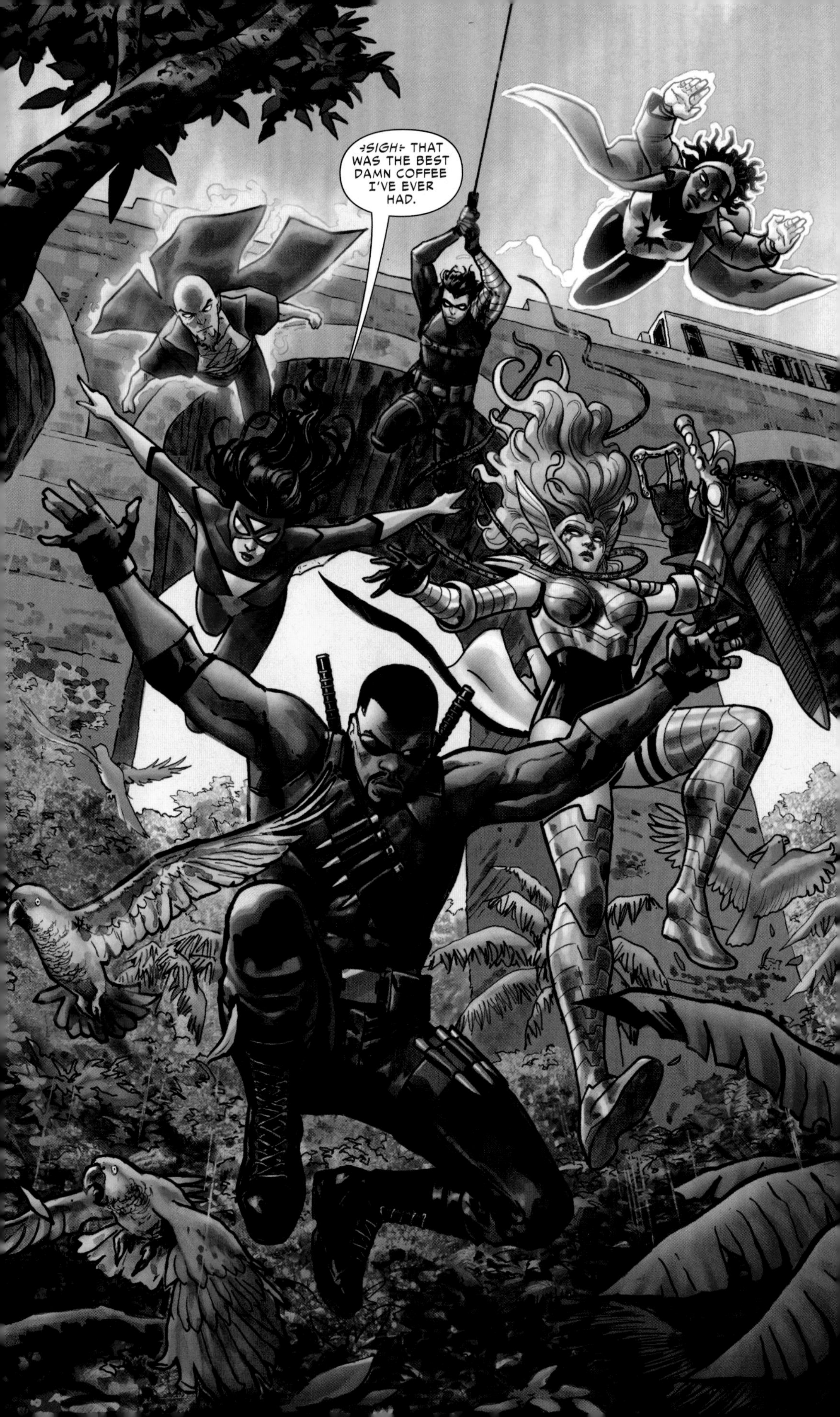

=SIGH= THAT WAS THE BEST DAMN COFFEE I'VE EVER HAD.

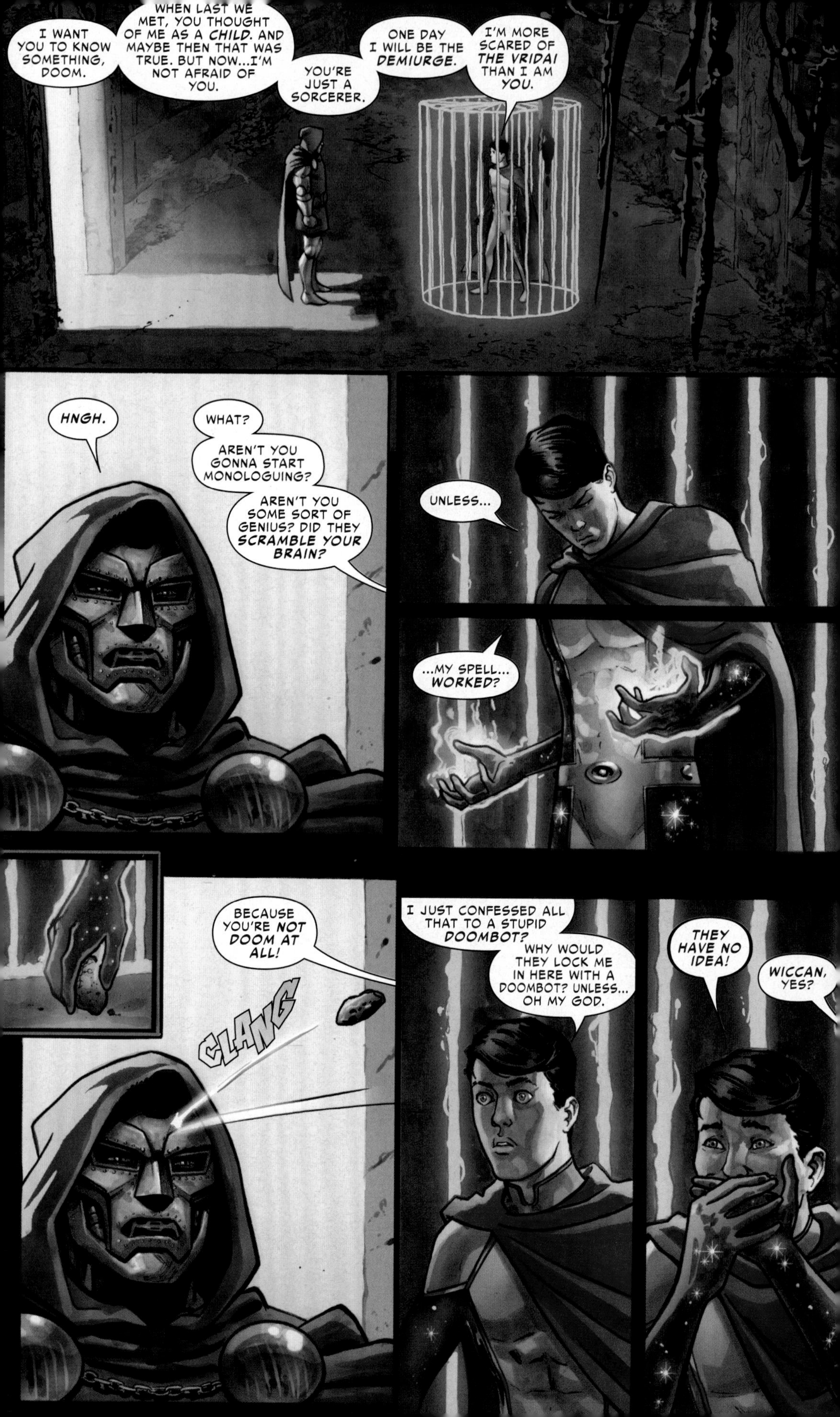
I WANT YOU TO KNOW SOMETHING, DOOM.
WHEN LAST WE MET, YOU THOUGHT OF ME AS A CHILD. AND MAYBE THEN THAT WAS TRUE. BUT NOW...I'M NOT AFRAID OF YOU.
YOU'RE JUST A SORCERER.
ONE DAY I WILL BE THE DEMIURGE.
I'M MORE SCARED OF THE VRIDAI THAN I AM YOU.
HNGH.
WHAT?
AREN'T YOU GONNA START MONOLOGUING?
AREN'T YOU SOME SORT OF GENIUS? DID THEY SCRAMBLE YOUR BRAIN?
UNLESS...
...MY SPELL... WORKED?
BECAUSE YOU'RE NOT DOOM AT ALL!
CLANG
I JUST CONFESSED ALL THAT TO A STUPID DOOMBOT?
WHY WOULD THEY LOCK ME IN HERE WITH A DOOMBOT? UNLESS... OH MY GOD.
THEY HAVE NO IDEA!
WICCAN, YES?

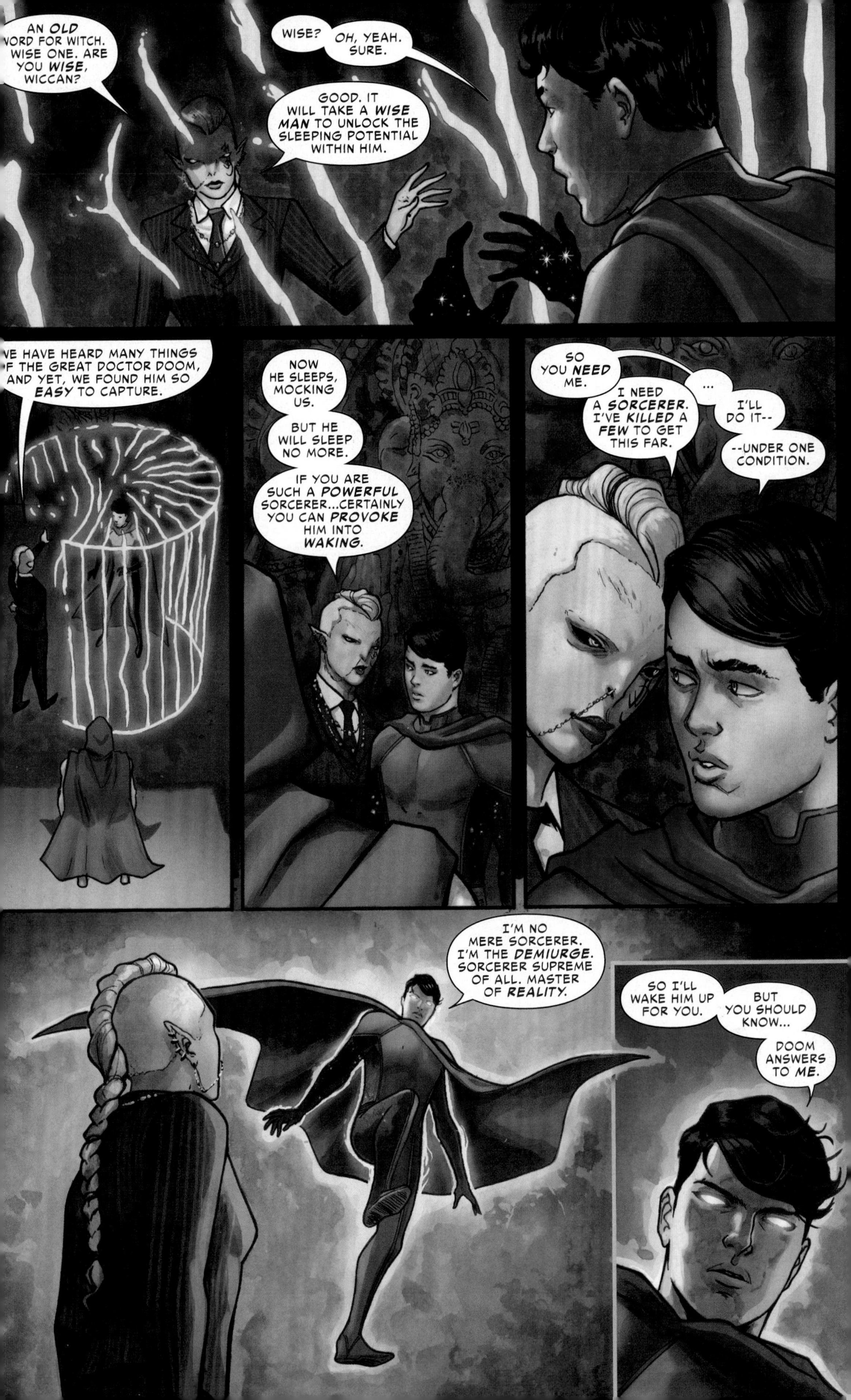
AN OLD WORD FOR WITCH. WISE ONE. ARE YOU WISE, WICCAN?
WISE?
OH, YEAH. SURE.
GOOD. IT WILL TAKE A WISE MAN TO UNLOCK THE SLEEPING POTENTIAL WITHIN HIM.
WE HAVE HEARD MANY THINGS OF THE GREAT DOCTOR DOOM, AND YET, WE FOUND HIM SO EASY TO CAPTURE.
NOW HE SLEEPS, MOCKING US.
BUT HE WILL SLEEP NO MORE.
IF YOU ARE SUCH A POWERFUL SORCERER...CERTAINLY YOU CAN PROVOKE HIM INTO WAKING.
SO YOU NEED ME.
I NEED A SORCERER. I'VE KILLED A FEW TO GET THIS FAR.
...
I'LL DO IT--
--UNDER ONE CONDITION.
I'M NO MERE SORCERER. I'M THE DEMIURGE. SORCERER SUPREME OF ALL. MASTER OF REALITY.
SO I'LL WAKE HIM UP FOR YOU.
BUT YOU SHOULD KNOW...
DOOM ANSWERS TO ME.

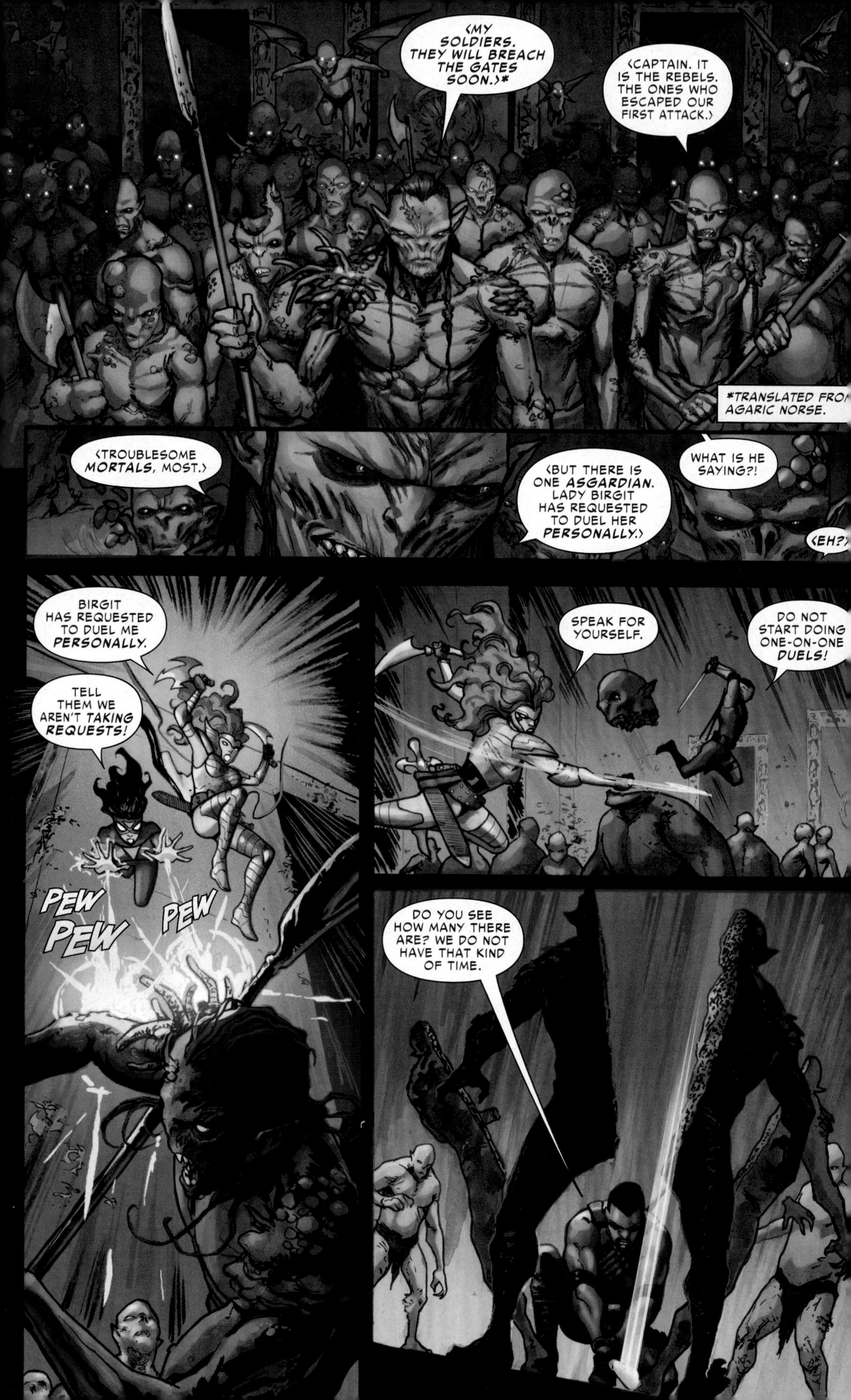
‹MY SOLDIERS. THEY WILL BREACH THE GATES SOON.›*
‹CAPTAIN. IT IS THE REBELS. THE ONES WHO ESCAPED OUR FIRST ATTACK.›
*TRANSLATED FROM AGARIC NORSE.
‹TROUBLESOME MORTALS, MOST.›
‹BUT THERE IS ONE ASGARDIAN. LADY BIRGIT HAS REQUESTED TO DUEL HER PERSONALLY.›
WHAT IS HE SAYING?!
‹EH?›
BIRGIT HAS REQUESTED TO DUEL ME PERSONALLY.
TELL THEM WE AREN'T TAKING REQUESTS!
PEW PEW
PEW
SPEAK FOR YOURSELF.
DO NOT START DOING ONE-ON-ONE DUELS!
DO YOU SEE HOW MANY THERE ARE? WE DO NOT HAVE THAT KIND OF TIME.

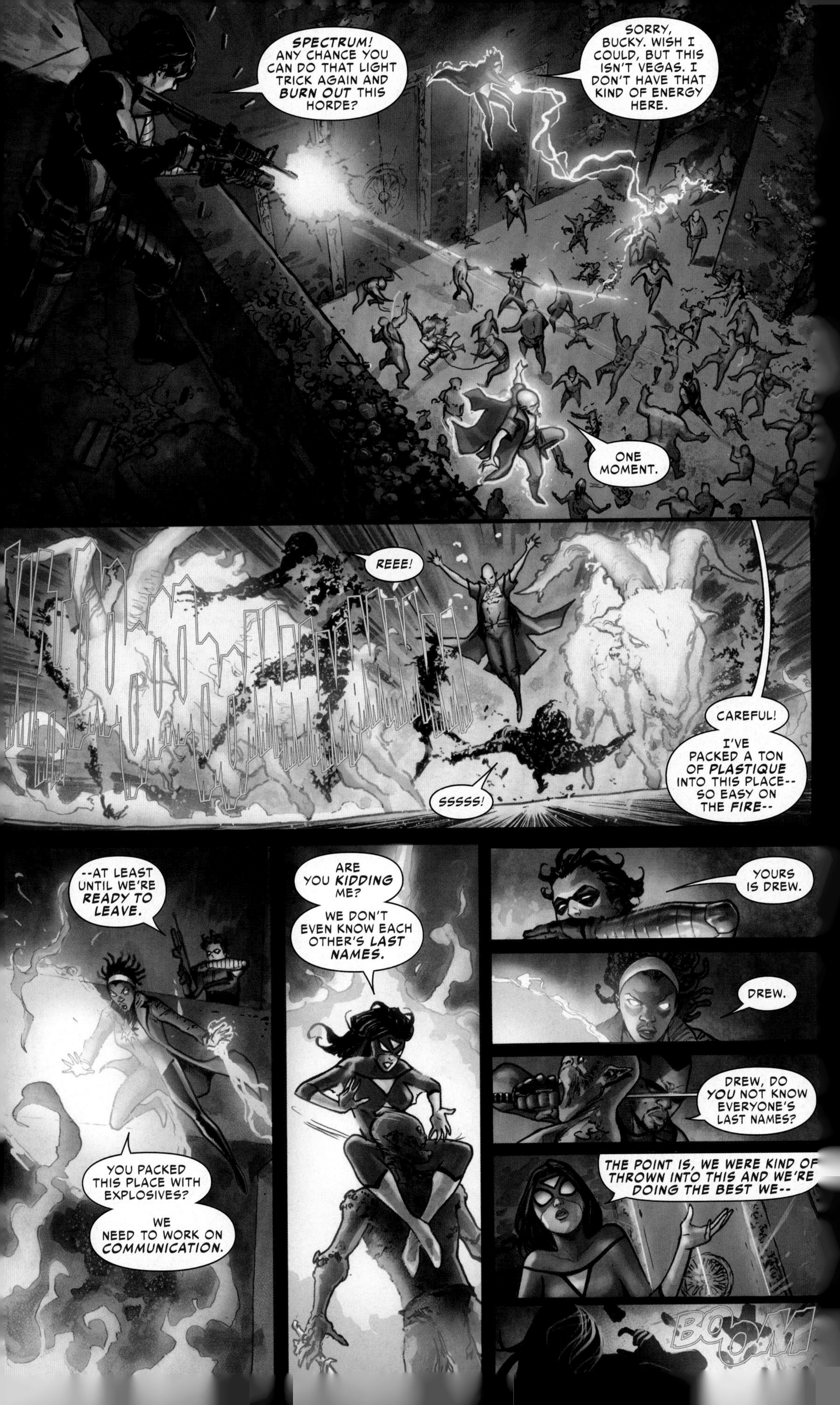

SPECTRUM! ANY CHANCE YOU CAN DO THAT LIGHT TRICK AGAIN AND BURN OUT THIS HORDE?
SORRY, BUCKY. WISH I COULD, BUT THIS ISN'T VEGAS. I DON'T HAVE THAT KIND OF ENERGY HERE.
ONE MOMENT.
REEE!
SSSSS!
CAREFUL!
I'VE PACKED A TON OF PLASTIQUE INTO THIS PLACE-- SO EASY ON THE FIRE--
--AT LEAST UNTIL WE'RE READY TO LEAVE.
YOU PACKED THIS PLACE WITH EXPLOSIVES?
WE NEED TO WORK ON COMMUNICATION.
ARE YOU KIDDING ME?
WE DON'T EVEN KNOW EACH OTHER'S LAST NAMES.
YOURS IS DREW.
DREW.
DREW, DO YOU NOT KNOW EVERYONE'S LAST NAMES?
THE POINT IS, WE WERE KIND OF THROWN INTO THIS AND WE'RE DOING THE BEST WE--
BOOM

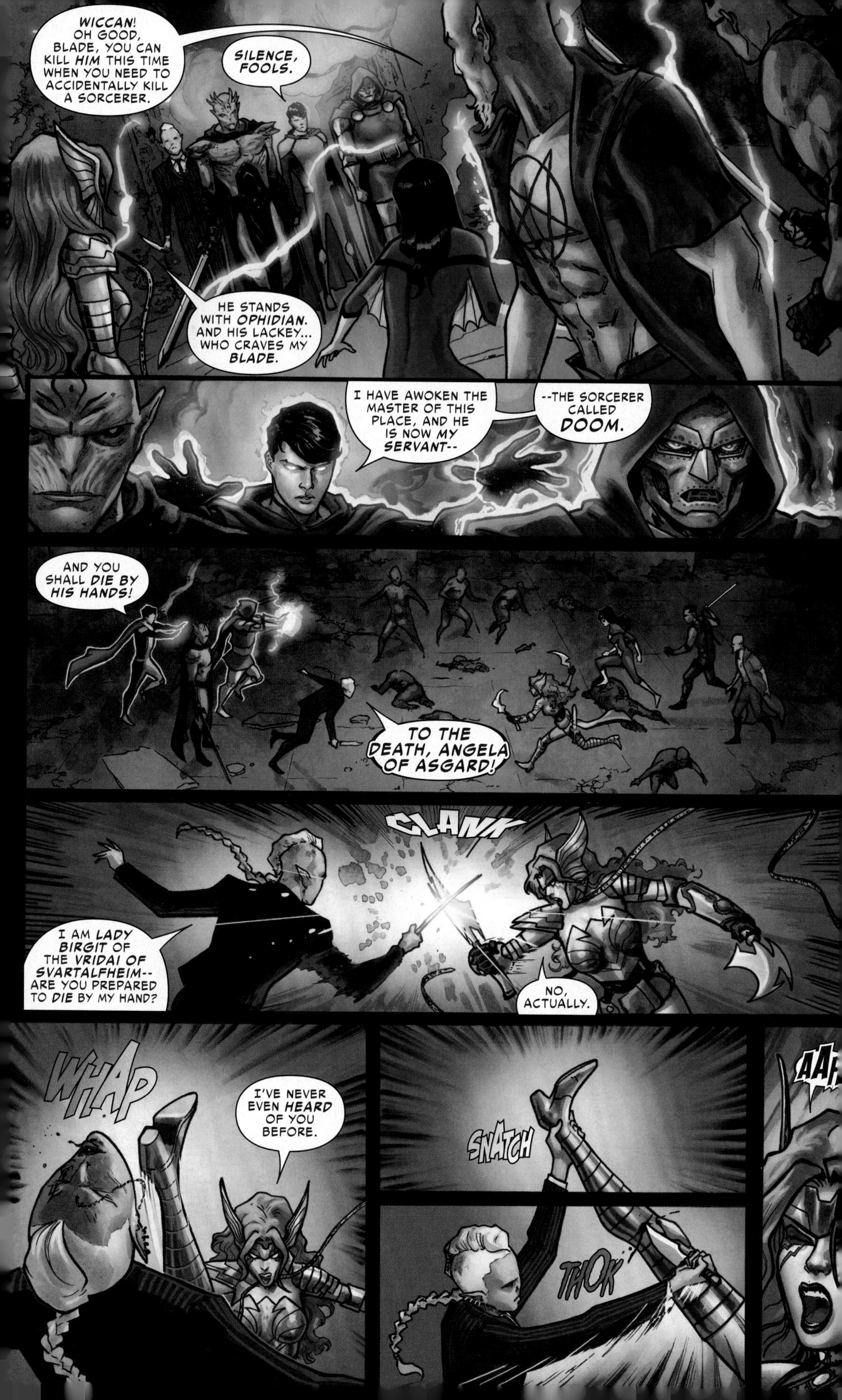

WICCAN! OH GOOD, BLADE, YOU CAN KILL HIM THIS TIME WHEN YOU NEED TO ACCIDENTALLY KILL A SORCERER.
SILENCE, FOOLS.
HE STANDS WITH OPHIDIAN. AND HIS LACKEY... WHO CRAVES MY BLADE.
I HAVE AWOKEN THE MASTER OF THIS PLACE, AND HE IS NOW MY SERVANT--
--THE SORCERER CALLED DOOM.
AND YOU SHALL DIE BY HIS HANDS!
TO THE DEATH, ANGELA OF ASGARD!
CLANK
I AM LADY BIRGIT OF THE VRIDAI OF SVARTALFHEIM-- ARE YOU PREPARED TO DIE BY MY HAND?
NO, ACTUALLY.
WHAP
I'VE NEVER EVEN HEARD OF YOU BEFORE.
SNATCH
THOK

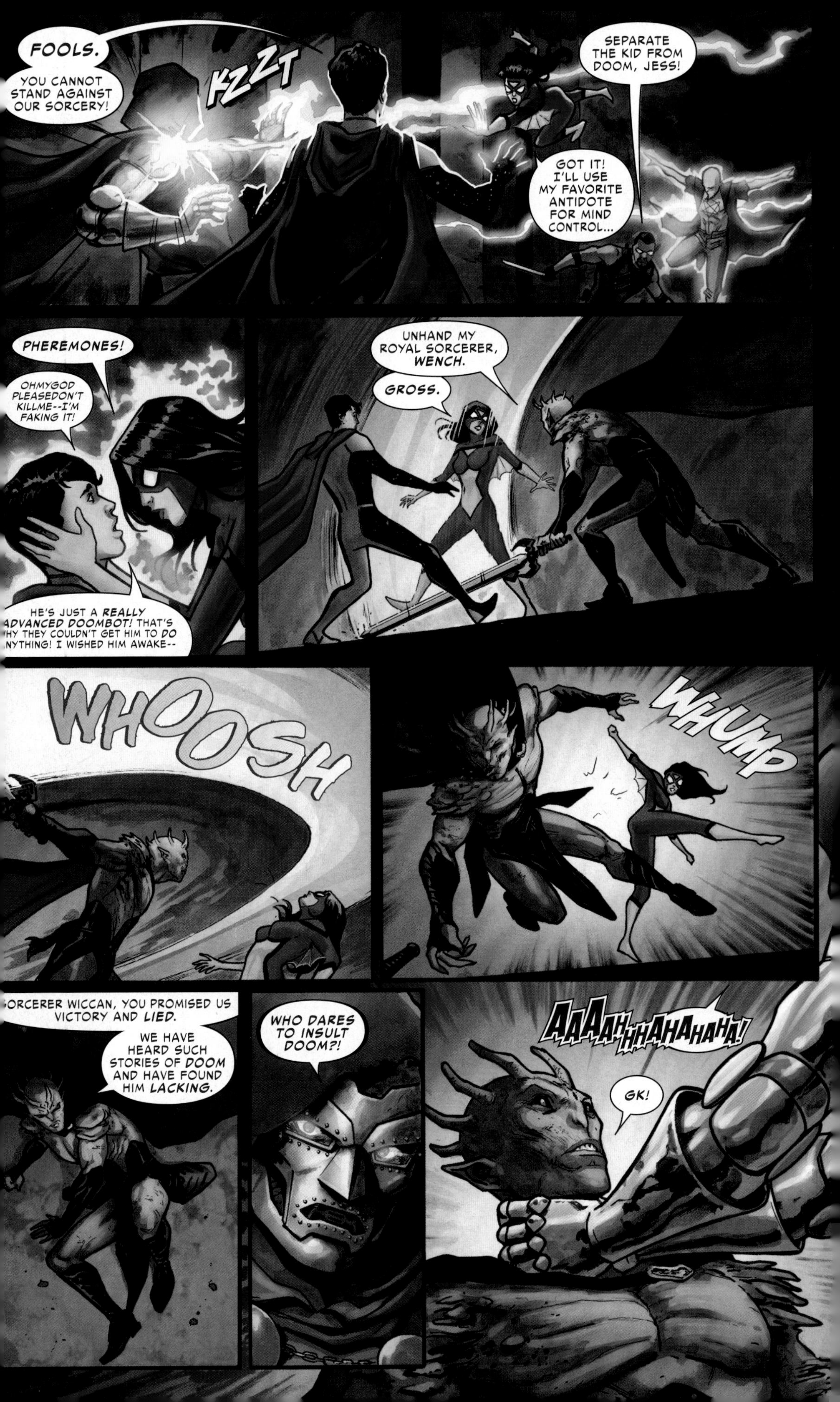
FOOLS.
YOU CANNOT STAND AGAINST OUR SORCERY!
KZZT
SEPARATE THE KID FROM DOOM, JESS!
GOT IT! I'LL USE MY FAVORITE ANTIDOTE FOR MIND CONTROL...
PHEREMONES!
OHMYGOD PLEASEDON'T KILLME--I'M FAKING IT!
HE'S JUST A REALLY ADVANCED DOOMBOT! THAT'S WHY THEY COULDN'T GET HIM TO DO ANYTHING! I WISHED HIM AWAKE--
UNHAND MY ROYAL SORCERER, WENCH.
GROSS.
WHOOSH
WHUMP
SORCERER WICCAN, YOU PROMISED US VICTORY AND LIED.
WE HAVE HEARD SUCH STORIES OF DOOM AND HAVE FOUND HIM LACKING.
WHO DARES TO INSULT DOOM?!
AAAAHHHAHAHAHA!
GK!

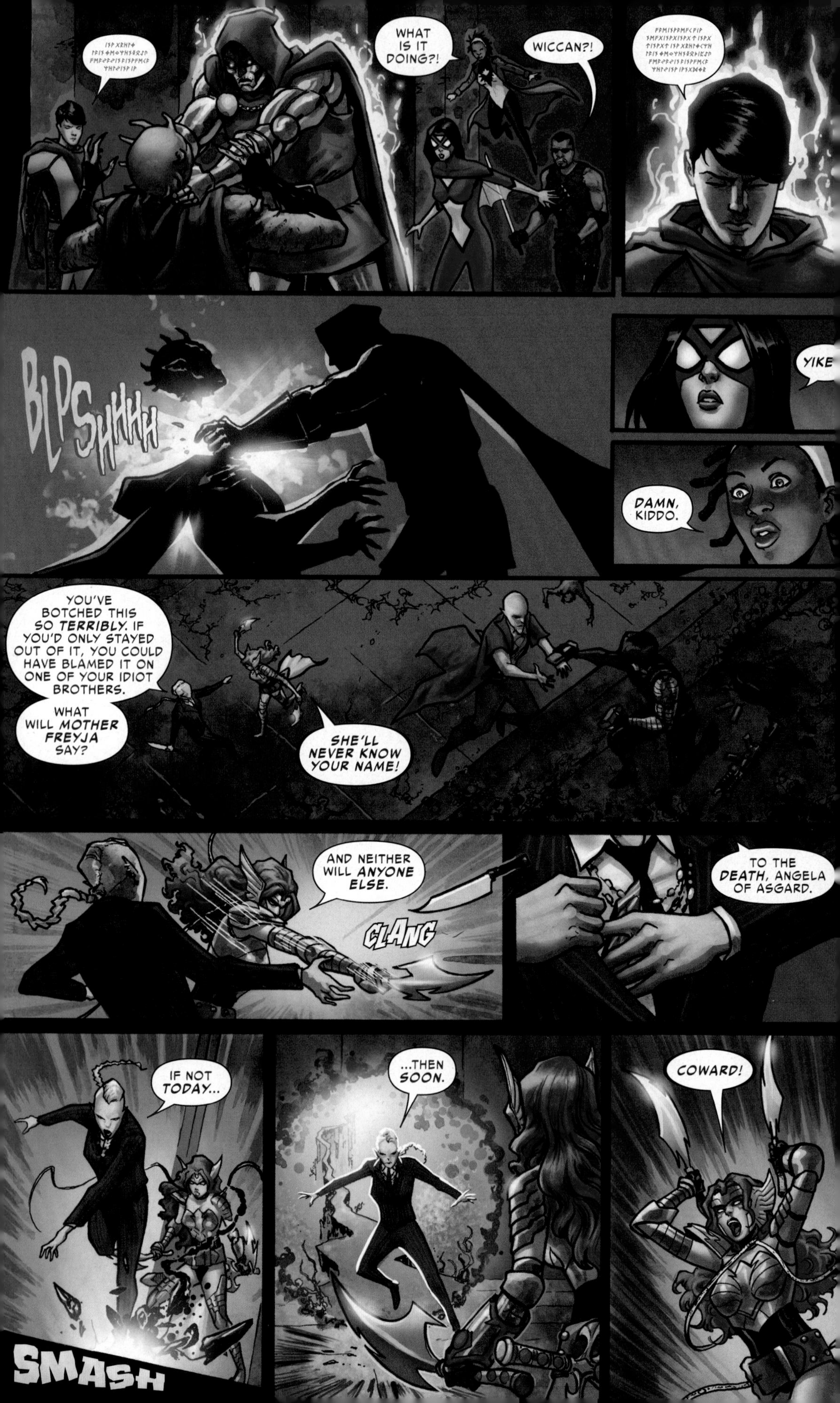
WHAT IS IT DOING?!
WICCAN?!
BLPSHHHH
YIKE
DAMN, KIDDO.
YOU'VE BOTCHED THIS SO TERRIBLY. IF YOU'D ONLY STAYED OUT OF IT, YOU COULD HAVE BLAMED IT ON ONE OF YOUR IDIOT BROTHERS.
WHAT WILL MOTHER FREYJA SAY?
SHE'LL NEVER KNOW YOUR NAME!
AND NEITHER WILL ANYONE ELSE.
CLANG
TO THE DEATH, ANGELA OF ASGARD.
IF NOT TODAY...
SMASH
...THEN SOON.
COWARD!

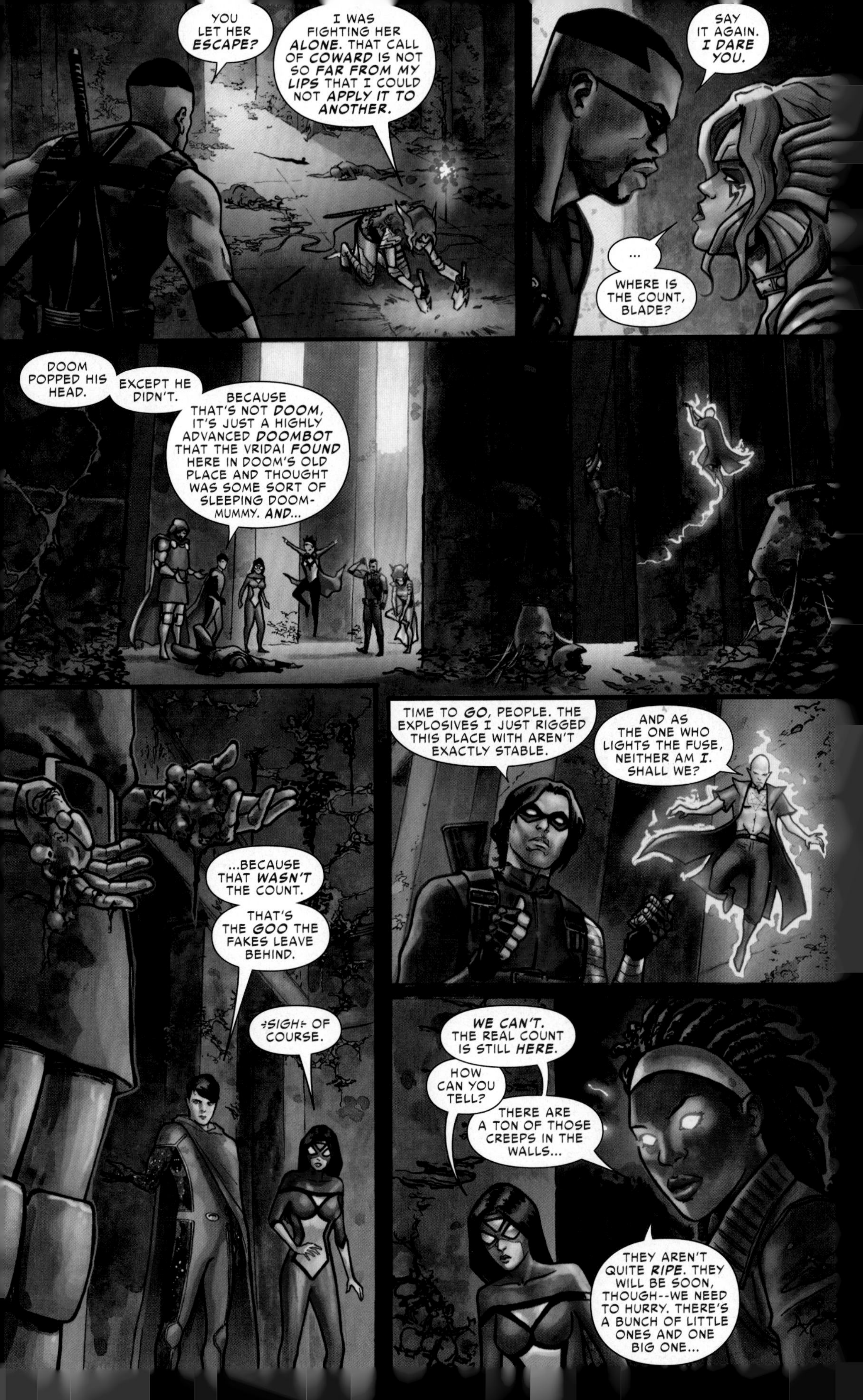
YOU LET HER ESCAPE?
I WAS FIGHTING HER ALONE. THAT CALL OF COWARD IS NOT SO FAR FROM MY LIPS THAT I COULD NOT APPLY IT TO ANOTHER.
SAY IT AGAIN. I DARE YOU.
...
WHERE IS THE COUNT, BLADE?
DOOM POPPED HIS HEAD.
EXCEPT HE DIDN'T.
BECAUSE THAT'S NOT DOOM, IT'S JUST A HIGHLY ADVANCED DOOMBOT THAT THE VRIDAI FOUND HERE IN DOOM'S OLD PLACE AND THOUGHT WAS SOME SORT OF SLEEPING DOOM-MUMMY. AND...
...BECAUSE THAT WASN'T THE COUNT.
THAT'S THE GOO THE FAKES LEAVE BEHIND.
-SIGH- OF COURSE.
TIME TO GO, PEOPLE. THE EXPLOSIVES I JUST RIGGED THIS PLACE WITH AREN'T EXACTLY STABLE.
AND AS THE ONE WHO LIGHTS THE FUSE, NEITHER AM I. SHALL WE?
WE CAN'T. THE REAL COUNT IS STILL HERE.
HOW CAN YOU TELL?
THERE ARE A TON OF THOSE CREEPS IN THE WALLS...
THEY AREN'T QUITE RIPE. THEY WILL BE SOON, THOUGH--WE NEED TO HURRY. THERE'S A BUNCH OF LITTLE ONES AND ONE BIG ONE...

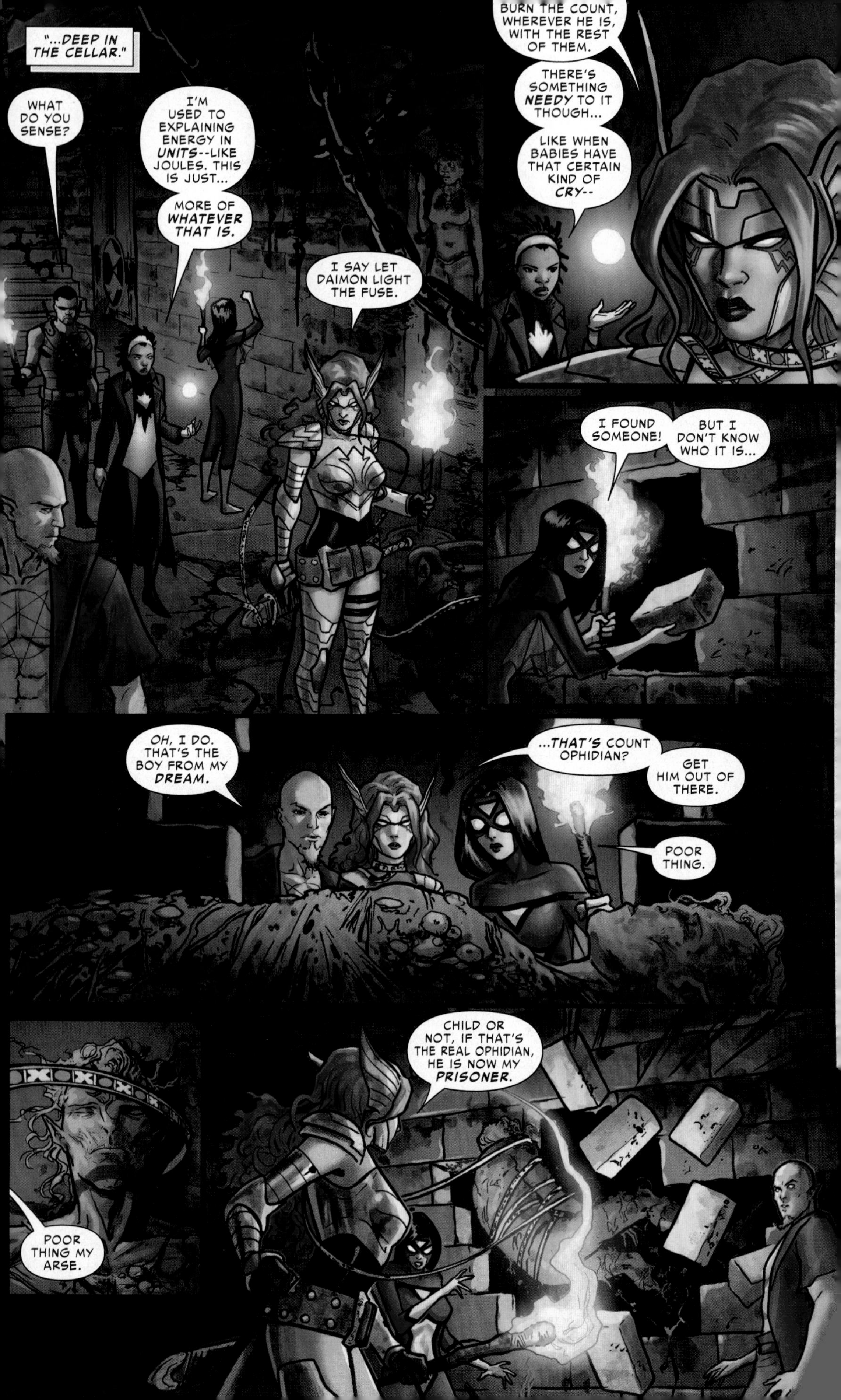
"...DEEP IN THE CELLAR."
WHAT DO YOU SENSE?
I'M USED TO EXPLAINING ENERGY IN UNITS--LIKE JOULES. THIS IS JUST...
MORE OF WHATEVER THAT IS.
I SAY LET DAIMON LIGHT THE FUSE.
BURN THE COUNT, WHEREVER HE IS, WITH THE REST OF THEM.
THERE'S SOMETHING NEEDY TO IT THOUGH...
LIKE WHEN BABIES HAVE THAT CERTAIN KIND OF CRY--
I FOUND SOMEONE!
BUT I DON'T KNOW WHO IT IS...
OH, I DO. THAT'S THE BOY FROM MY DREAM.
...THAT'S COUNT OPHIDIAN?
GET HIM OUT OF THERE.
POOR THING.
POOR THING MY ARSE.
CHILD OR NOT, IF THAT'S THE REAL OPHIDIAN, HE IS NOW MY PRISONER.

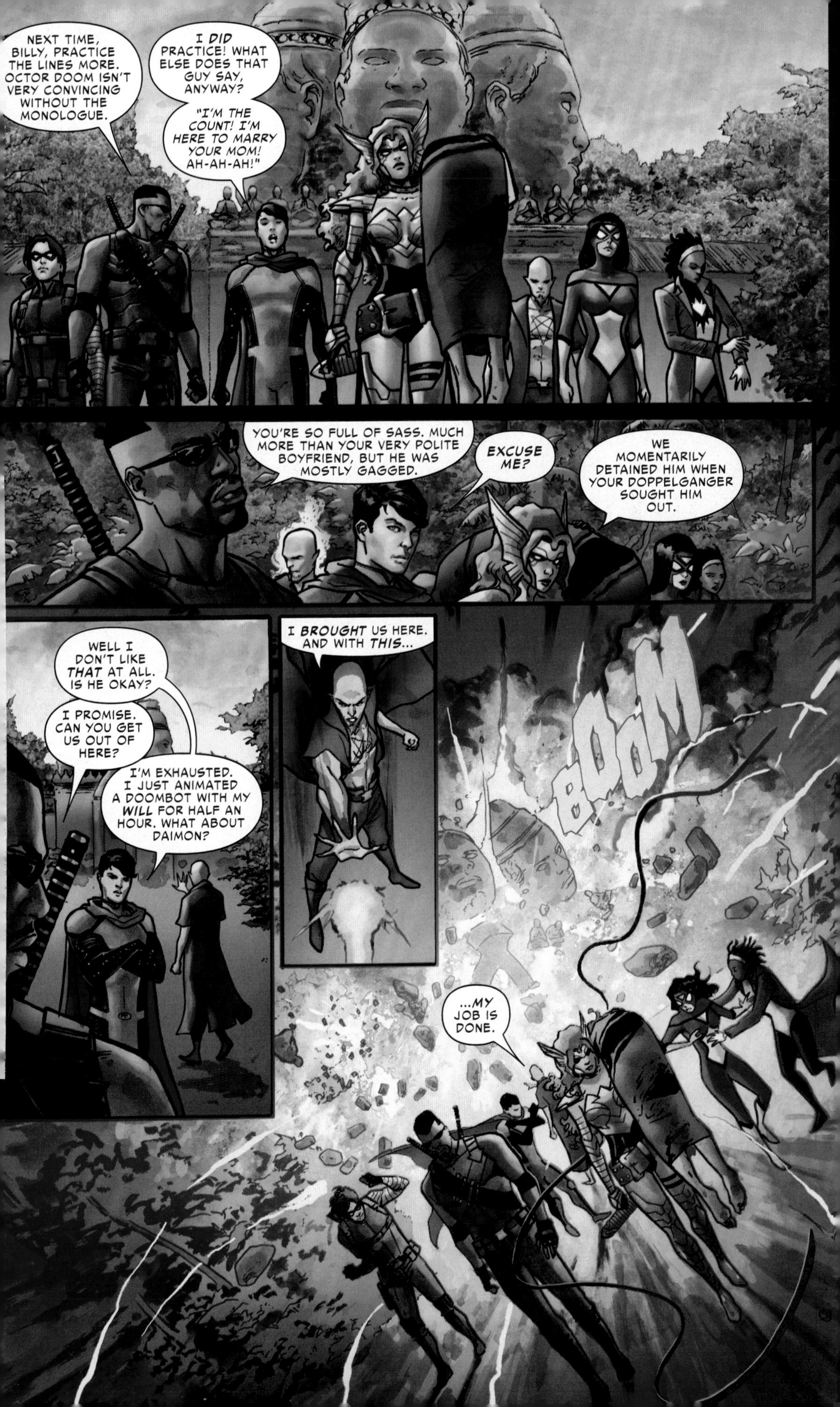
NEXT TIME, BILLY, PRACTICE THE LINES MORE. OCTOR DOOM ISN'T VERY CONVINCING WITHOUT THE MONOLOGUE.
I *DID* PRACTICE! WHAT ELSE DOES THAT GUY SAY, ANYWAY?
"I'M THE COUNT! I'M HERE TO MARRY YOUR MOM! AH-AH-AH!"
YOU'RE SO FULL OF SASS. MUCH MORE THAN YOUR VERY POLITE BOYFRIEND, BUT HE WAS MOSTLY GAGGED.
EXCUSE ME?
WE MOMENTARILY DETAINED HIM WHEN YOUR DOPPELGANGER SOUGHT HIM OUT.
WELL I DON'T LIKE *THAT* AT ALL. IS HE OKAY?
I PROMISE. CAN YOU GET US OUT OF HERE?
I'M EXHAUSTED. I JUST ANIMATED A DOOMBOT WITH MY *WILL* FOR HALF AN HOUR. WHAT ABOUT DAIMON?
I *BROUGHT* US HERE. AND WITH *THIS*...
BOOM
...MY JOB IS DONE.

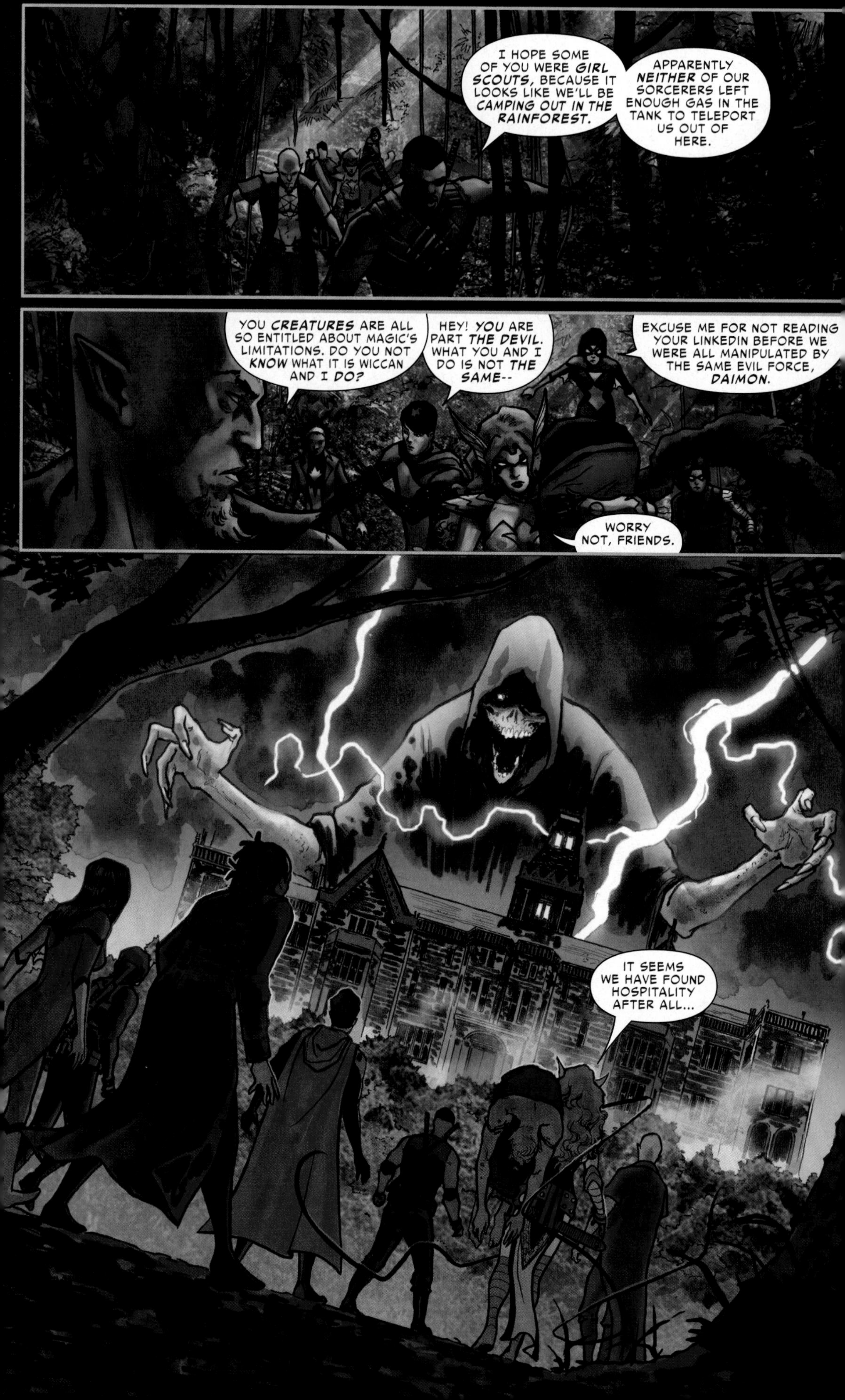
I HOPE SOME OF YOU WERE GIRL SCOUTS, BECAUSE IT LOOKS LIKE WE'LL BE CAMPING OUT IN THE RAINFOREST.
APPARENTLY NEITHER OF OUR SORCERERS LEFT ENOUGH GAS IN THE TANK TO TELEPORT US OUT OF HERE.
YOU CREATURES ARE ALL SO ENTITLED ABOUT MAGIC'S LIMITATIONS. DO YOU NOT KNOW WHAT IT IS WICCAN AND I DO?
HEY! YOU ARE PART THE DEVIL. WHAT YOU AND I DO IS NOT THE SAME--
EXCUSE ME FOR NOT READING YOUR LINKEDIN BEFORE WE WERE ALL MANIPULATED BY THE SAME EVIL FORCE, DAIMON.
WORRY NOT, FRIENDS.
IT SEEMS WE HAVE FOUND HOSPITALITY AFTER ALL...

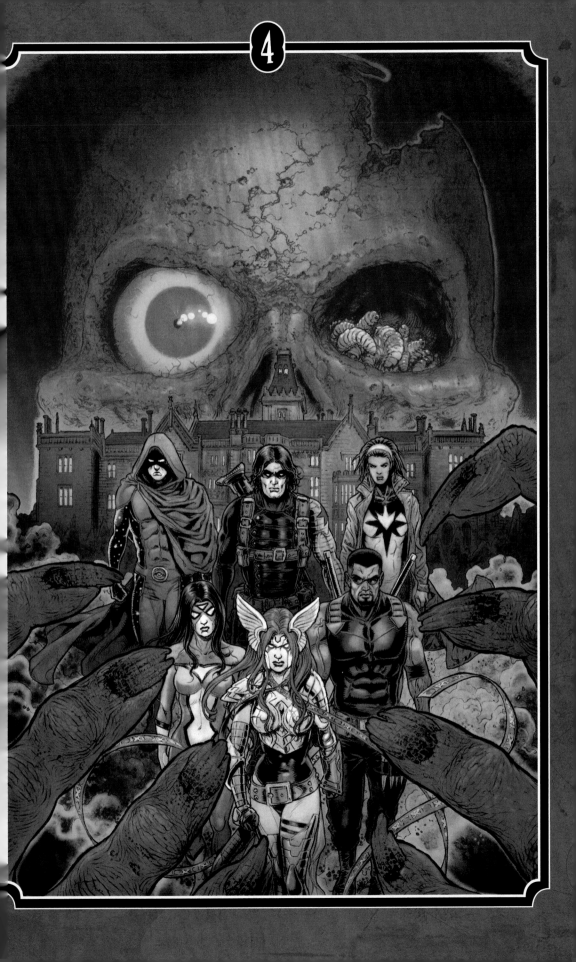

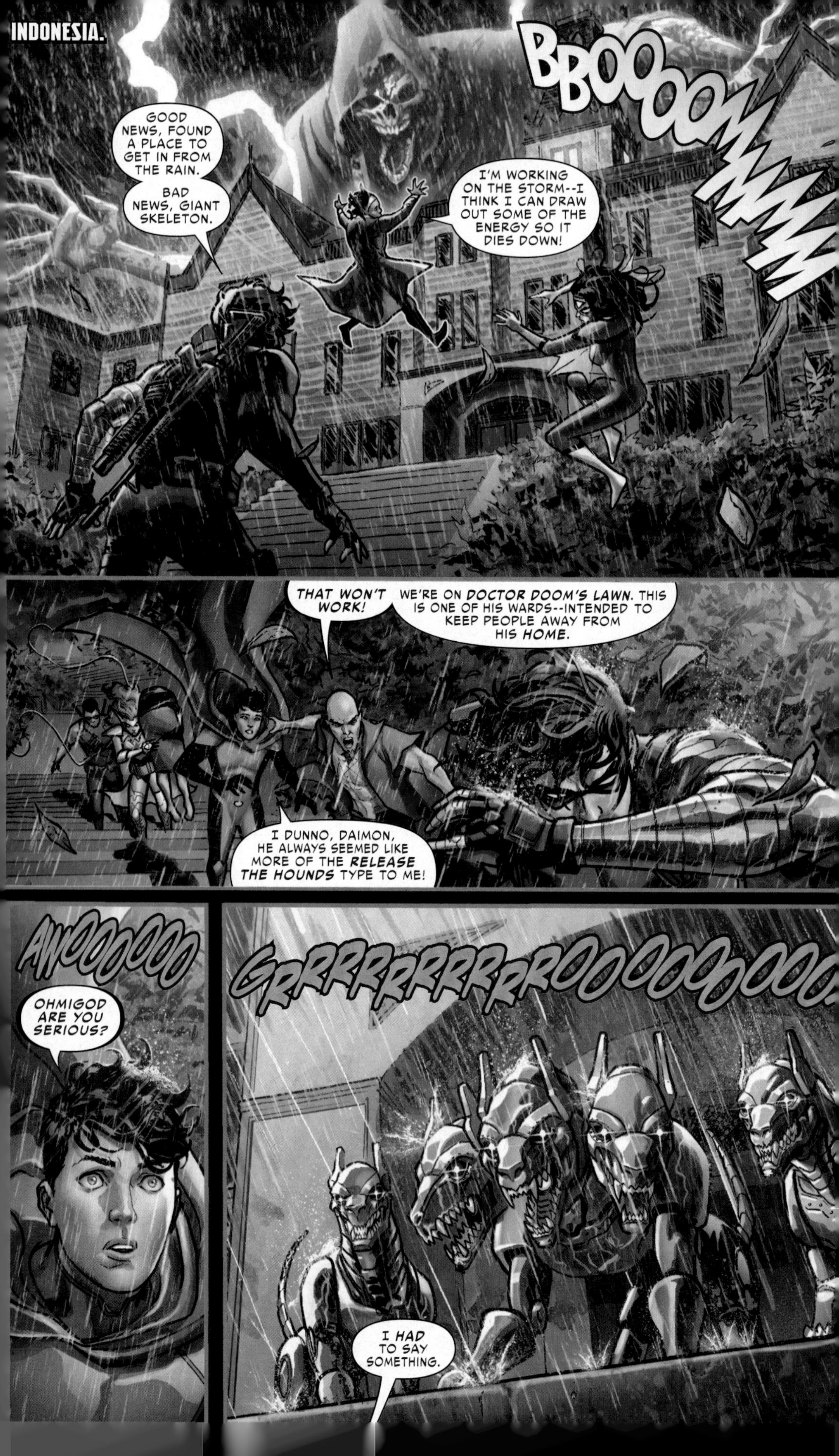
INDONESIA.
GOOD NEWS, FOUND A PLACE TO GET IN FROM THE RAIN.
BAD NEWS, GIANT SKELETON.
I'M WORKING ON THE STORM--I THINK I CAN DRAW OUT SOME OF THE ENERGY SO IT DIES DOWN!
BBOOOOOMMMM
THAT WON'T WORK!
WE'RE ON DOCTOR DOOM'S LAWN. THIS IS ONE OF HIS WARDS--INTENDED TO KEEP PEOPLE AWAY FROM HIS HOME.
I DUNNO, DAIMON, HE ALWAYS SEEMED LIKE MORE OF THE RELEASE THE HOUNDS TYPE TO ME!
AWOOOOOO
OHMIGOD ARE YOU SERIOUS?
GRRRRRRRRROOOOOOOOO
I HAD TO SAY SOMETHING.

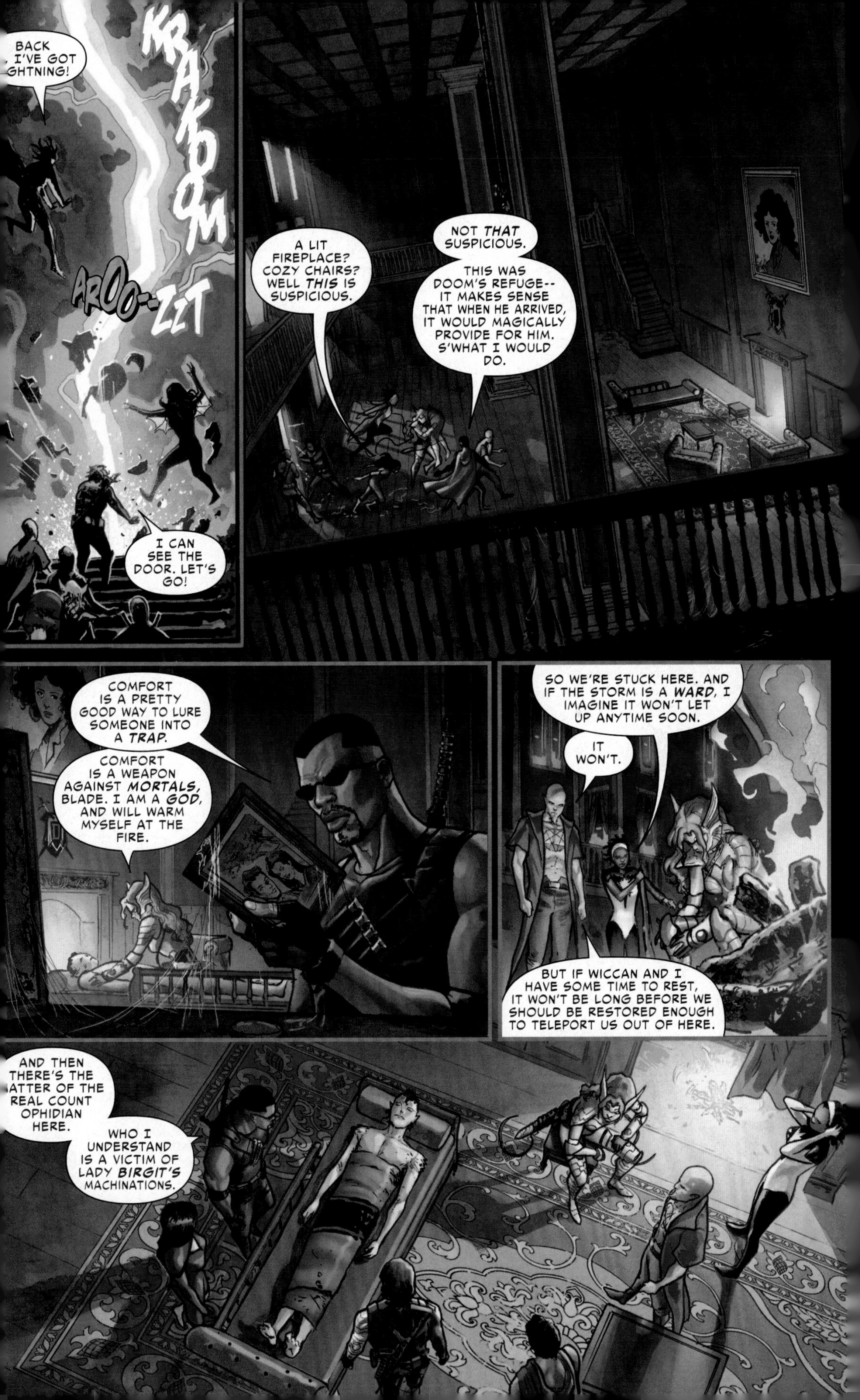

BACK
, I'VE GOT
GHTNING!
KRAKOOM
AROO--ZZT
I CAN SEE THE DOOR. LET'S GO!
A LIT FIREPLACE? COZY CHAIRS? WELL THIS IS SUSPICIOUS.
NOT THAT SUSPICIOUS.
THIS WAS DOOM'S REFUGE-- IT MAKES SENSE THAT WHEN HE ARRIVED, IT WOULD MAGICALLY PROVIDE FOR HIM. S'WHAT I WOULD DO.
COMFORT IS A PRETTY GOOD WAY TO LURE SOMEONE INTO A TRAP.
COMFORT IS A WEAPON AGAINST MORTALS, BLADE. I AM A GOD, AND WILL WARM MYSELF AT THE FIRE.
SO WE'RE STUCK HERE. AND IF THE STORM IS A WARD, I IMAGINE IT WON'T LET UP ANYTIME SOON.
IT WON'T.
BUT IF WICCAN AND I HAVE SOME TIME TO REST, IT WON'T BE LONG BEFORE WE SHOULD BE RESTORED ENOUGH TO TELEPORT US OUT OF HERE.
AND THEN THERE'S THE ATTER OF THE REAL COUNT OPHIDIAN HERE.
WHO I UNDERSTAND IS A VICTIM OF LADY BIRGIT'S MACHINATIONS.

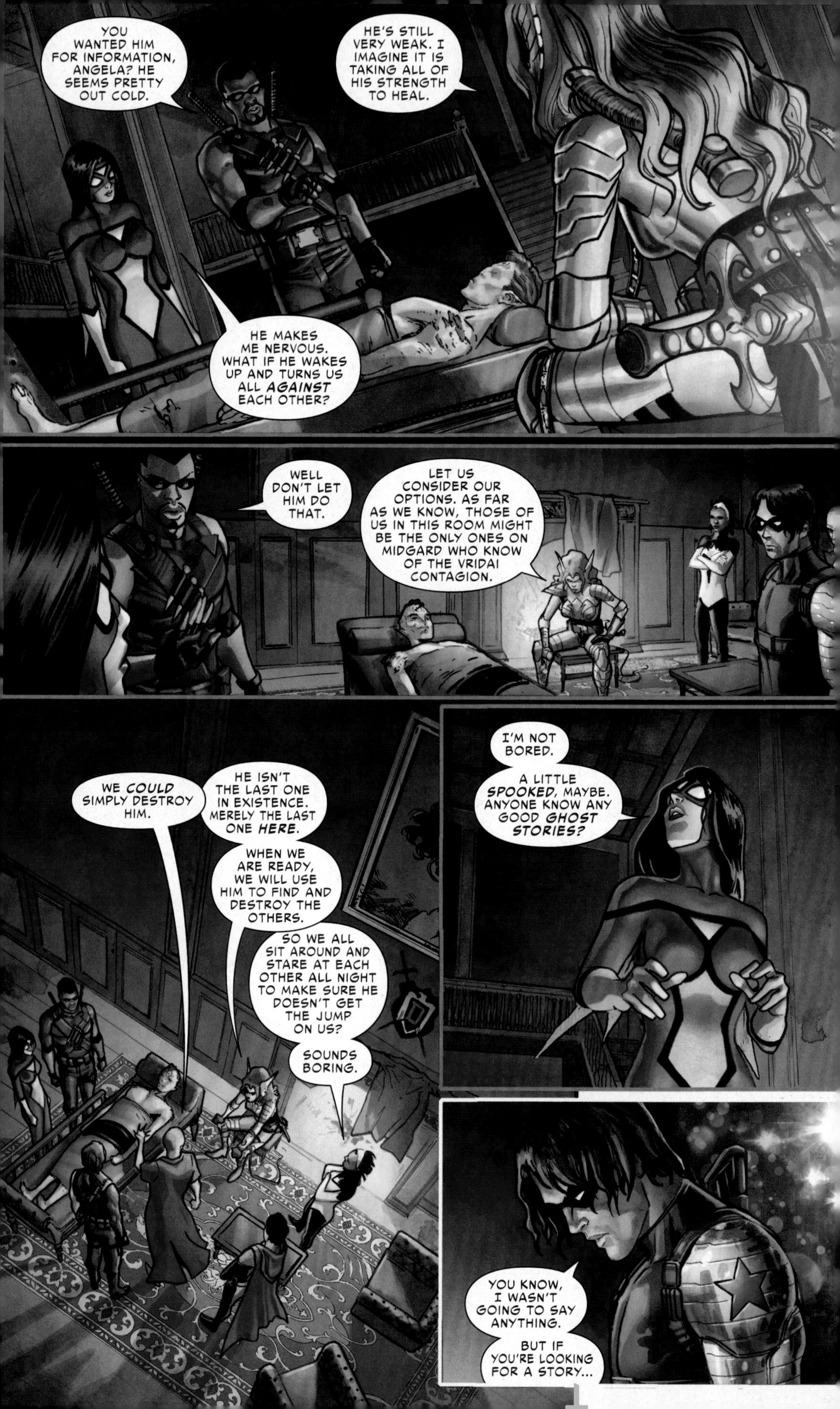
YOU WANTED HIM FOR INFORMATION, ANGELA? HE SEEMS PRETTY OUT COLD.
HE'S STILL VERY WEAK. I IMAGINE IT IS TAKING ALL OF HIS STRENGTH TO HEAL.
HE MAKES ME NERVOUS. WHAT IF HE WAKES UP AND TURNS US ALL *AGAINST* EACH OTHER?
WELL DON'T LET HIM DO THAT.
LET US CONSIDER OUR OPTIONS. AS FAR AS WE KNOW, THOSE OF US IN THIS ROOM MIGHT BE THE ONLY ONES ON MIDGARD WHO KNOW OF THE VRIDAI CONTAGION.
WE *COULD* SIMPLY DESTROY HIM.
HE ISN'T THE LAST ONE IN EXISTENCE. MERELY THE LAST ONE *HERE*.
WHEN WE ARE READY, WE WILL USE HIM TO FIND AND DESTROY THE OTHERS.
SO WE ALL SIT AROUND AND STARE AT EACH OTHER ALL NIGHT TO MAKE SURE HE DOESN'T GET THE JUMP ON US?
SOUNDS BORING.
I'M NOT BORED.
A LITTLE *SPOOKED*, MAYBE. ANYONE KNOW ANY GOOD *GHOST STORIES?*
YOU KNOW, I WASN'T GOING TO SAY ANYTHING.
BUT IF YOU'RE LOOKING FOR A STORY...

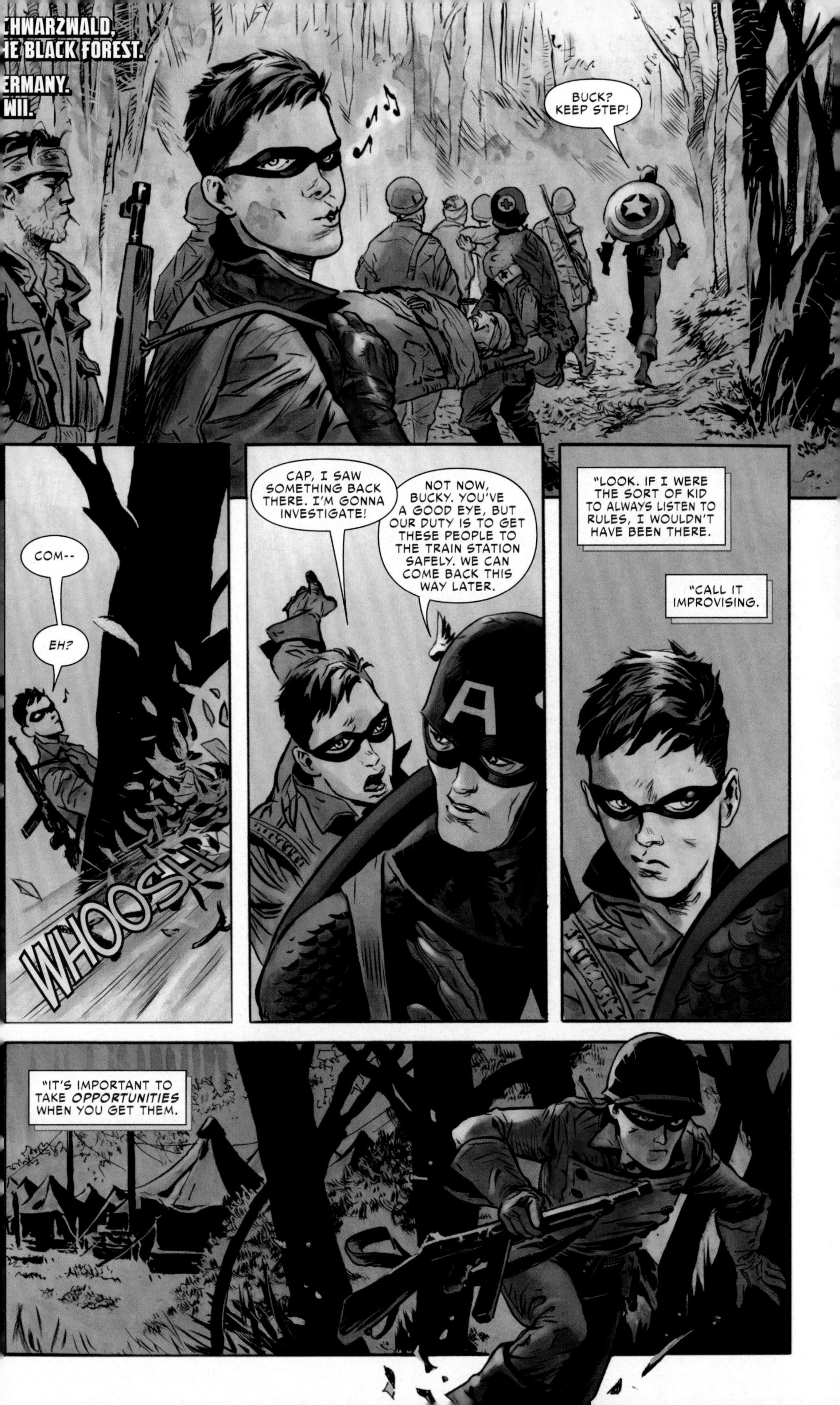
CHWARZWALD,
HE BLACK FOREST.
ERMANY.
WII.
BUCK? KEEP STEP!
COM--
EH?
WHOOSH
CAP, I SAW SOMETHING BACK THERE. I'M GONNA INVESTIGATE!
NOT NOW, BUCKY. YOU'VE A GOOD EYE, BUT OUR DUTY IS TO GET THESE PEOPLE TO THE TRAIN STATION SAFELY. WE CAN COME BACK THIS WAY LATER.
"LOOK. IF I WERE THE SORT OF KID TO ALWAYS LISTEN TO RULES, I WOULDN'T HAVE BEEN THERE.
"CALL IT IMPROVISING.
"IT'S IMPORTANT TO TAKE *OPPORTUNITIES* WHEN YOU GET THEM.

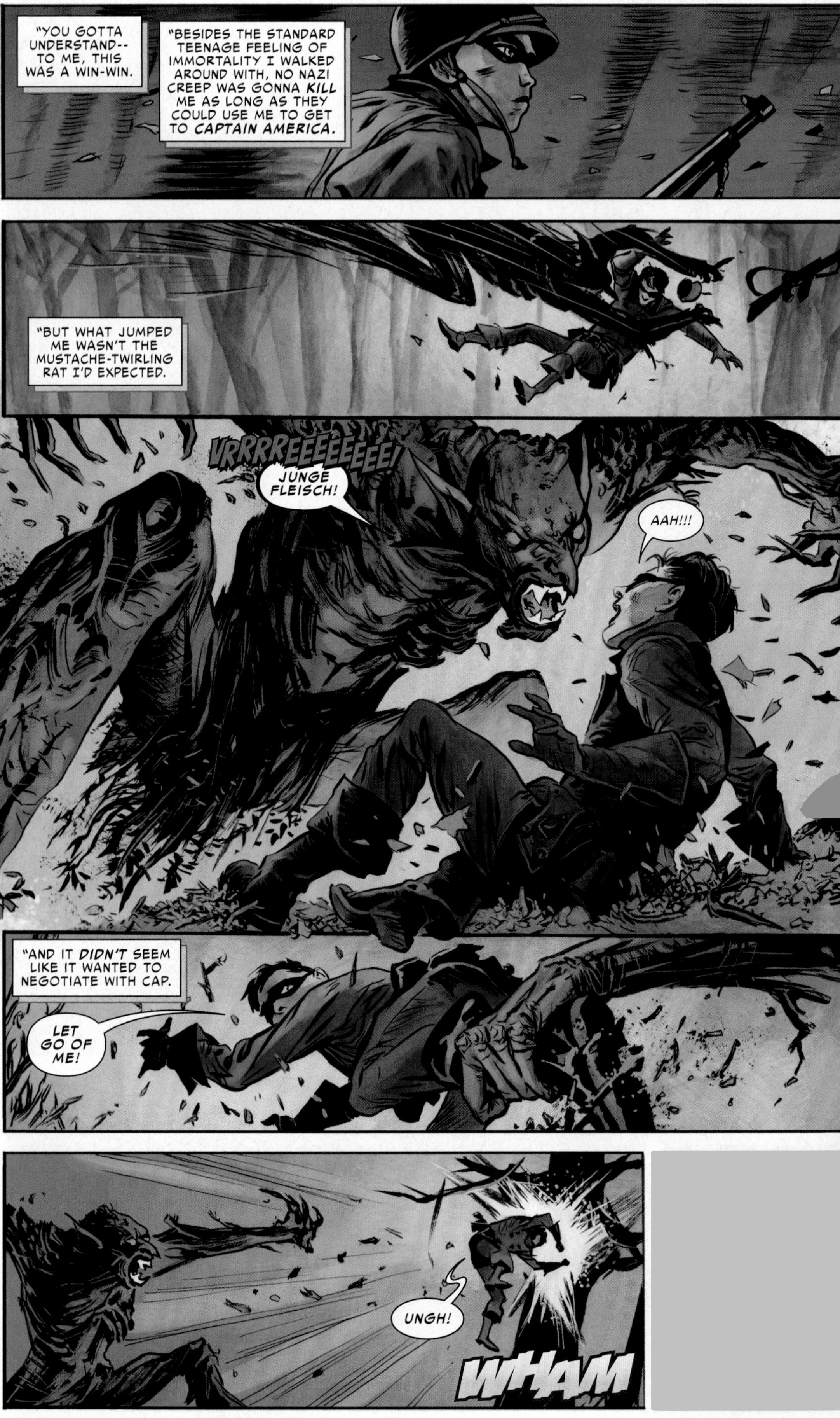

"YOU GOTTA UNDERSTAND-- TO ME, THIS WAS A WIN-WIN.
"BESIDES THE STANDARD TEENAGE FEELING OF IMMORTALITY I WALKED AROUND WITH, NO NAZI CREEP WAS GONNA KILL ME AS LONG AS THEY COULD USE ME TO GET TO CAPTAIN AMERICA.
"BUT WHAT JUMPED ME WASN'T THE MUSTACHE-TWIRLING RAT I'D EXPECTED.
VRRRREEEEEEEEE!
JUNGE FLEISCH!
AAH!!!
"AND IT DIDN'T SEEM LIKE IT WANTED TO NEGOTIATE WITH CAP.
LET GO OF ME!
UNGH!
WHAM

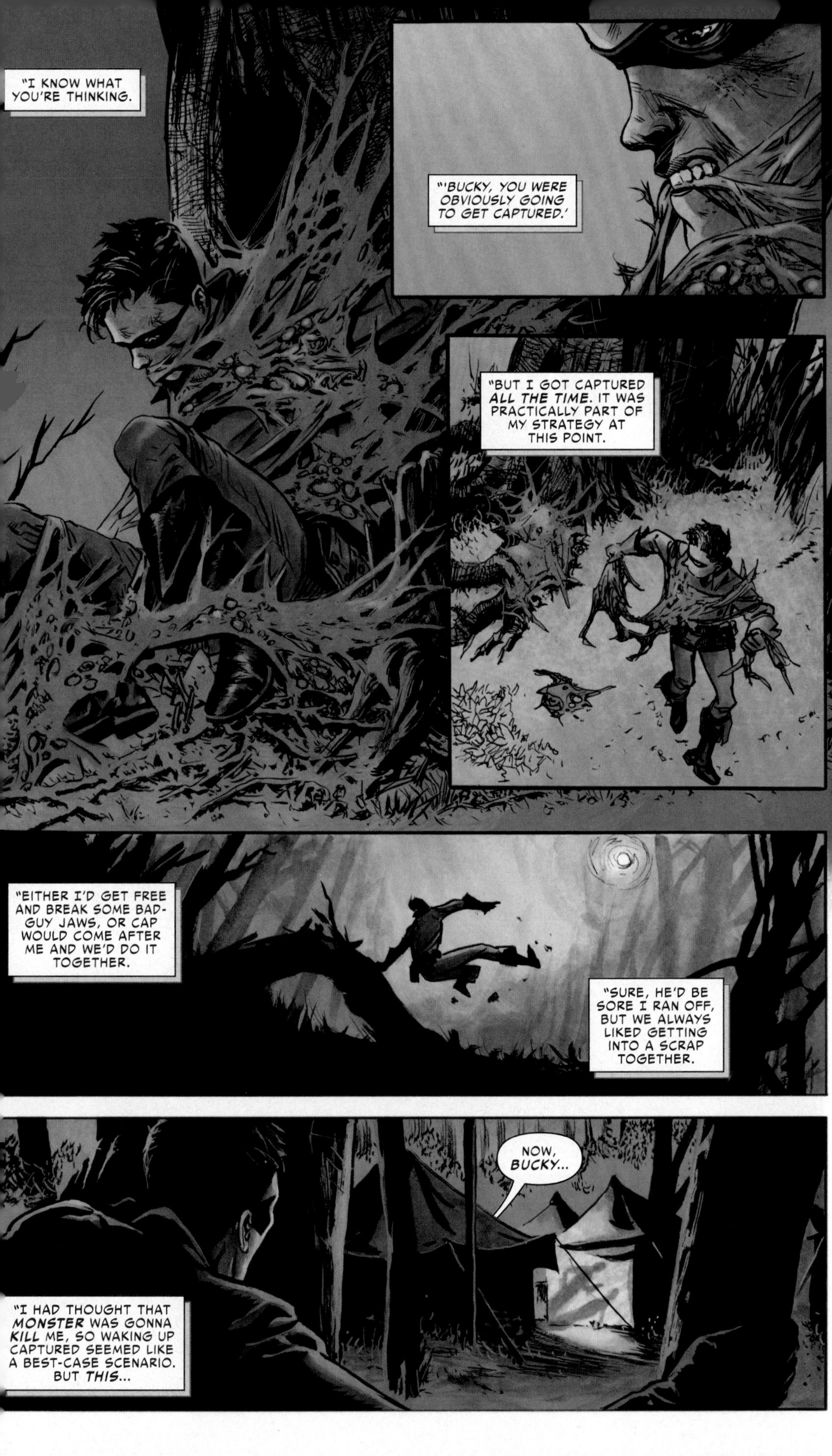
"I KNOW WHAT YOU'RE THINKING.
"'BUCKY, YOU WERE OBVIOUSLY GOING TO GET CAPTURED.'
"BUT I GOT CAPTURED ALL THE TIME. IT WAS PRACTICALLY PART OF MY STRATEGY AT THIS POINT.
"EITHER I'D GET FREE AND BREAK SOME BAD-GUY JAWS, OR CAP WOULD COME AFTER ME AND WE'D DO IT TOGETHER.
"SURE, HE'D BE SORE I RAN OFF, BUT WE ALWAYS LIKED GETTING INTO A SCRAP TOGETHER.
NOW, BUCKY...
"I HAD THOUGHT THAT MONSTER WAS GONNA KILL ME, SO WAKING UP CAPTURED SEEMED LIKE A BEST-CASE SCENARIO. BUT THIS...

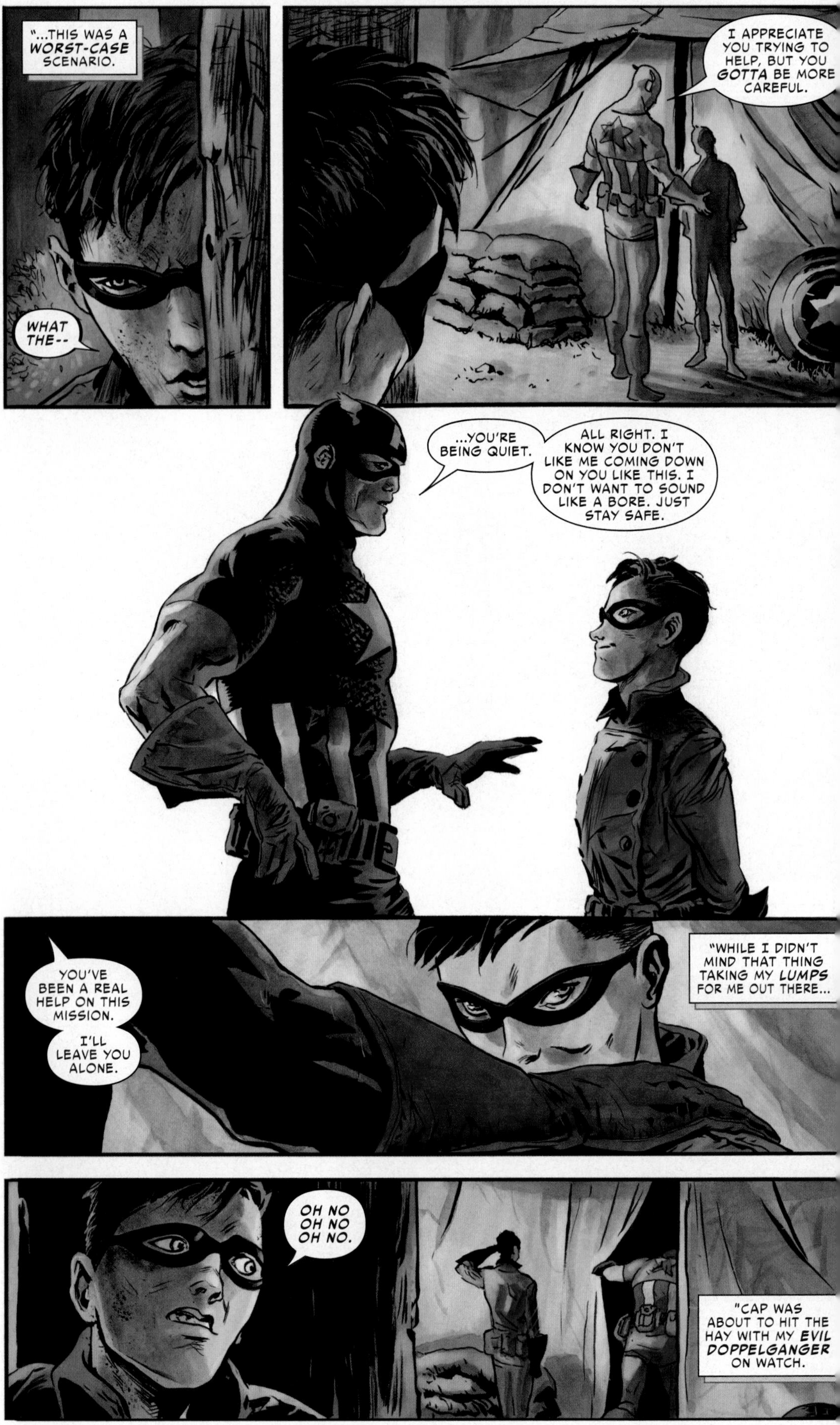
"...THIS WAS A WORST-CASE SCENARIO.
WHAT THE--
I APPRECIATE YOU TRYING TO HELP, BUT YOU GOTTA BE MORE CAREFUL.
...YOU'RE BEING QUIET.
ALL RIGHT. I KNOW YOU DON'T LIKE ME COMING DOWN ON YOU LIKE THIS. I DON'T WANT TO SOUND LIKE A BORE. JUST STAY SAFE.
YOU'VE BEEN A REAL HELP ON THIS MISSION.
I'LL LEAVE YOU ALONE.
"WHILE I DIDN'T MIND THAT THING TAKING MY LUMPS FOR ME OUT THERE...
OH NO OH NO OH NO.
"CAP WAS ABOUT TO HIT THE HAY WITH MY EVIL DOPPELGANGER ON WATCH.

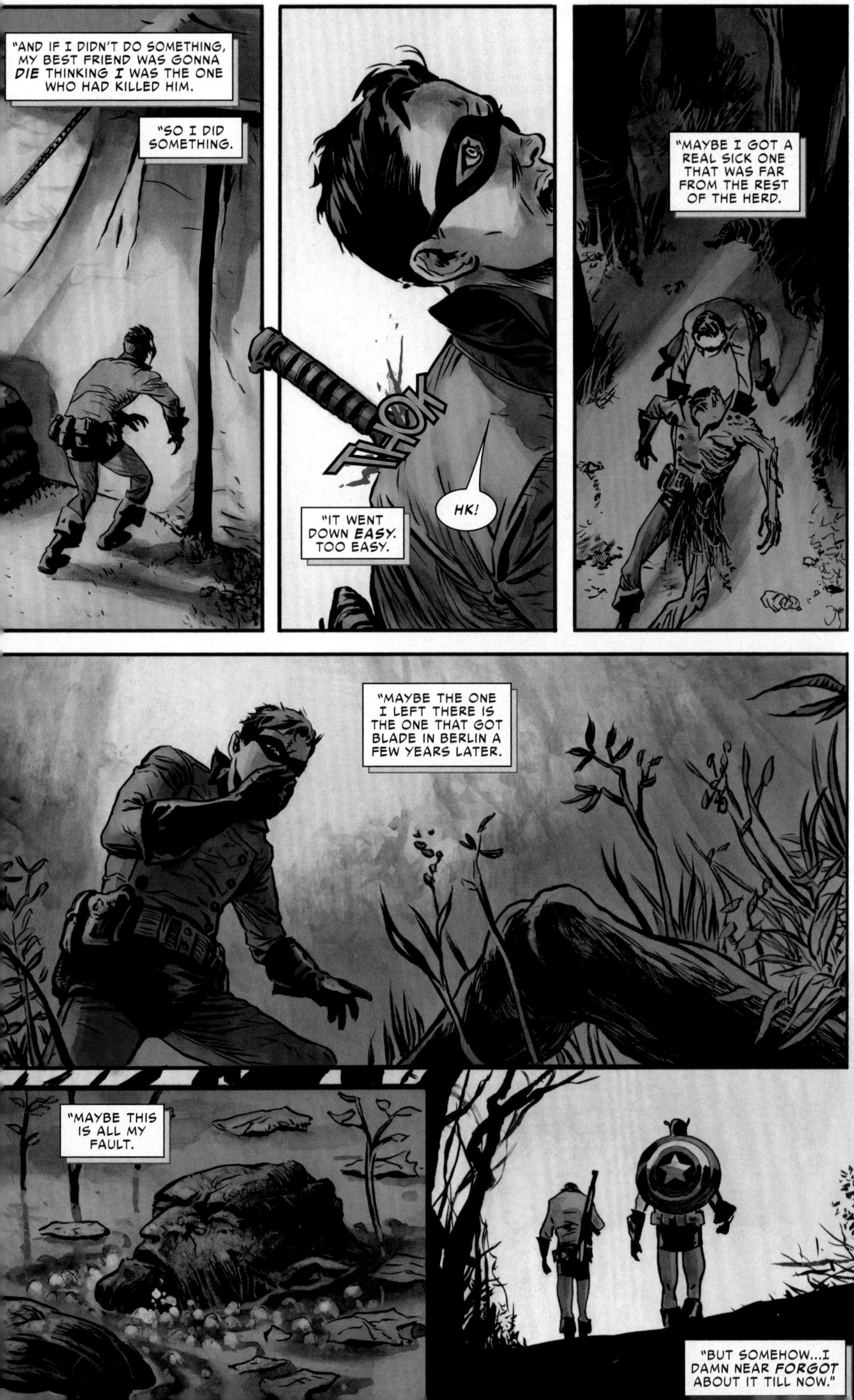
"AND IF I DIDN'T DO SOMETHING, MY BEST FRIEND WAS GONNA ***DIE*** THINKING ***I*** WAS THE ONE WHO HAD KILLED HIM.
"SO I DID SOMETHING.
THOK
"IT WENT DOWN ***EASY***. TOO EASY.
HK!
"MAYBE I GOT A REAL SICK ONE THAT WAS FAR FROM THE REST OF THE HERD.
"MAYBE THE ONE I LEFT THERE IS THE ONE THAT GOT BLADE IN BERLIN A FEW YEARS LATER.
"MAYBE THIS IS ALL MY FAULT.
"BUT SOMEHOW...I DAMN NEAR ***FORGOT*** ABOUT IT TILL NOW."

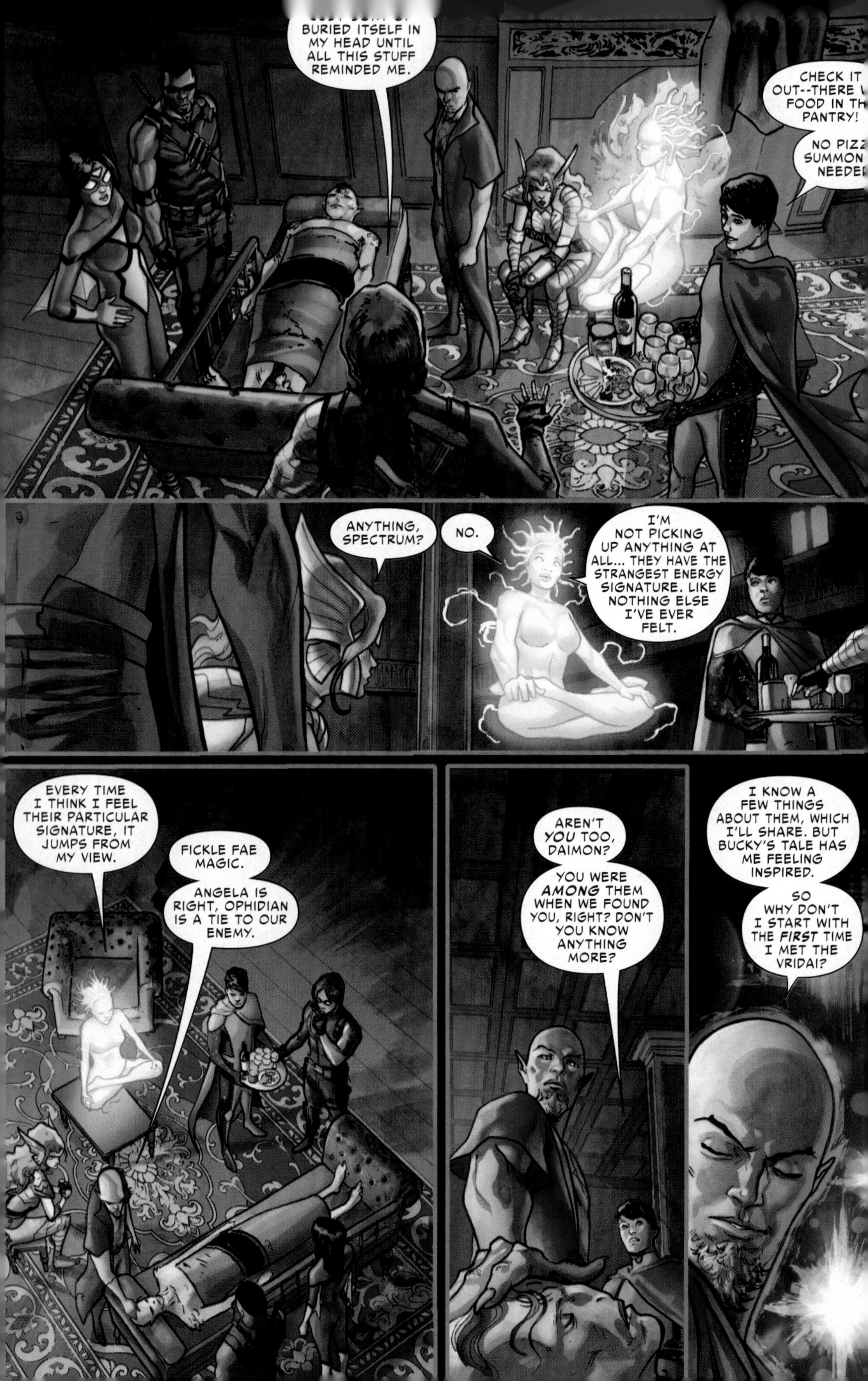
BURIED ITSELF IN MY HEAD UNTIL ALL THIS STUFF REMINDED ME.
CHECK IT OUT--THERE FOOD IN TH PANTRY!
NO PIZZ SUMMON NEEDE
ANYTHING, SPECTRUM?
NO.
I'M NOT PICKING UP ANYTHING AT ALL... THEY HAVE THE STRANGEST ENERGY SIGNATURE. LIKE NOTHING ELSE I'VE EVER FELT.
EVERY TIME I THINK I FEEL THEIR PARTICULAR SIGNATURE, IT JUMPS FROM MY VIEW.
FICKLE FAE MAGIC.
ANGELA IS RIGHT, OPHIDIAN IS A TIE TO OUR ENEMY.
AREN'T YOU TOO, DAIMON?
YOU WERE AMONG THEM WHEN WE FOUND YOU, RIGHT? DON'T YOU KNOW ANYTHING MORE?
I KNOW A FEW THINGS ABOUT THEM, WHICH I'LL SHARE. BUT BUCKY'S TALE HAS ME FEELING INSPIRED.
SO WHY DON'T I START WITH THE FIRST TIME I MET THE VRIDAI?

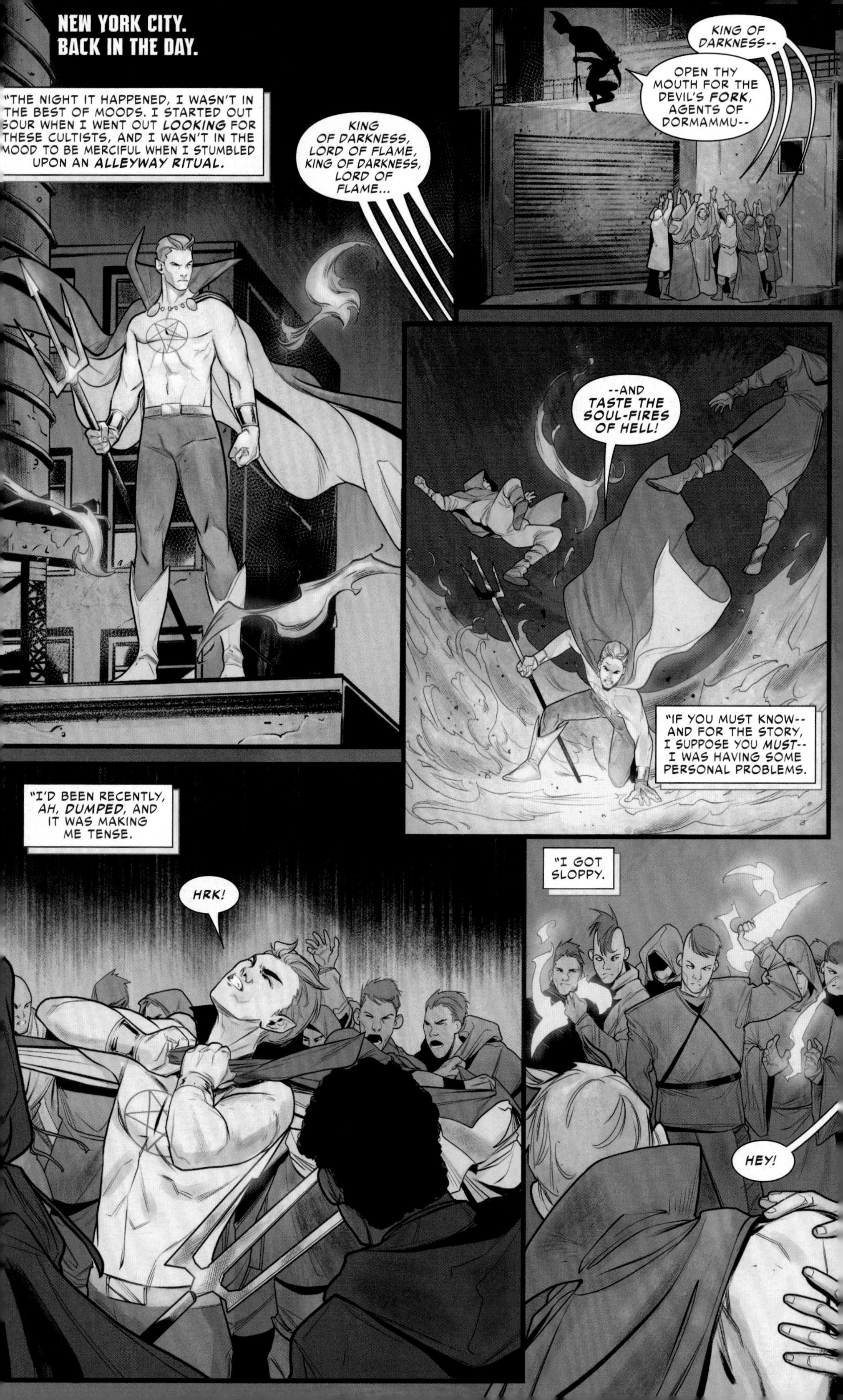
NEW YORK CITY.
BACK IN THE DAY.
"THE NIGHT IT HAPPENED, I WASN'T IN THE BEST OF MOODS. I STARTED OUT SOUR WHEN I WENT OUT LOOKING FOR THESE CULTISTS, AND I WASN'T IN THE MOOD TO BE MERCIFUL WHEN I STUMBLED UPON AN ALLEYWAY RITUAL.
KING OF DARKNESS, LORD OF FLAME, KING OF DARKNESS, LORD OF FLAME...
KING OF DARKNESS--
OPEN THY MOUTH FOR THE DEVIL'S FORK, AGENTS OF DORMAMMU--
--AND TASTE THE SOUL-FIRES OF HELL!
"IF YOU MUST KNOW--AND FOR THE STORY, I SUPPOSE YOU MUST--I WAS HAVING SOME PERSONAL PROBLEMS.
"I'D BEEN RECENTLY, AH, DUMPED, AND IT WAS MAKING ME TENSE.
HRK!
"I GOT SLOPPY.
HEY!

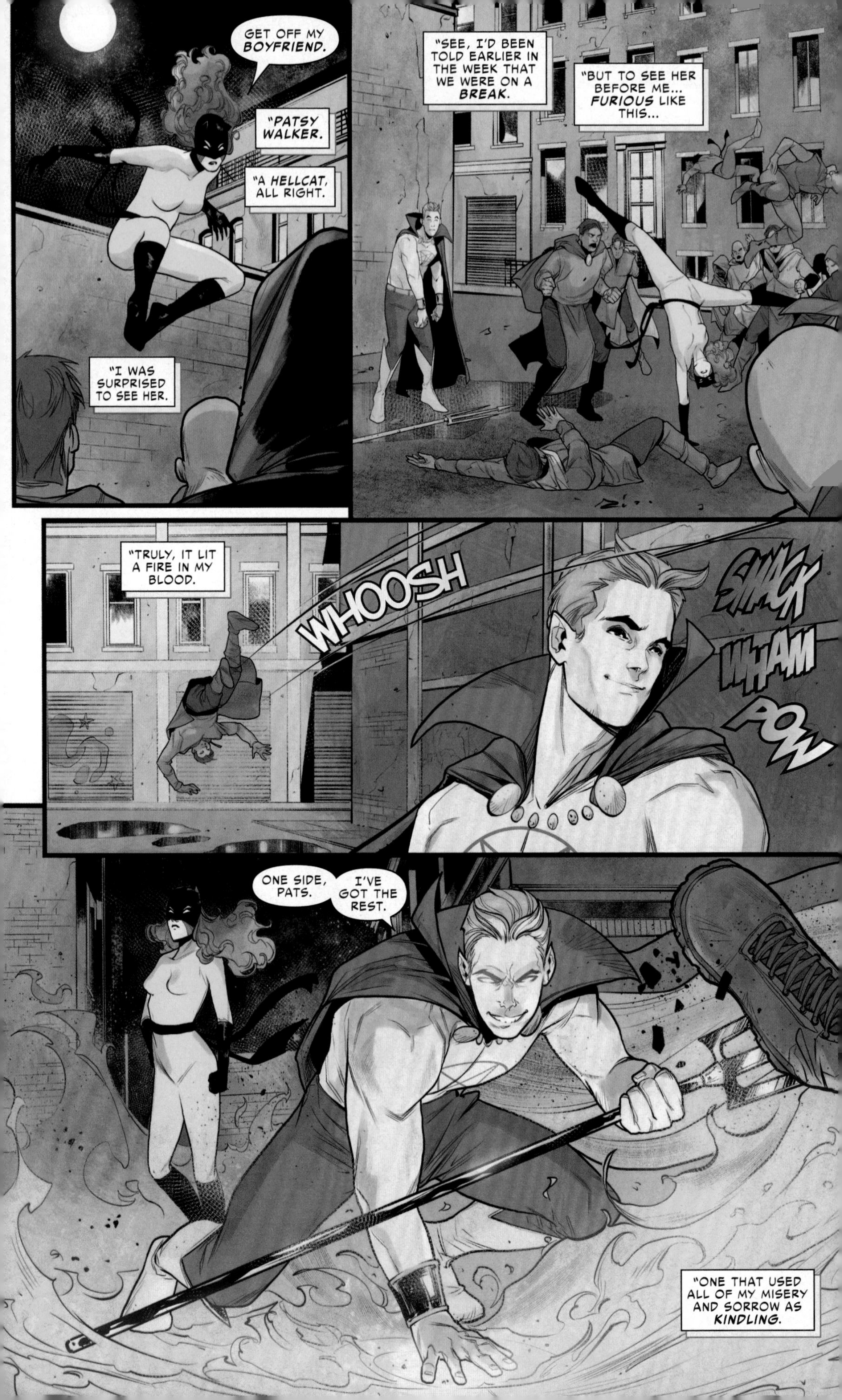
GET OFF MY BOYFRIEND.
"PATSY WALKER.
"A HELLCAT, ALL RIGHT.
"I WAS SURPRISED TO SEE HER.
"SEE, I'D BEEN TOLD EARLIER IN THE WEEK THAT WE WERE ON A BREAK.
"BUT TO SEE HER BEFORE ME... FURIOUS LIKE THIS...
"TRULY, IT LIT A FIRE IN MY BLOOD.
WHOOSH
SMACK
WHAM
POW
ONE SIDE, PATS.
I'VE GOT THE REST.
"ONE THAT USED ALL OF MY MISERY AND SORROW AS KINDLING.

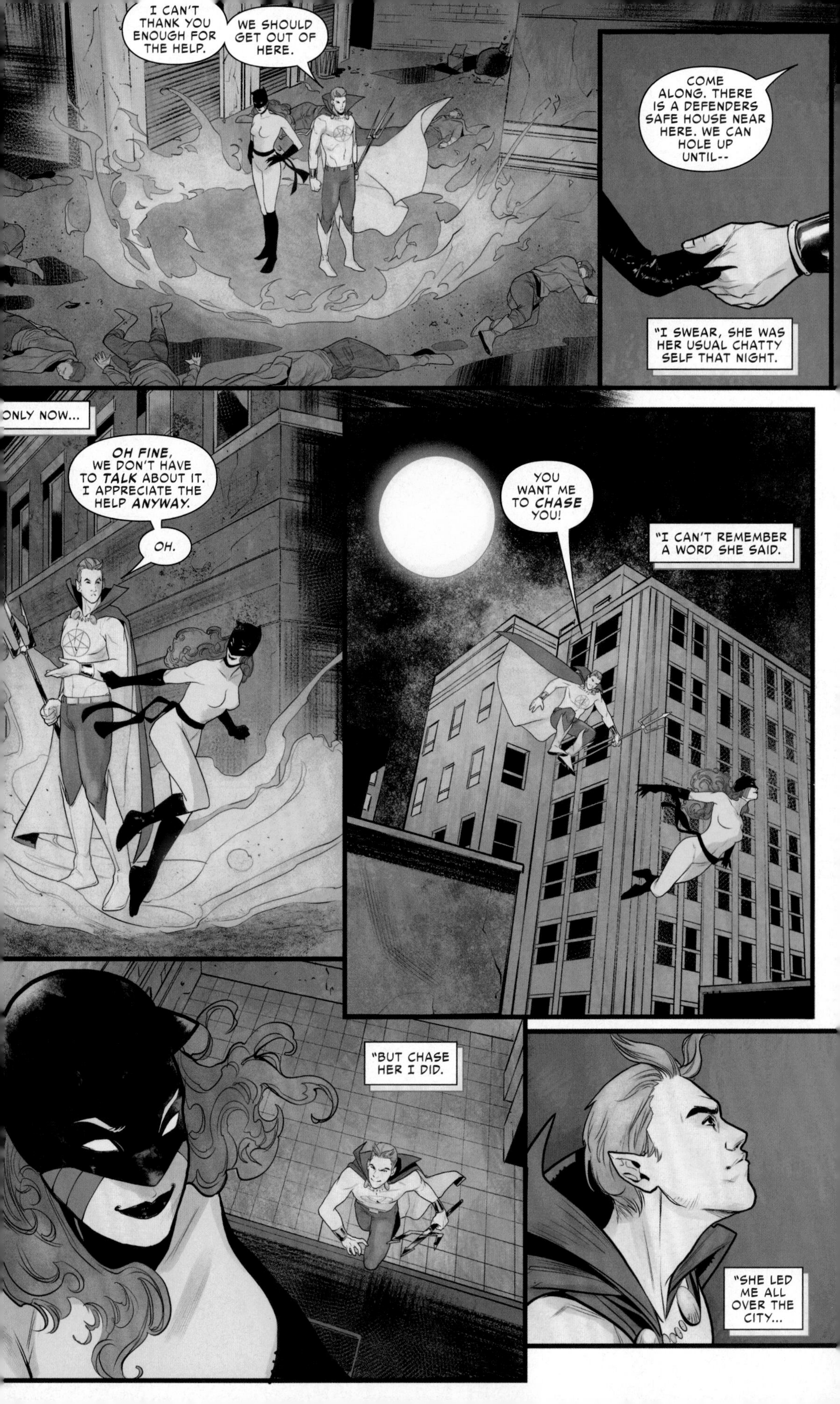

I CAN'T THANK YOU ENOUGH FOR THE HELP.
WE SHOULD GET OUT OF HERE.
COME ALONG. THERE IS A DEFENDERS SAFE HOUSE NEAR HERE. WE CAN HOLE UP UNTIL--
"I SWEAR, SHE WAS HER USUAL CHATTY SELF THAT NIGHT.
ONLY NOW...
OH FINE, WE DON'T HAVE TO TALK ABOUT IT. I APPRECIATE THE HELP ANYWAY.
OH.
YOU WANT ME TO CHASE YOU!
"I CAN'T REMEMBER A WORD SHE SAID.
"BUT CHASE HER I DID.
"SHE LED ME ALL OVER THE CITY...

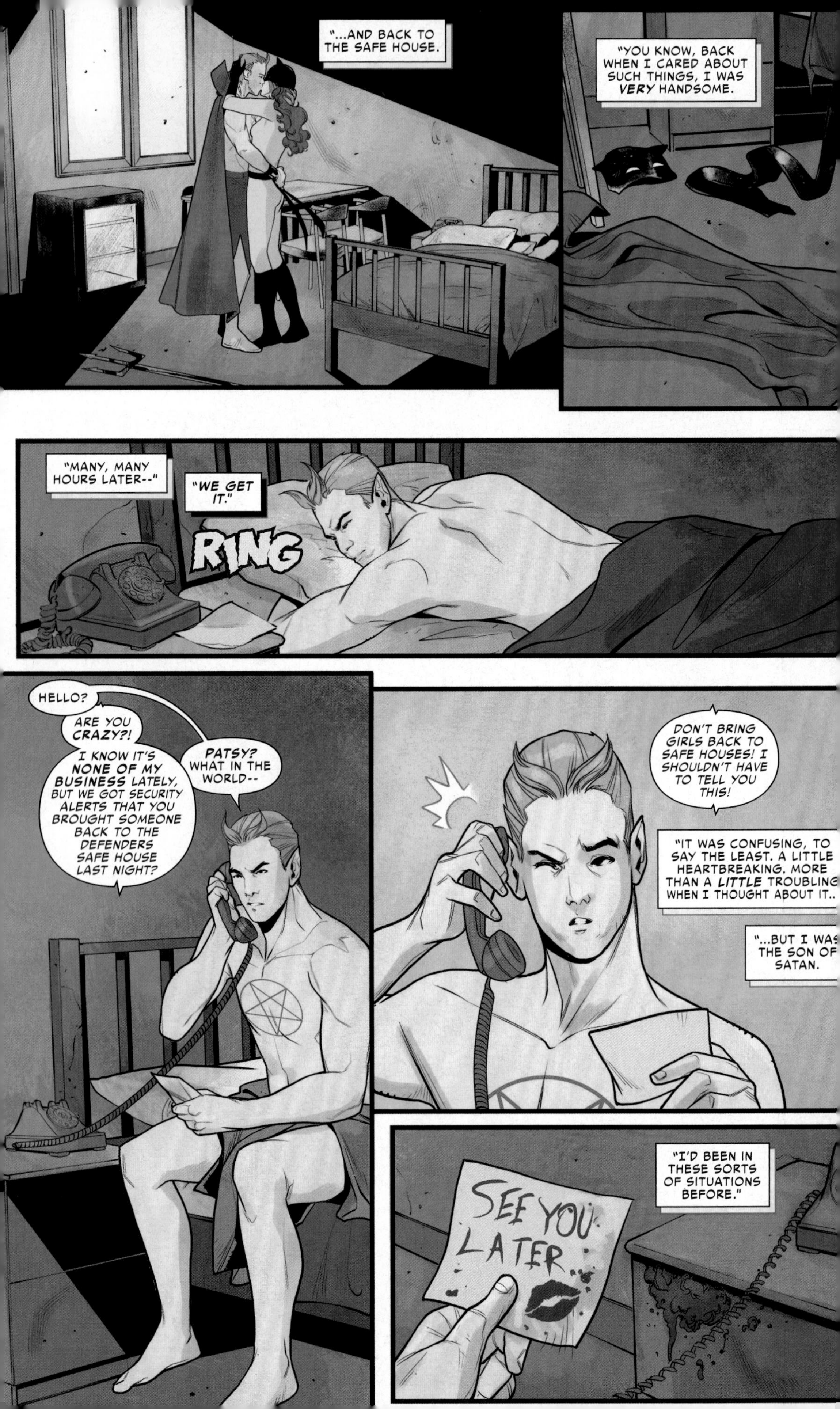
"...AND BACK TO THE SAFE HOUSE.
"YOU KNOW, BACK WHEN I CARED ABOUT SUCH THINGS, I WAS VERY HANDSOME.
"MANY, MANY HOURS LATER--"
"WE GET IT."
RING
HELLO?
PATSY? WHAT IN THE WORLD--
ARE YOU CRAZY?!
I KNOW IT'S NONE OF MY BUSINESS LATELY, BUT WE GOT SECURITY ALERTS THAT YOU BROUGHT SOMEONE BACK TO THE DEFENDERS SAFE HOUSE LAST NIGHT?
DON'T BRING GIRLS BACK TO SAFE HOUSES! I SHOULDN'T HAVE TO TELL YOU THIS!
"IT WAS CONFUSING, TO SAY THE LEAST. A LITTLE HEARTBREAKING. MORE THAN A LITTLE TROUBLING WHEN I THOUGHT ABOUT IT...
"...BUT I WAS THE SON OF SATAN.
"I'D BEEN IN THESE SORTS OF SITUATIONS BEFORE."
SEE YOU LATER...

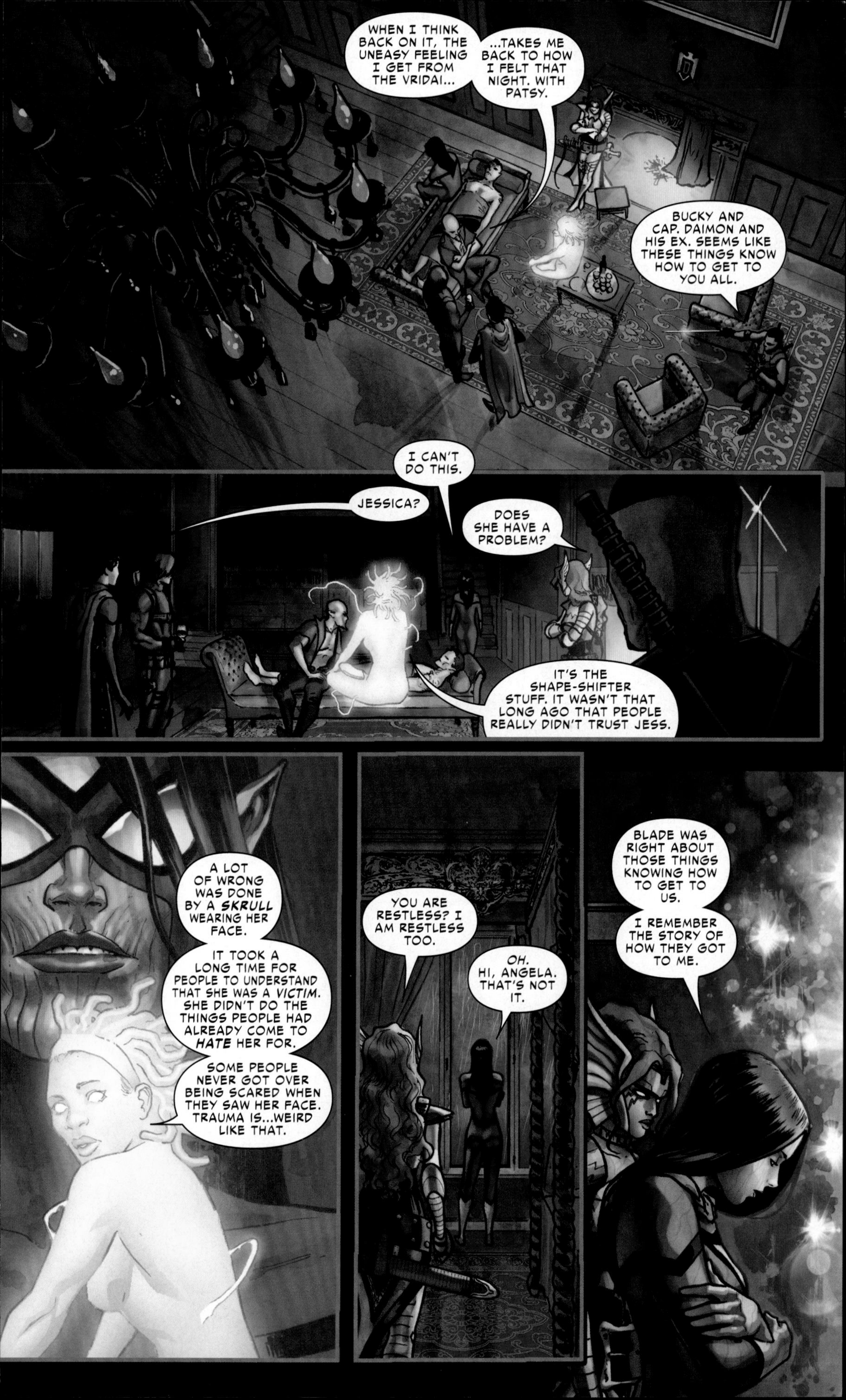
WHEN I THINK BACK ON IT, THE UNEASY FEELING I GET FROM THE VRIDAI...
...TAKES ME BACK TO HOW I FELT THAT NIGHT. WITH PATSY.
BUCKY AND CAP. DAIMON AND HIS EX. SEEMS LIKE THESE THINGS KNOW HOW TO GET TO YOU ALL.
I CAN'T DO THIS.
JESSICA?
DOES SHE HAVE A PROBLEM?
IT'S THE SHAPE-SHIFTER STUFF. IT WASN'T THAT LONG AGO THAT PEOPLE REALLY DIDN'T TRUST JESS.
A LOT OF WRONG WAS DONE BY A *SKRULL* WEARING HER FACE.
IT TOOK A LONG TIME FOR PEOPLE TO UNDERSTAND THAT SHE WAS A *VICTIM*. SHE DIDN'T DO THE THINGS PEOPLE HAD ALREADY COME TO *HATE* HER FOR.
SOME PEOPLE NEVER GOT OVER BEING SCARED WHEN THEY SAW HER FACE. TRAUMA IS...WEIRD LIKE THAT.
YOU ARE RESTLESS? I AM RESTLESS TOO.
OH. HI, ANGELA. THAT'S NOT IT.
BLADE WAS RIGHT ABOUT THOSE THINGS KNOWING HOW TO GET TO US.
I REMEMBER THE STORY OF HOW THEY GOT TO ME.

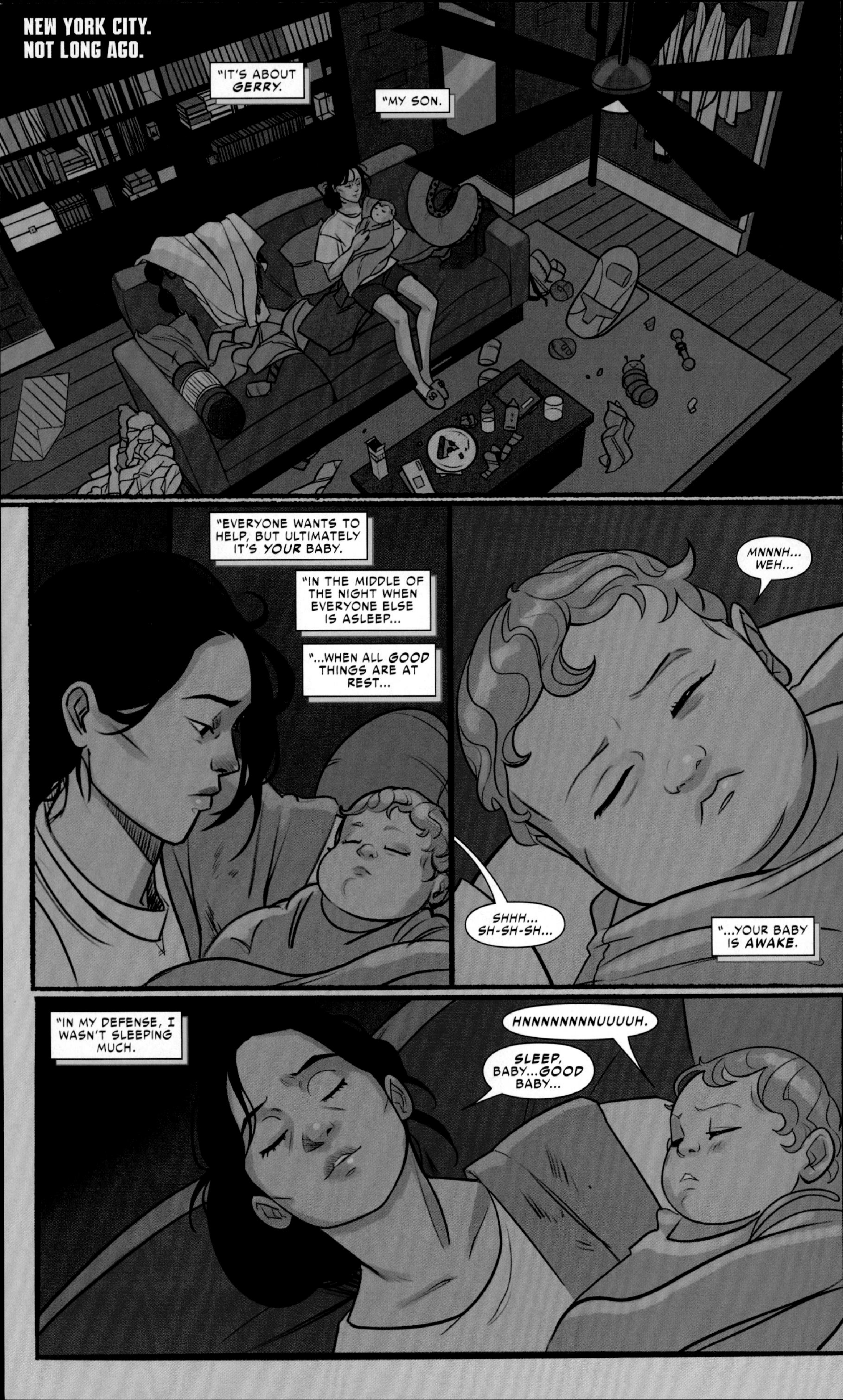
NEW YORK CITY.
NOT LONG AGO.
"IT'S ABOUT GERRY.
"MY SON.
"EVERYONE WANTS TO HELP, BUT ULTIMATELY IT'S YOUR BABY.
"IN THE MIDDLE OF THE NIGHT WHEN EVERYONE ELSE IS ASLEEP...
"...WHEN ALL GOOD THINGS ARE AT REST...
MNNNH... WEH...
SHHH... SH-SH-SH...
"...YOUR BABY IS AWAKE.
"IN MY DEFENSE, I WASN'T SLEEPING MUCH.
HNNNNNNNNUUUUH.
SLEEP, BABY...GOOD BABY...

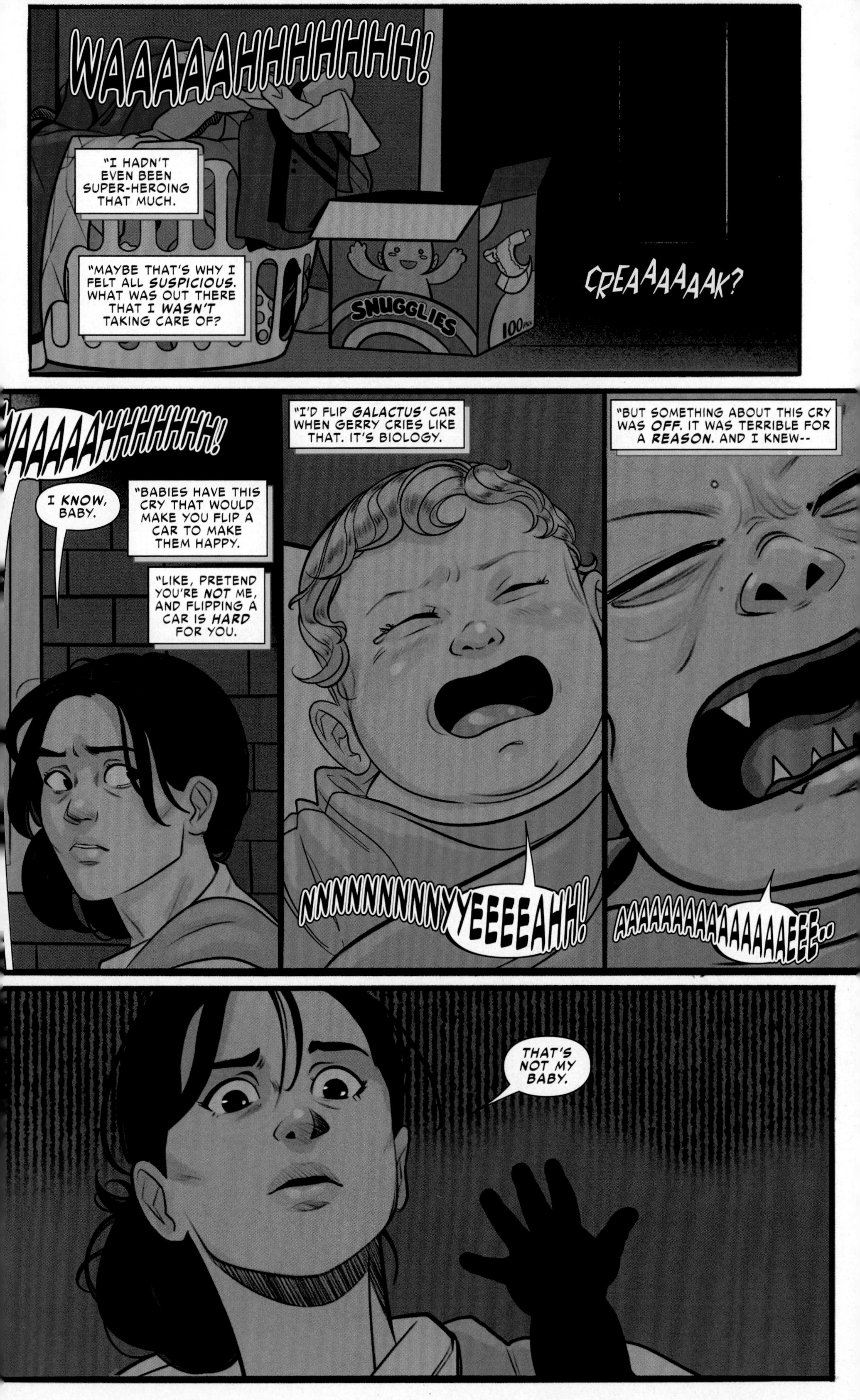
WAAAAAHHHHHHH!
"I HADN'T EVEN BEEN SUPER-HEROING THAT MUCH.
"MAYBE THAT'S WHY I FELT ALL SUSPICIOUS. WHAT WAS OUT THERE THAT I WASN'T TAKING CARE OF?
SNUGGLIES
100 PACK
CREAAAAAAK?
WAAAAAHHHHHHH!
I KNOW, BABY.
"BABIES HAVE THIS CRY THAT WOULD MAKE YOU FLIP A CAR TO MAKE THEM HAPPY.
"LIKE, PRETEND YOU'RE NOT ME, AND FLIPPING A CAR IS HARD FOR YOU.
"I'D FLIP GALACTUS' CAR WHEN GERRY CRIES LIKE THAT. IT'S BIOLOGY.
NNNNNNNNNNYEEEEAHH!
"BUT SOMETHING ABOUT THIS CRY WAS OFF. IT WAS TERRIBLE FOR A REASON. AND I KNEW--
AAAAAAAAAAAAAAEEE..
THAT'S NOT MY BABY.

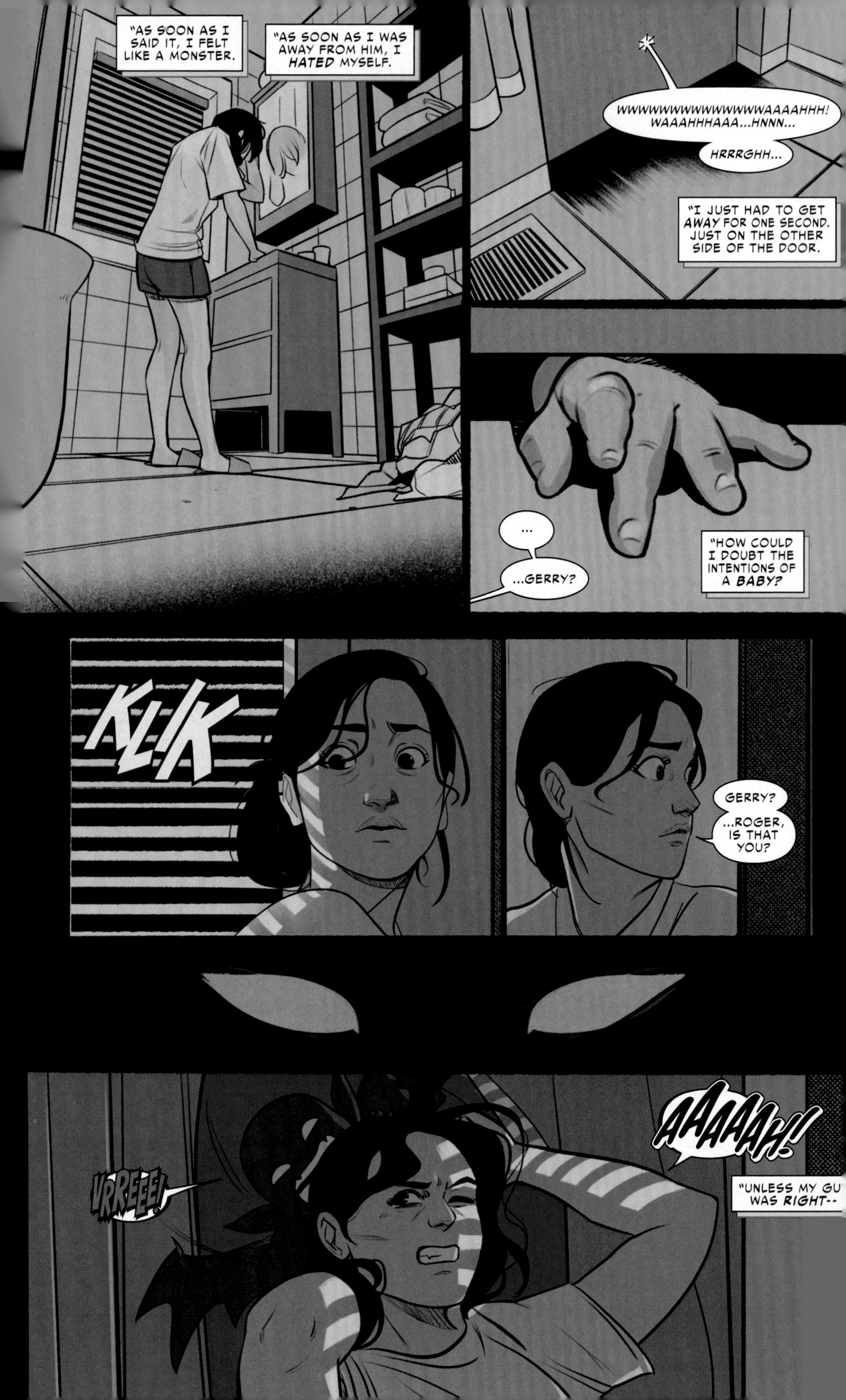
"AS SOON AS I SAID IT, I FELT LIKE A MONSTER.
"AS SOON AS I WAS AWAY FROM HIM, I HATED MYSELF.
WWWWWWWWWWWWWWWAAAAHHH! WAAAHHHAAA...HNNN...
HRRRGHH...
"I JUST HAD TO GET AWAY FOR ONE SECOND. JUST ON THE OTHER SIDE OF THE DOOR.
...
...GERRY?
"HOW COULD I DOUBT THE INTENTIONS OF A BABY?
KLIK
GERRY? ...ROGER, IS THAT YOU?
AAAAAH!
VRREEE!
"UNLESS MY GU
WAS RIGHT--

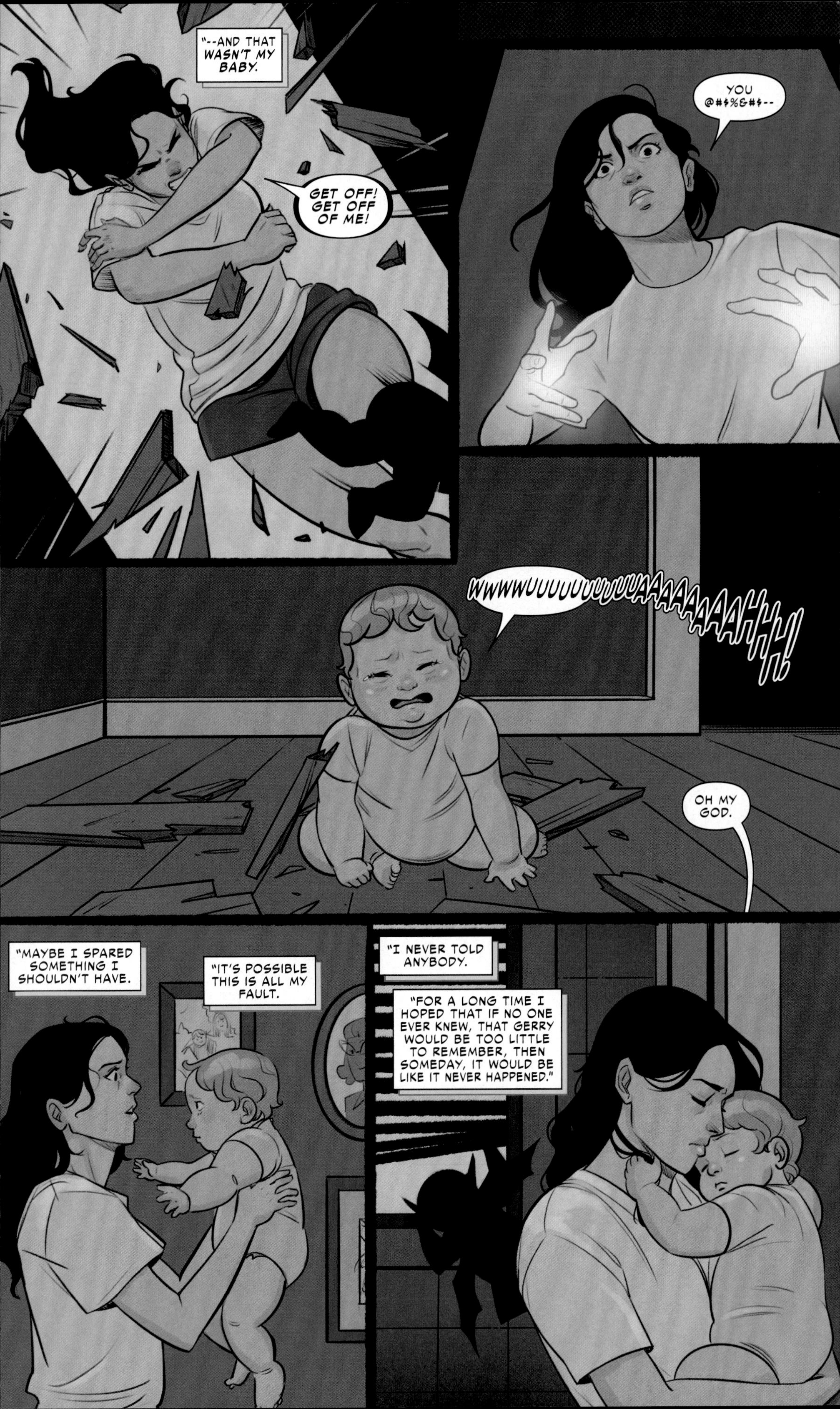
"--AND THAT WASN'T MY BABY.
GET OFF! GET OFF OF ME!
YOU @#$%&#$--
WWWWUUUUUUUUUAAAAAAAAAHHH!
OH MY GOD.
"MAYBE I SPARED SOMETHING I SHOULDN'T HAVE.
"IT'S POSSIBLE THIS IS ALL MY FAULT.
"I NEVER TOLD ANYBODY.
"FOR A LONG TIME I HOPED THAT IF NO ONE EVER KNEW, THAT GERRY WOULD BE TOO LITTLE TO REMEMBER, THEN SOMEDAY, IT WOULD BE LIKE IT NEVER HAPPENED."

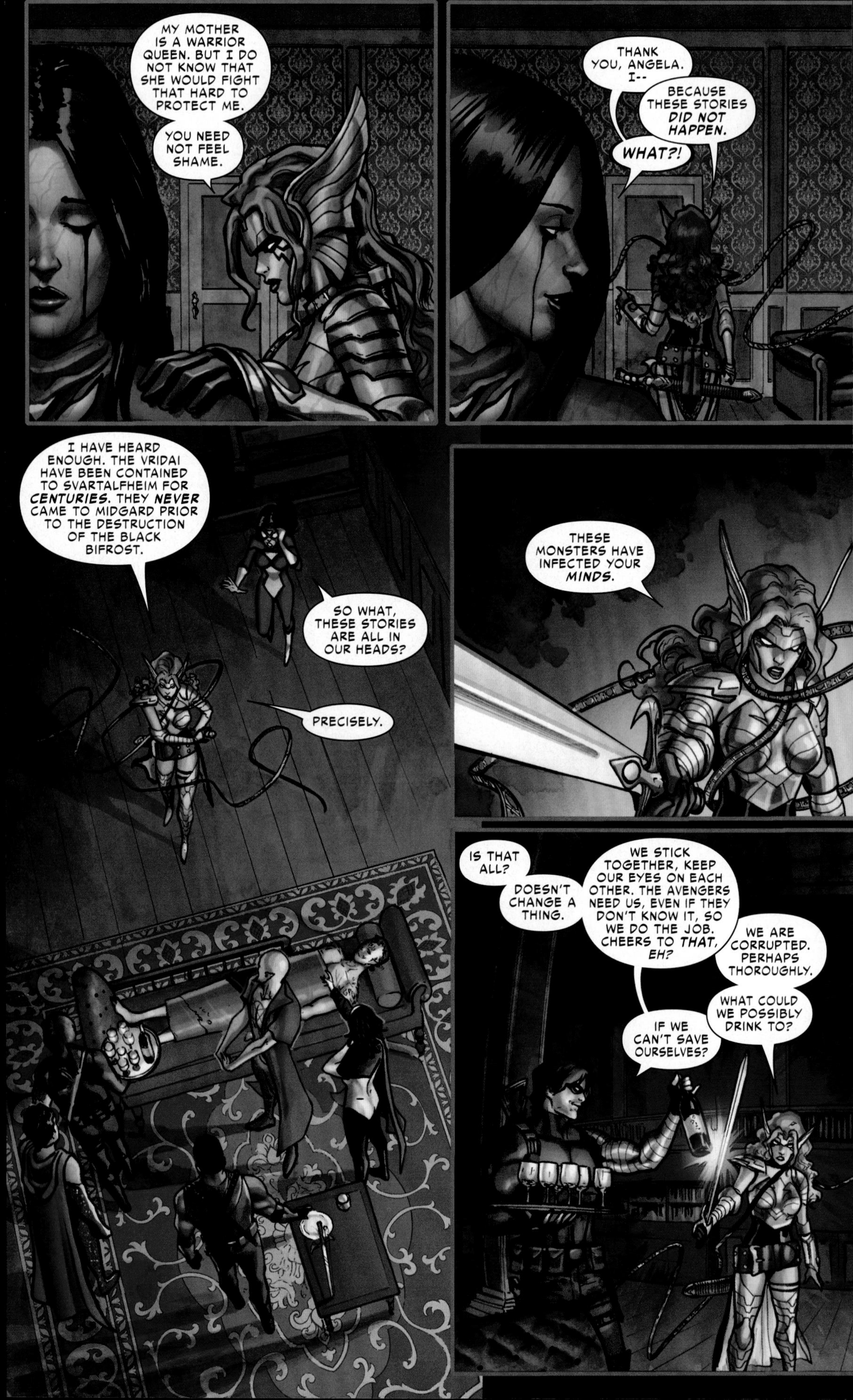
MY MOTHER IS A WARRIOR QUEEN. BUT I DO NOT KNOW THAT SHE WOULD FIGHT THAT HARD TO PROTECT ME.
YOU NEED NOT FEEL SHAME.
THANK YOU, ANGELA. I--
BECAUSE THESE STORIES *DID NOT HAPPEN*.
WHAT?!
I HAVE HEARD ENOUGH. THE VRIDAI HAVE BEEN CONTAINED TO SVARTALFHEIM FOR *CENTURIES*. THEY *NEVER* CAME TO MIDGARD PRIOR TO THE DESTRUCTION OF THE BLACK BIFROST.
SO WHAT, THESE STORIES ARE ALL IN OUR HEADS?
PRECISELY.
THESE MONSTERS HAVE INFECTED YOUR *MINDS*.
IS THAT ALL?
DOESN'T CHANGE A THING.
WE STICK TOGETHER, KEEP OUR EYES ON EACH OTHER. THE AVENGERS NEED US, EVEN IF THEY DON'T KNOW IT, SO WE DO THE JOB. CHEERS TO *THAT*, *EH?*
WE ARE CORRUPTED. PERHAPS THOROUGHLY.
WHAT COULD WE POSSIBLY DRINK TO?
IF WE CAN'T SAVE OURSELVES?

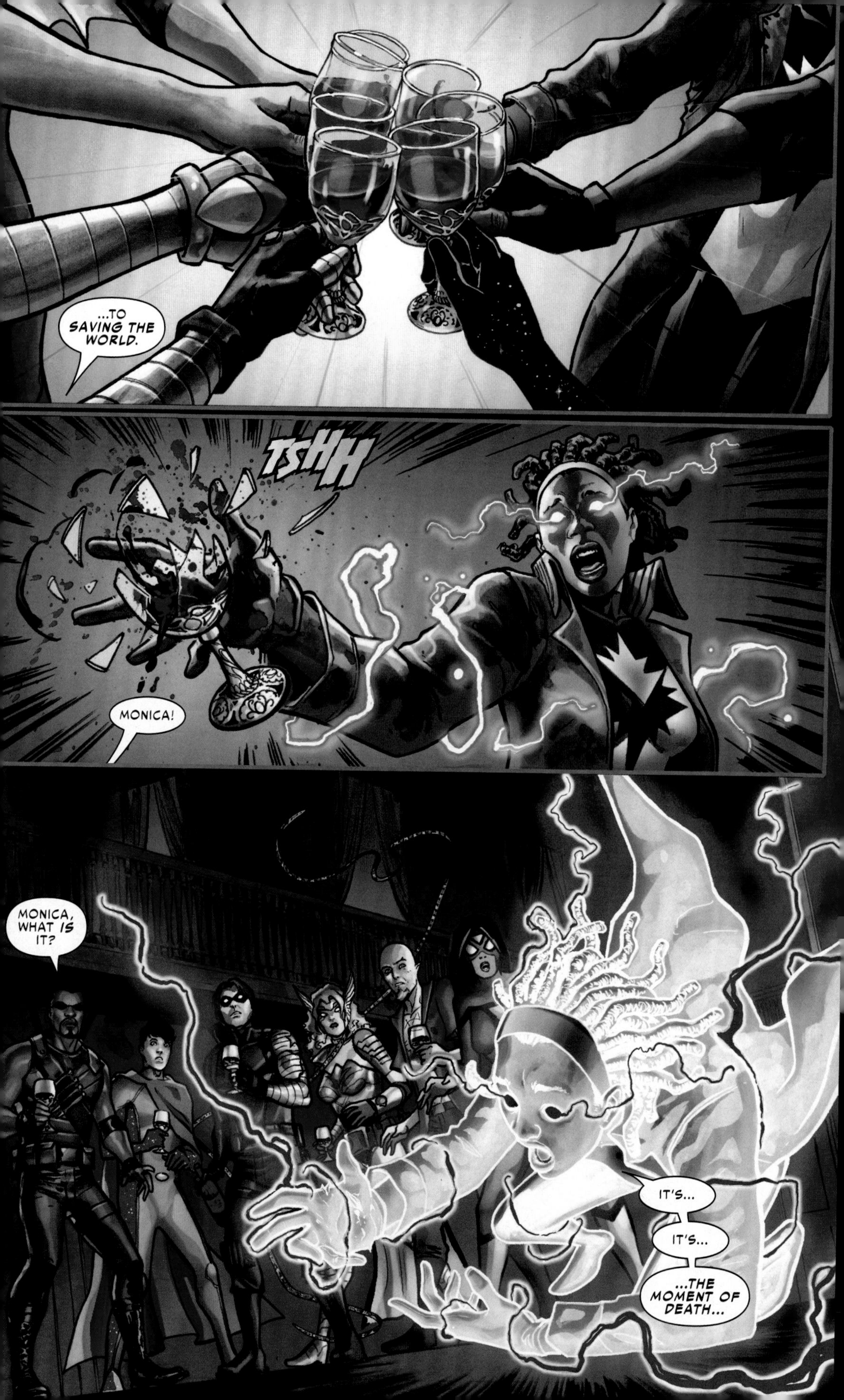
...TO SAVING THE WORLD.
TSHH
MONICA!
MONICA, WHAT IS IT?
IT'S...
IT'S...
...THE MOMENT OF DEATH...

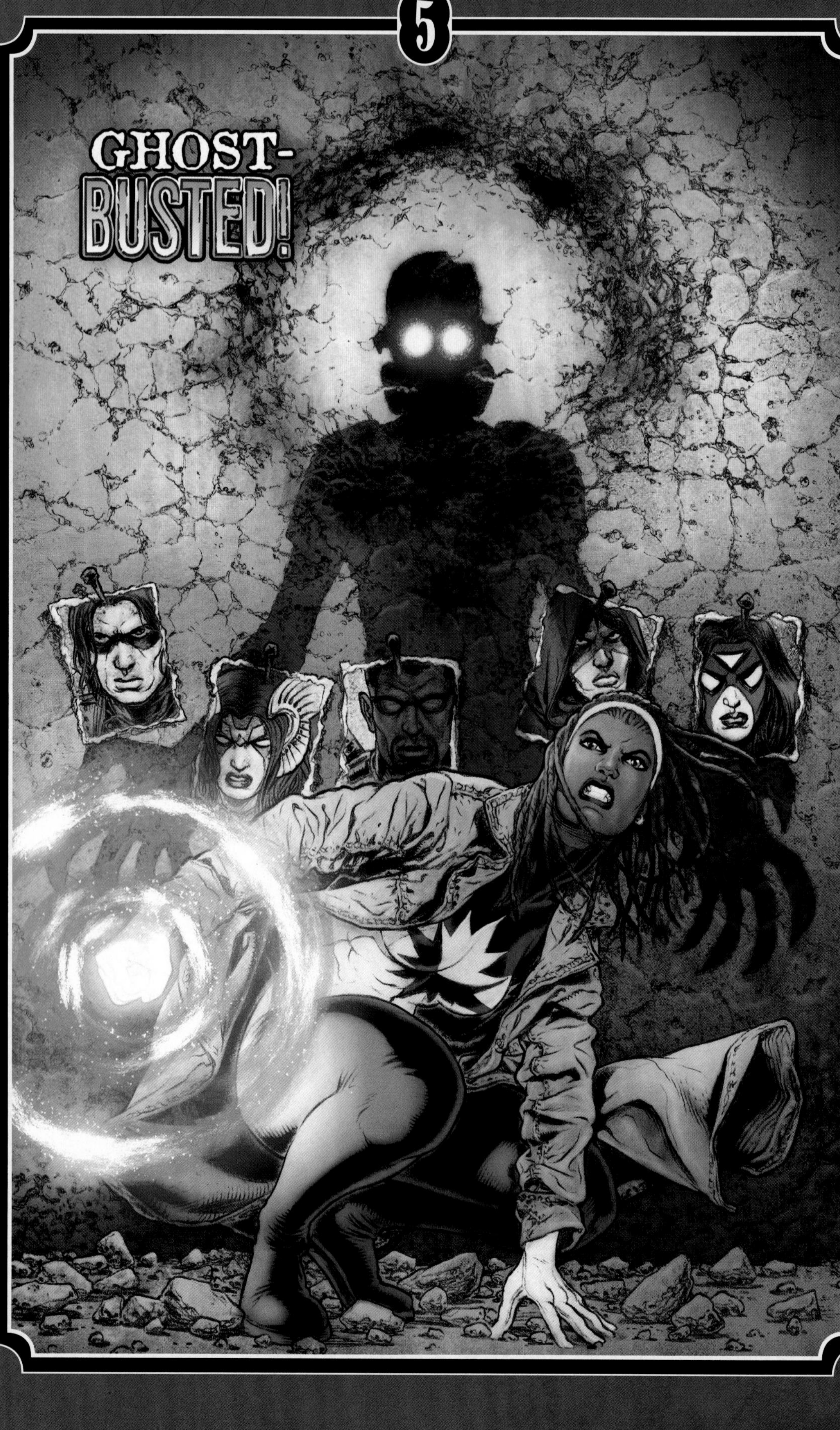
5
GHOST-
BUSTED!

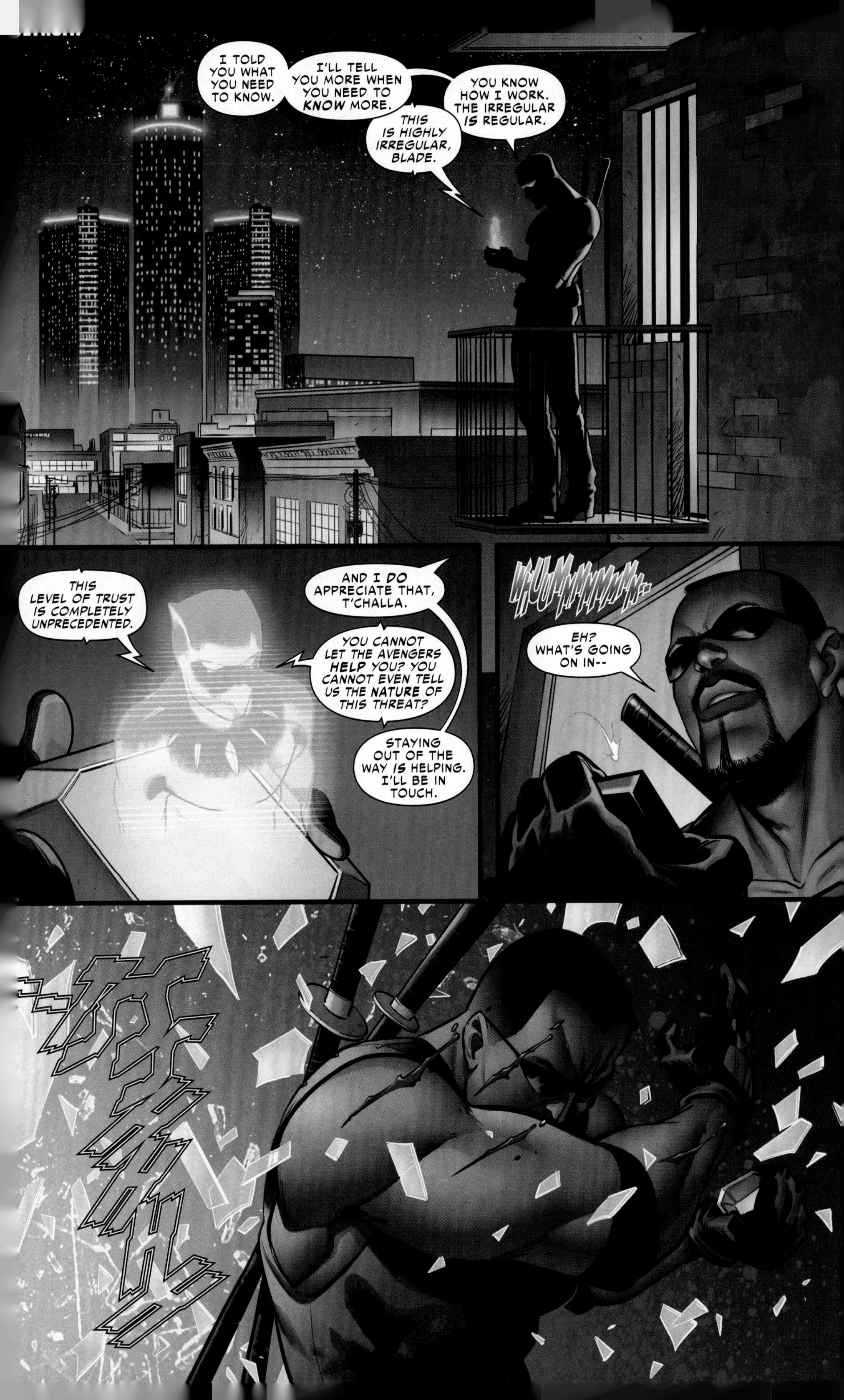
I TOLD YOU WHAT YOU NEED TO KNOW.
I'LL TELL YOU MORE WHEN YOU NEED TO KNOW MORE.
THIS IS HIGHLY IRREGULAR, BLADE.
YOU KNOW HOW I WORK. THE IRREGULAR IS REGULAR.
THIS LEVEL OF TRUST IS COMPLETELY UNPRECEDENTED.
AND I DO APPRECIATE THAT, T'CHALLA.
YOU CANNOT LET THE AVENGERS HELP YOU? YOU CANNOT EVEN TELL US THE NATURE OF THIS THREAT?
STAYING OUT OF THE WAY IS HELPING. I'LL BE IN TOUCH.
WHUMMMMMMM--
EH? WHAT'S GOING ON IN--

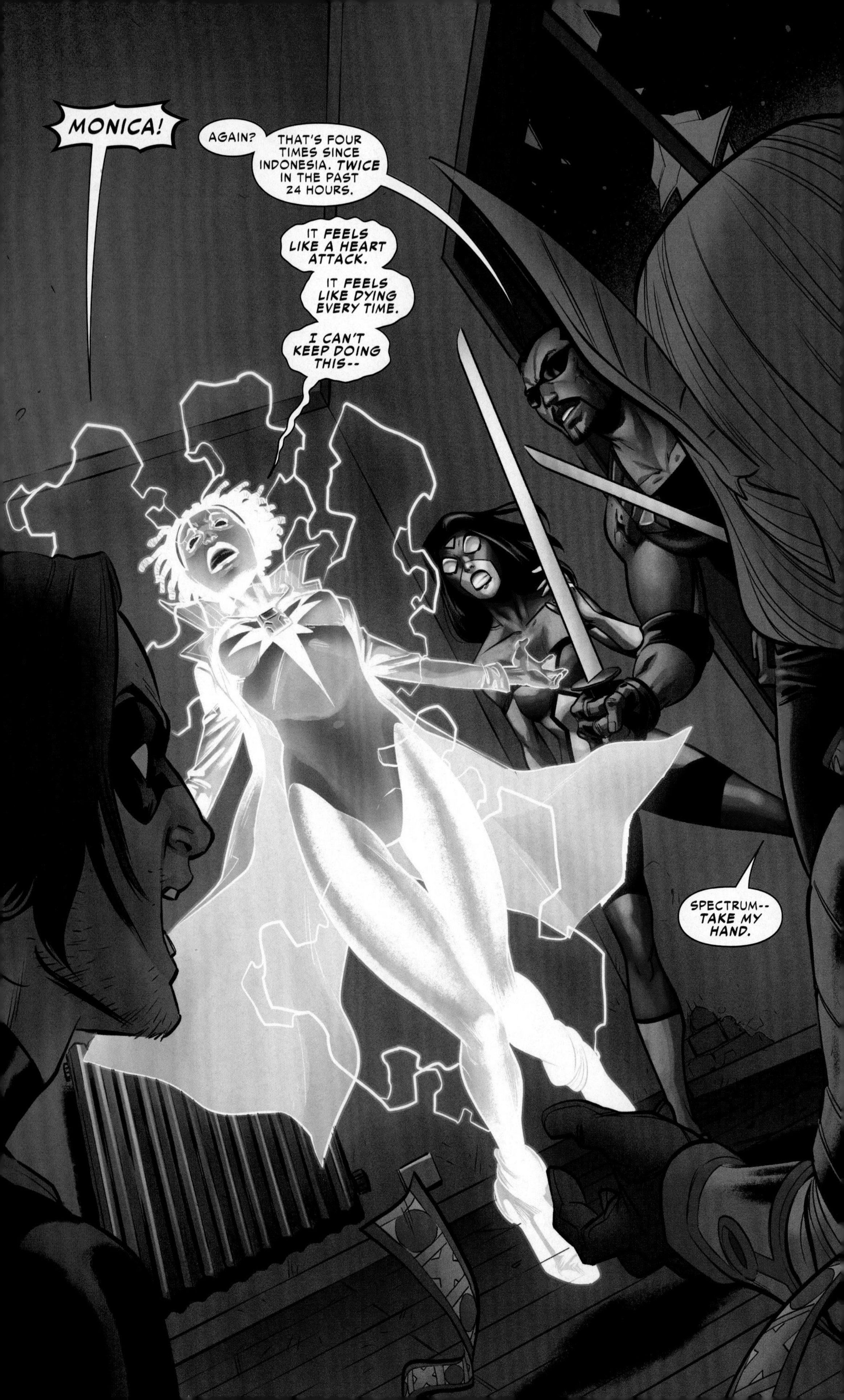

MONICA!
AGAIN?
THAT'S FOUR TIMES SINCE INDONESIA. TWICE IN THE PAST 24 HOURS.
IT FEELS LIKE A HEART ATTACK.
IT FEELS LIKE DYING EVERY TIME.
I CAN'T KEEP DOING THIS--
SPECTRUM--TAKE MY HAND.

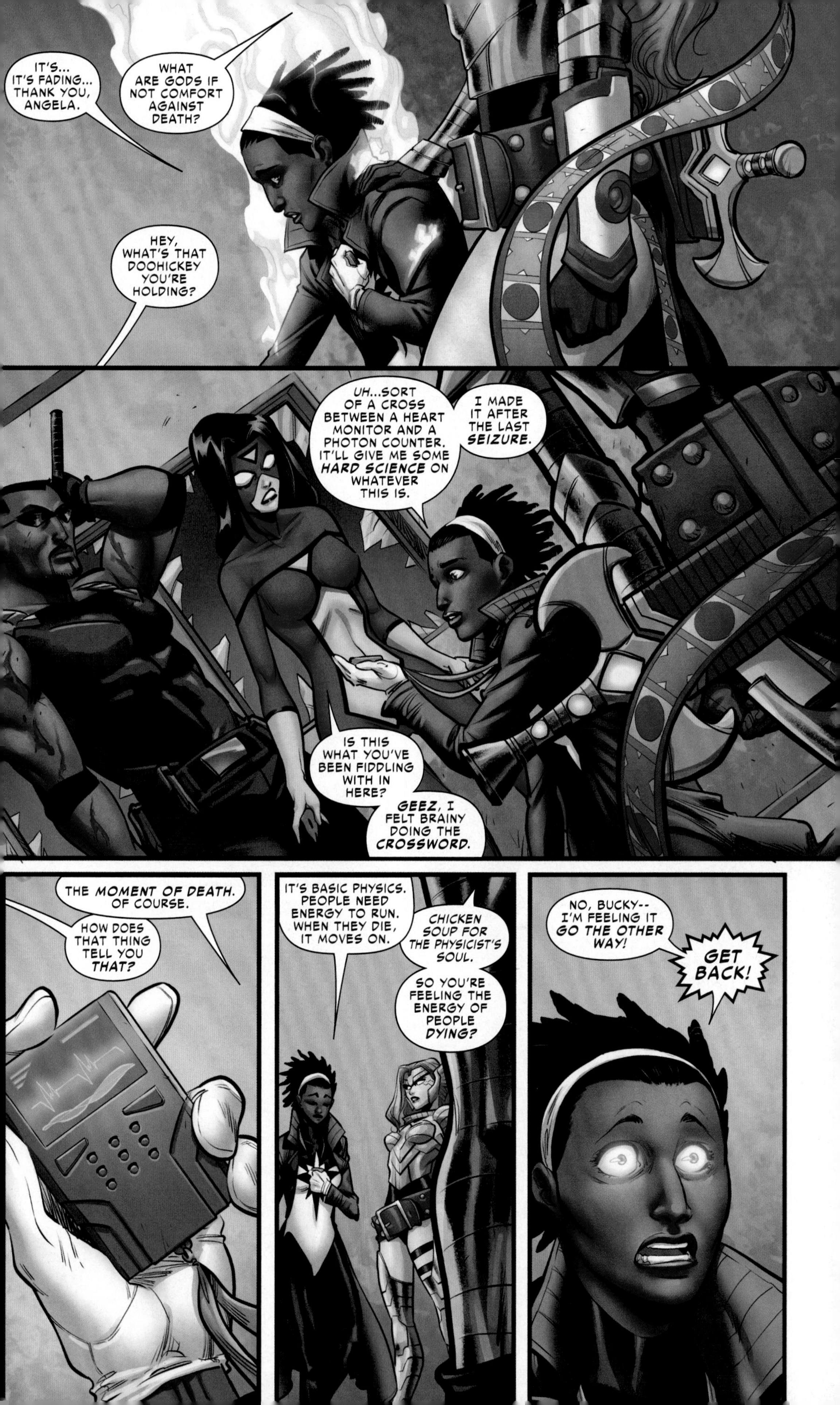

IT'S... IT'S FADING... THANK YOU, ANGELA.
WHAT ARE GODS IF NOT COMFORT AGAINST DEATH?
HEY, WHAT'S THAT DOOHICKEY YOU'RE HOLDING?
UH...SORT OF A CROSS BETWEEN A HEART MONITOR AND A PHOTON COUNTER. IT'LL GIVE ME SOME HARD SCIENCE ON WHATEVER THIS IS.
I MADE IT AFTER THE LAST SEIZURE.
IS THIS WHAT YOU'VE BEEN FIDDLING WITH IN HERE?
GEEZ, I FELT BRAINY DOING THE CROSSWORD.
THE MOMENT OF DEATH. OF COURSE.
HOW DOES THAT THING TELL YOU THAT?
IT'S BASIC PHYSICS. PEOPLE NEED ENERGY TO RUN. WHEN THEY DIE, IT MOVES ON.
CHICKEN SOUP FOR THE PHYSICIST'S SOUL.
SO YOU'RE FEELING THE ENERGY OF PEOPLE DYING?
NO, BUCKY-- I'M FEELING IT GO THE OTHER WAY!
GET BACK!

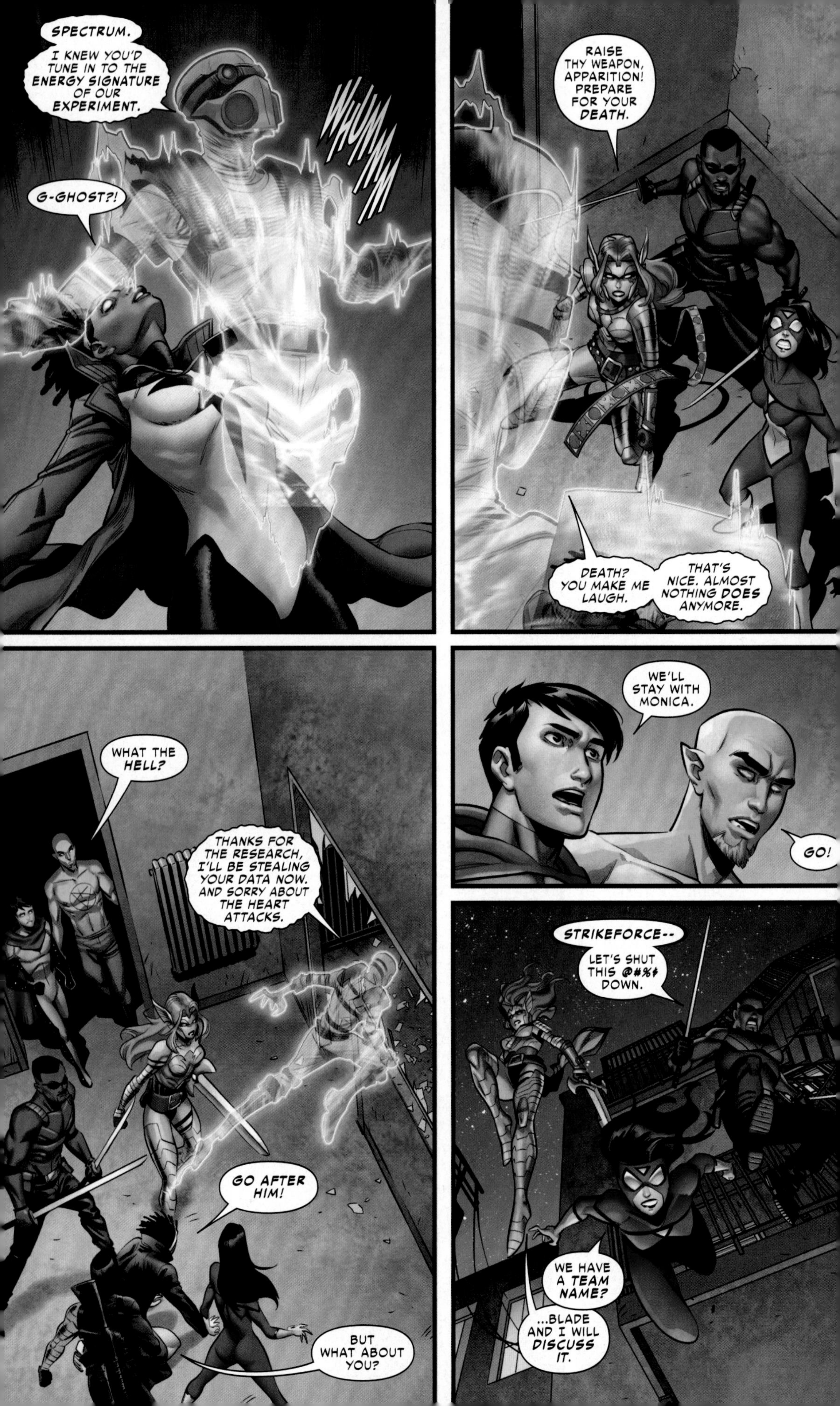

SPECTRUM.
I KNEW YOU'D TUNE IN TO THE ENERGY SIGNATURE OF OUR EXPERIMENT.
WHUMMM
G-GHOST?!
RAISE THY WEAPON, APPARITION! PREPARE FOR YOUR DEATH.
DEATH? YOU MAKE ME LAUGH.
THAT'S NICE. ALMOST NOTHING DOES ANYMORE.
WHAT THE HELL?
THANKS FOR THE RESEARCH, I'LL BE STEALING YOUR DATA NOW. AND SORRY ABOUT THE HEART ATTACKS.
GO AFTER HIM!
BUT WHAT ABOUT YOU?
WE'LL STAY WITH MONICA.
GO!
STRIKEFORCE--
LET'S SHUT THIS @#%$ DOWN.
WE HAVE A TEAM NAME?
...BLADE AND I WILL DISCUSS IT.

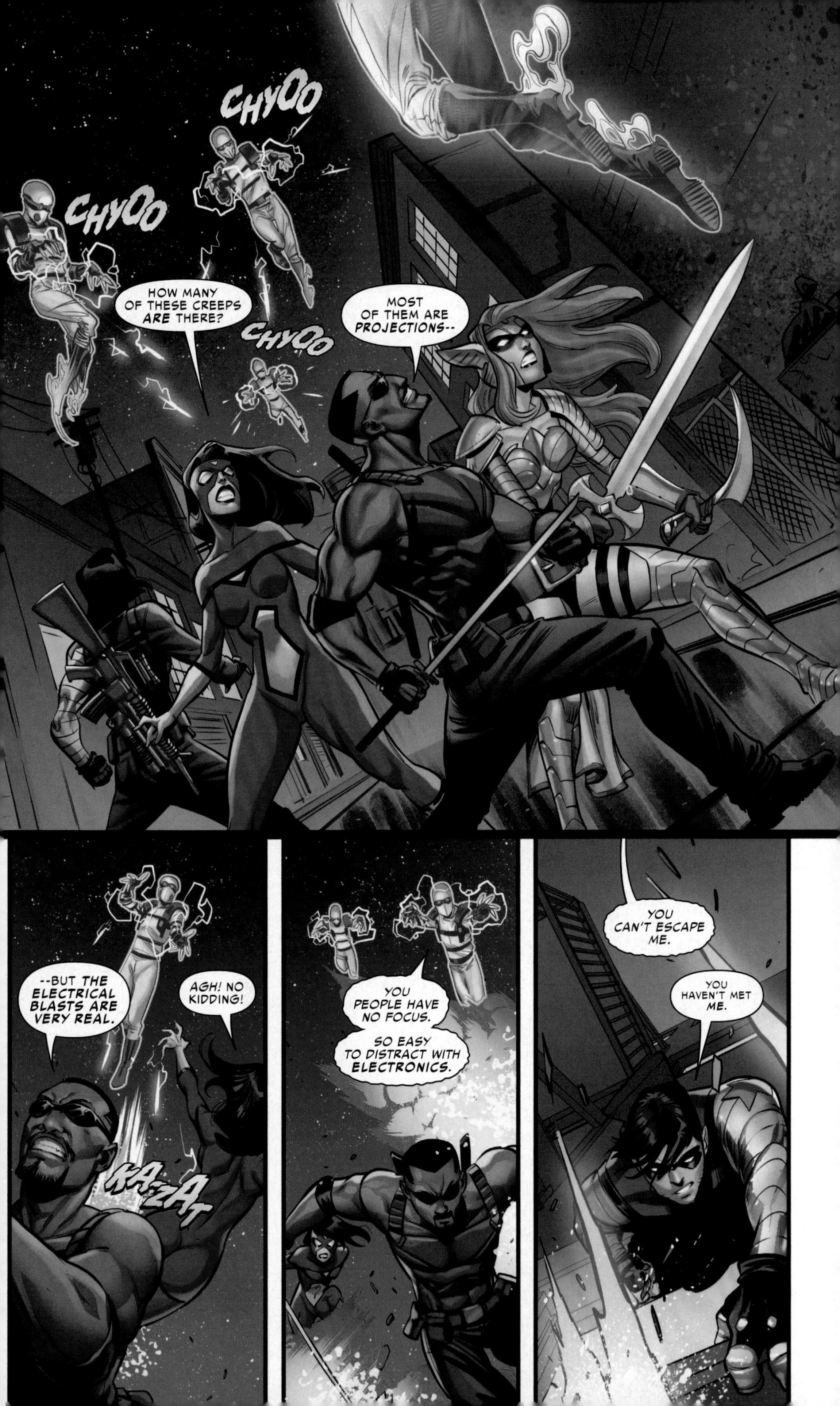
CHYOO
CHYOO
HOW MANY OF THESE CREEPS ARE THERE?
CHYOO
MOST OF THEM ARE PROJECTIONS--
--BUT THE ELECTRICAL BLASTS ARE VERY REAL.
AGH! NO KIDDING!
KA-ZAT
YOU PEOPLE HAVE NO FOCUS.
SO EASY TO DISTRACT WITH ELECTRONICS.
YOU CAN'T ESCAPE ME.
YOU HAVEN'T MET ME.

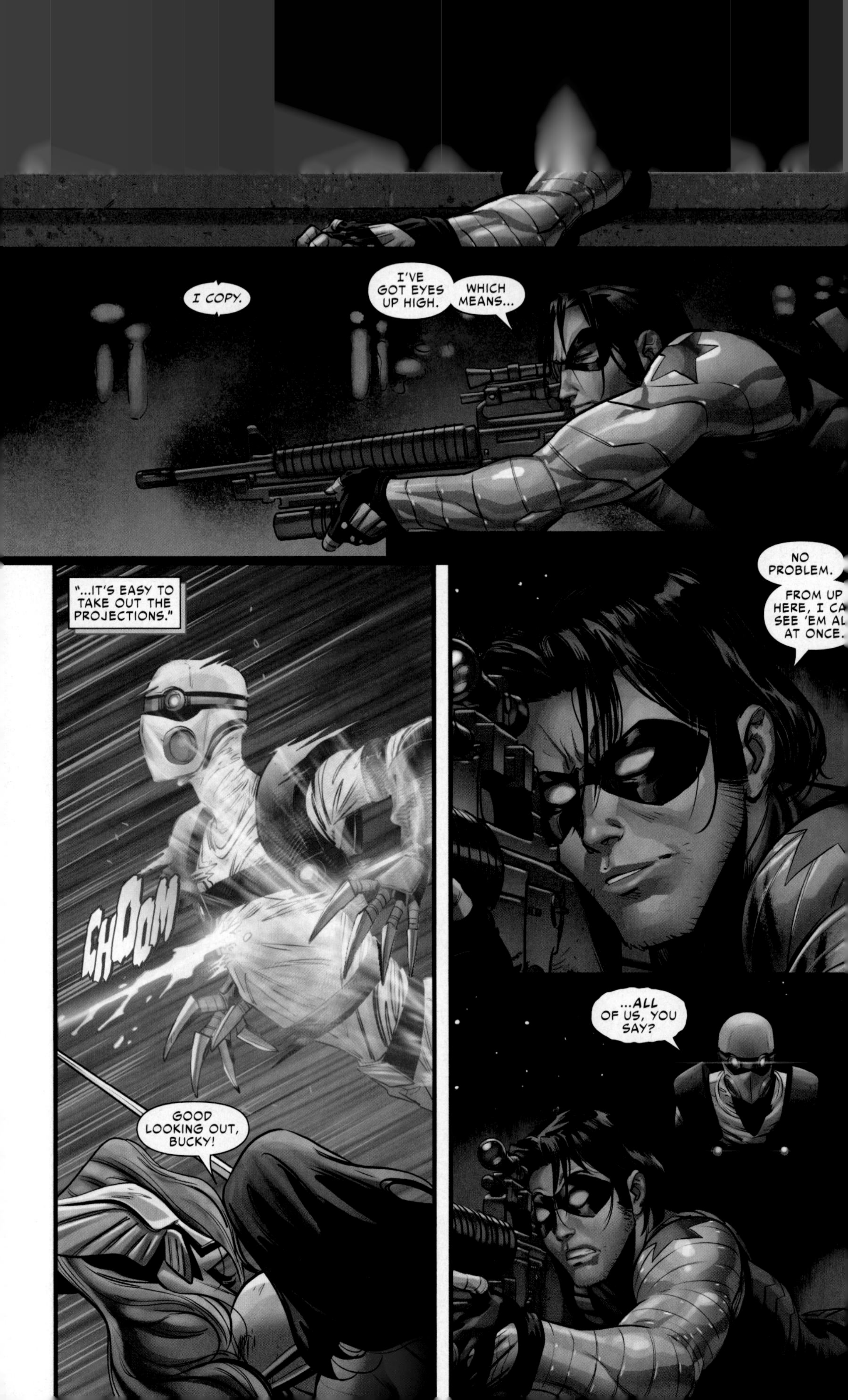
I COPY.
I'VE GOT EYES UP HIGH.
WHICH MEANS...
"...IT'S EASY TO TAKE OUT THE PROJECTIONS."
NO PROBLEM.
FROM UP HERE, I CA SEE 'EM AL AT ONCE.
CHOOM
GOOD LOOKING OUT, BUCKY!
...ALL OF US, YOU SAY?

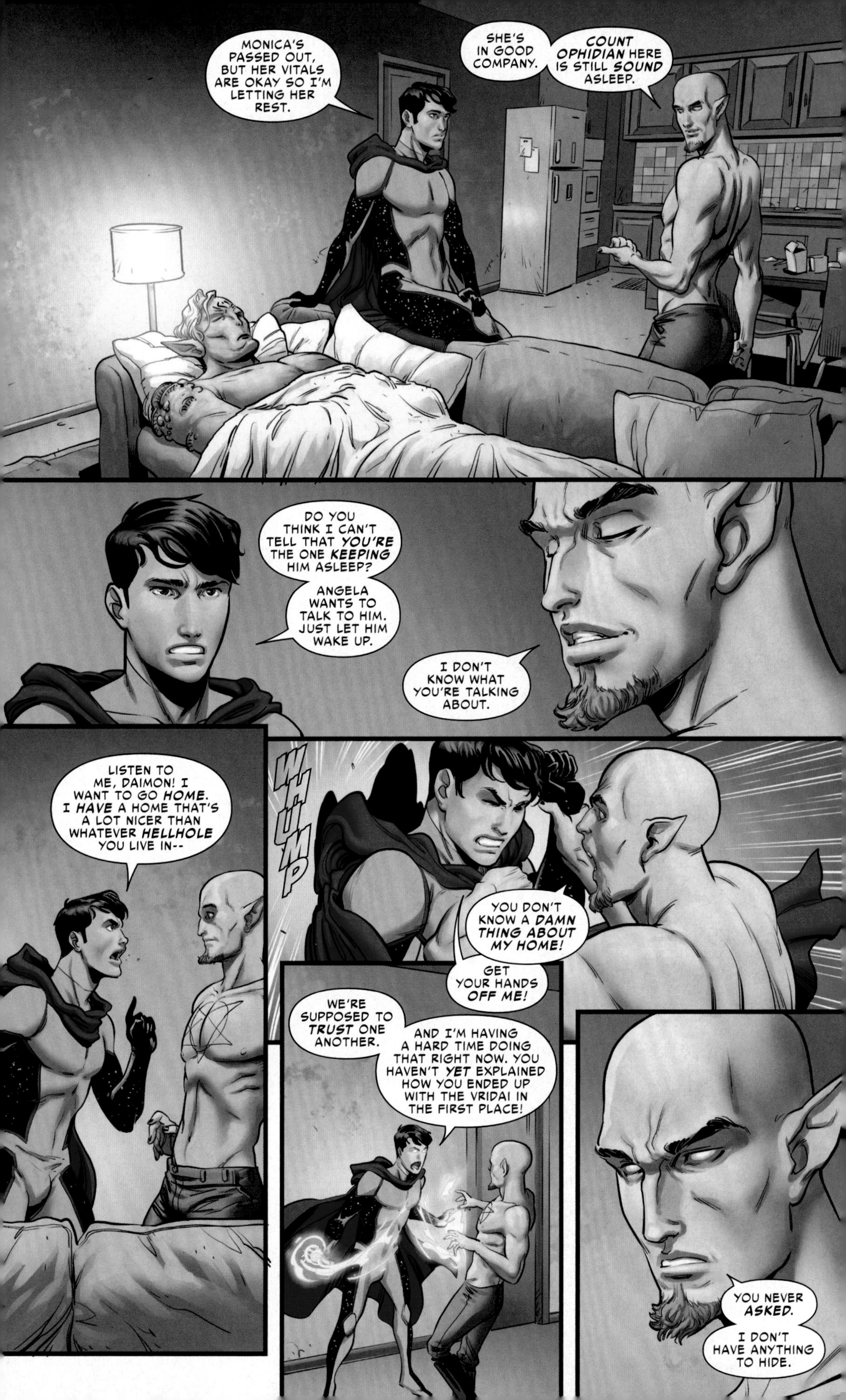

MONICA'S PASSED OUT, BUT HER VITALS ARE OKAY SO I'M LETTING HER REST.
SHE'S IN GOOD COMPANY.
COUNT OPHIDIAN HERE IS STILL SOUND ASLEEP.
DO YOU THINK I CAN'T TELL THAT YOU'RE THE ONE KEEPING HIM ASLEEP?
ANGELA WANTS TO TALK TO HIM. JUST LET HIM WAKE UP.
I DON'T KNOW WHAT YOU'RE TALKING ABOUT.
LISTEN TO ME, DAIMON! I WANT TO GO HOME. I HAVE A HOME THAT'S A LOT NICER THAN WHATEVER HELLHOLE YOU LIVE IN--
WHUMP
YOU DON'T KNOW A DAMN THING ABOUT MY HOME!
GET YOUR HANDS OFF ME!
WE'RE SUPPOSED TO TRUST ONE ANOTHER.
AND I'M HAVING A HARD TIME DOING THAT RIGHT NOW. YOU HAVEN'T YET EXPLAINED HOW YOU ENDED UP WITH THE VRIDAI IN THE FIRST PLACE!
YOU NEVER ASKED.
I DON'T HAVE ANYTHING TO HIDE.

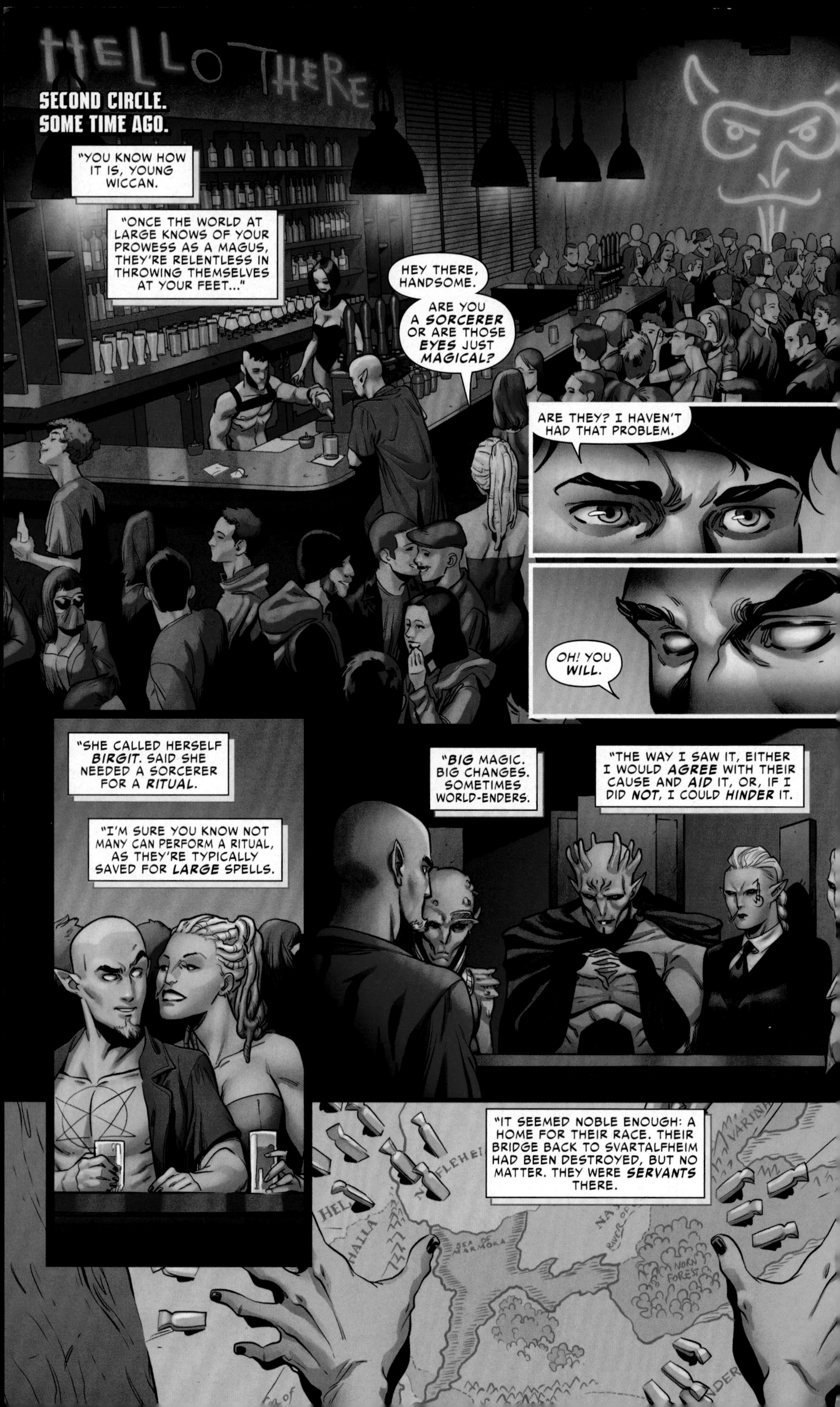
HELLO THERE
SECOND CIRCLE. SOME TIME AGO.
"YOU KNOW HOW IT IS, YOUNG WICCAN.
"ONCE THE WORLD AT LARGE KNOWS OF YOUR PROWESS AS A MAGUS, THEY'RE RELENTLESS IN THROWING THEMSELVES AT YOUR FEET..."
HEY THERE, HANDSOME.
ARE YOU A SORCERER OR ARE THOSE EYES JUST MAGICAL?
ARE THEY? I HAVEN'T HAD THAT PROBLEM.
OH! YOU WILL.
"SHE CALLED HERSELF BIRGIT. SAID SHE NEEDED A SORCERER FOR A RITUAL.
"I'M SURE YOU KNOW NOT MANY CAN PERFORM A RITUAL, AS THEY'RE TYPICALLY SAVED FOR LARGE SPELLS.
"BIG MAGIC. BIG CHANGES. SOMETIMES WORLD-ENDERS.
"THE WAY I SAW IT, EITHER I WOULD AGREE WITH THEIR CAUSE AND AID IT, OR, IF I DID NOT, I COULD HINDER IT.
"IT SEEMED NOBLE ENOUGH: A HOME FOR THEIR RACE. THEIR BRIDGE BACK TO SVARTALFHEIM HAD BEEN DESTROYED, BUT NO MATTER. THEY WERE SERVANTS THERE.
SEA OF MARMORA
NORN FOREST

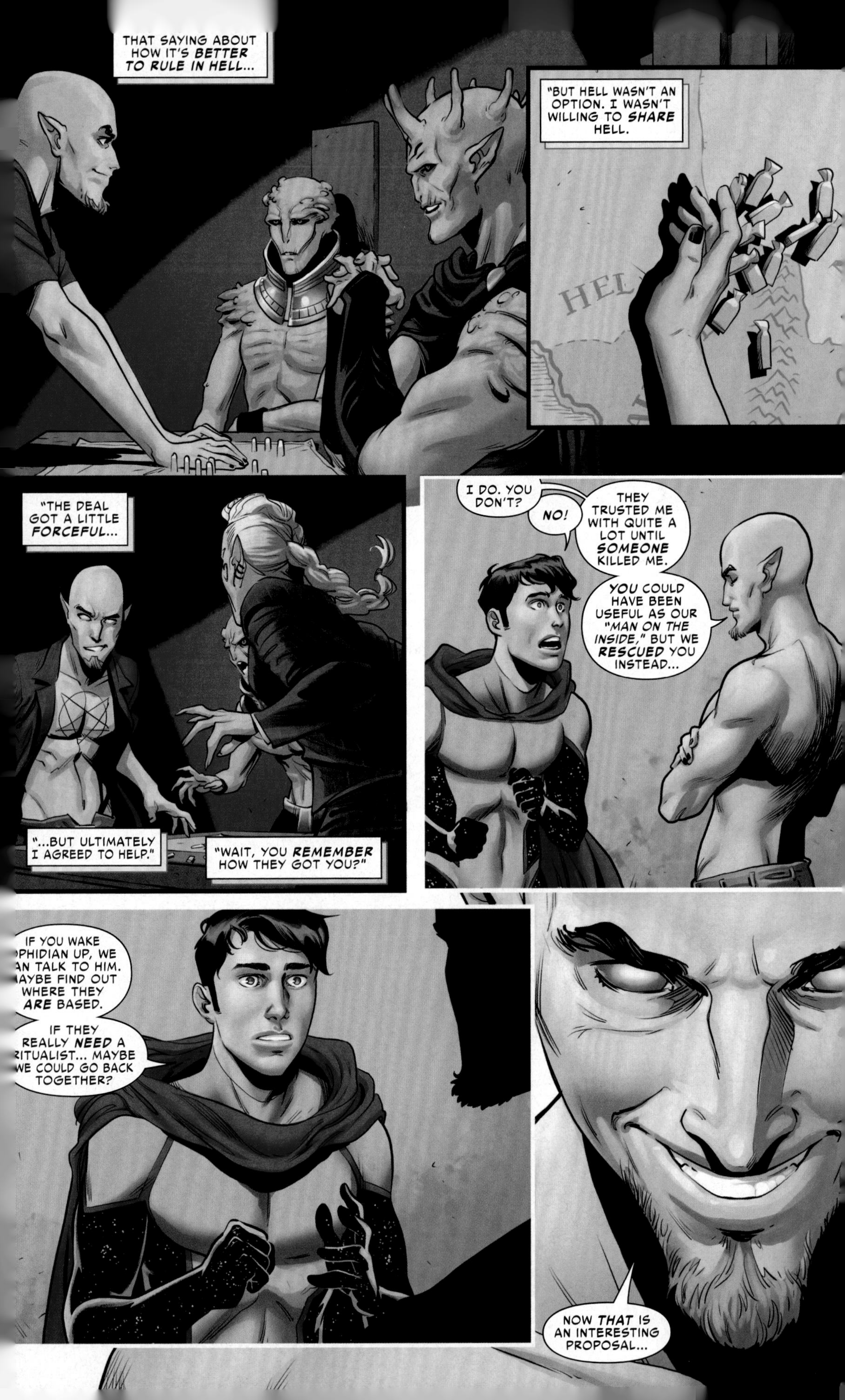

THAT SAYING ABOUT HOW IT'S *BETTER TO RULE IN HELL*...
"BUT HELL WASN'T AN OPTION. I WASN'T WILLING TO *SHARE* HELL.
HEL
"THE DEAL GOT A LITTLE *FORCEFUL*...
"...BUT ULTIMATELY I AGREED TO HELP."
"WAIT, YOU *REMEMBER* HOW THEY GOT YOU?"
I DO. YOU DON'T?
NO!
THEY TRUSTED ME WITH QUITE A LOT UNTIL *SOMEONE* KILLED ME.
YOU COULD HAVE BEEN USEFUL AS OUR "*MAN ON THE INSIDE*," BUT WE *RESCUED* YOU INSTEAD...
IF YOU WAKE OPHIDIAN UP, WE CAN TALK TO HIM. MAYBE FIND OUT WHERE THEY *ARE* BASED.
IF THEY REALLY *NEED* A RITUALIST... MAYBE WE COULD GO BACK TOGETHER?
NOW *THAT* IS AN INTERESTING PROPOSAL...

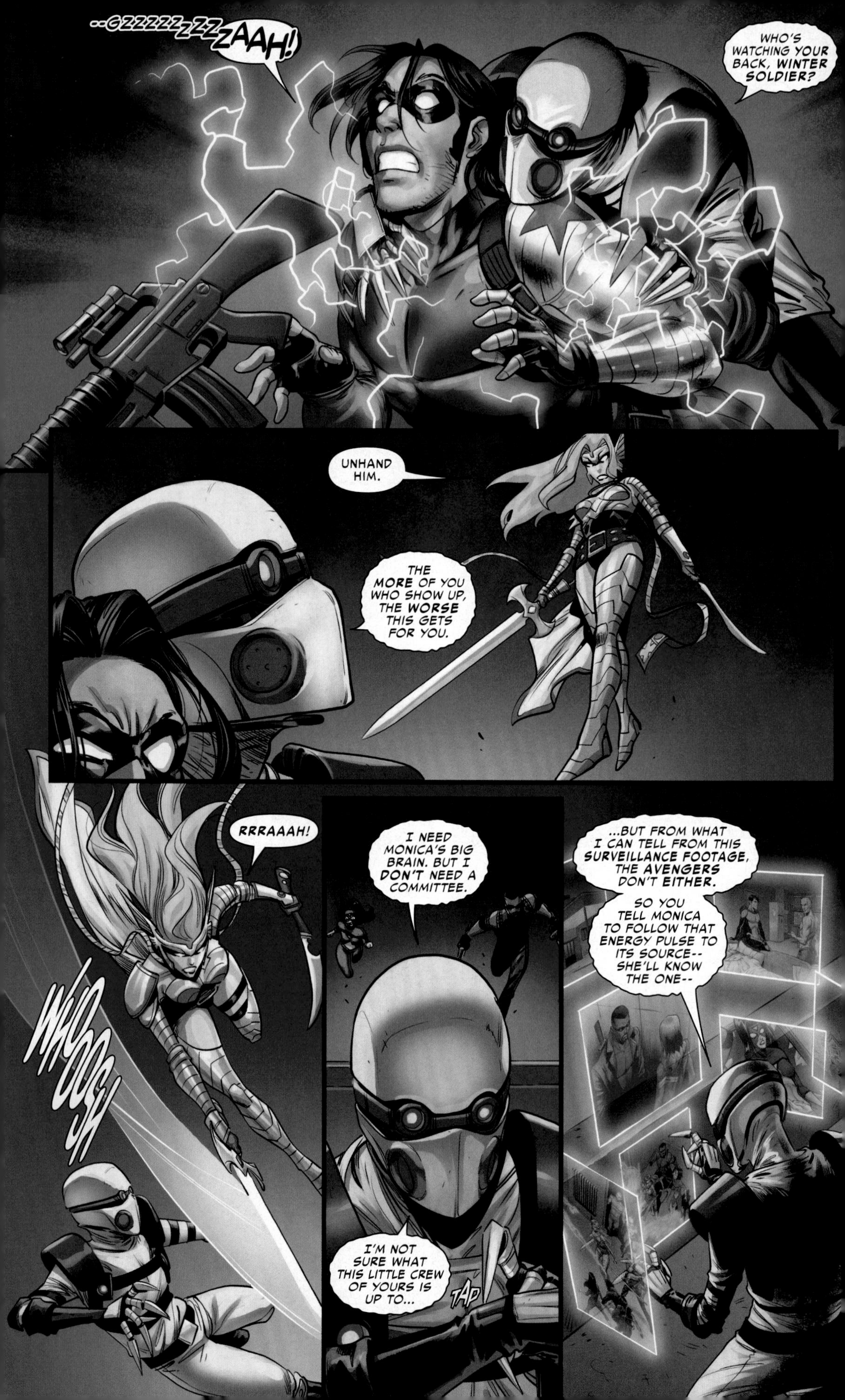
--GZZZZZZZZZAAH!
WHO'S WATCHING YOUR BACK, WINTER SOLDIER?
UNHAND HIM.
THE MORE OF YOU WHO SHOW UP, THE WORSE THIS GETS FOR YOU.
RRRAAAH!
WHOOSH
I NEED MONICA'S BIG BRAIN. BUT I DON'T NEED A COMMITTEE.
I'M NOT SURE WHAT THIS LITTLE CREW OF YOURS IS UP TO...
TAP
...BUT FROM WHAT I CAN TELL FROM THIS SURVEILLANCE FOOTAGE, THE AVENGERS DON'T EITHER.
SO YOU TELL MONICA TO FOLLOW THAT ENERGY PULSE TO ITS SOURCE-- SHE'LL KNOW THE ONE--

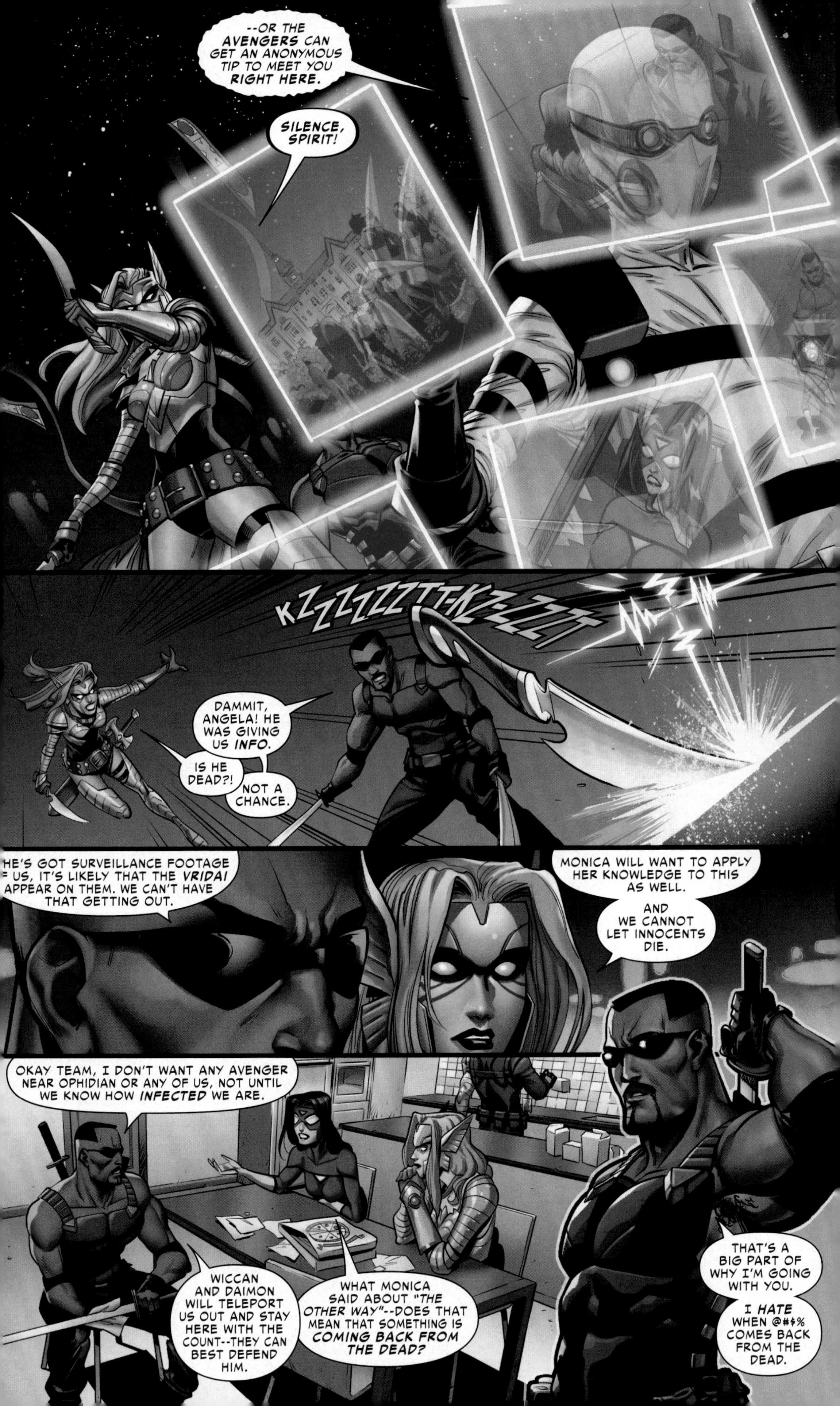
--OR THE AVENGERS CAN GET AN ANONYMOUS TIP TO MEET YOU RIGHT HERE.
SILENCE, SPIRIT!
KZZZZZZTT-KZ-ZZZT
DAMMIT, ANGELA! HE WAS GIVING US INFO.
IS HE DEAD?!
NOT A CHANCE.
HE'S GOT SURVEILLANCE FOOTAGE OF US, IT'S LIKELY THAT THE VRIDAI APPEAR ON THEM. WE CAN'T HAVE THAT GETTING OUT.
MONICA WILL WANT TO APPLY HER KNOWLEDGE TO THIS AS WELL.
AND WE CANNOT LET INNOCENTS DIE.
OKAY TEAM, I DON'T WANT ANY AVENGER NEAR OPHIDIAN OR ANY OF US, NOT UNTIL WE KNOW HOW INFECTED WE ARE.
WICCAN AND DAIMON WILL TELEPORT US OUT AND STAY HERE WITH THE COUNT--THEY CAN BEST DEFEND HIM.
WHAT MONICA SAID ABOUT "THE OTHER WAY"--DOES THAT MEAN THAT SOMETHING IS COMING BACK FROM THE DEAD?
THAT'S A BIG PART OF WHY I'M GOING WITH YOU.
I HATE WHEN @#$% COMES BACK FROM THE DEAD.

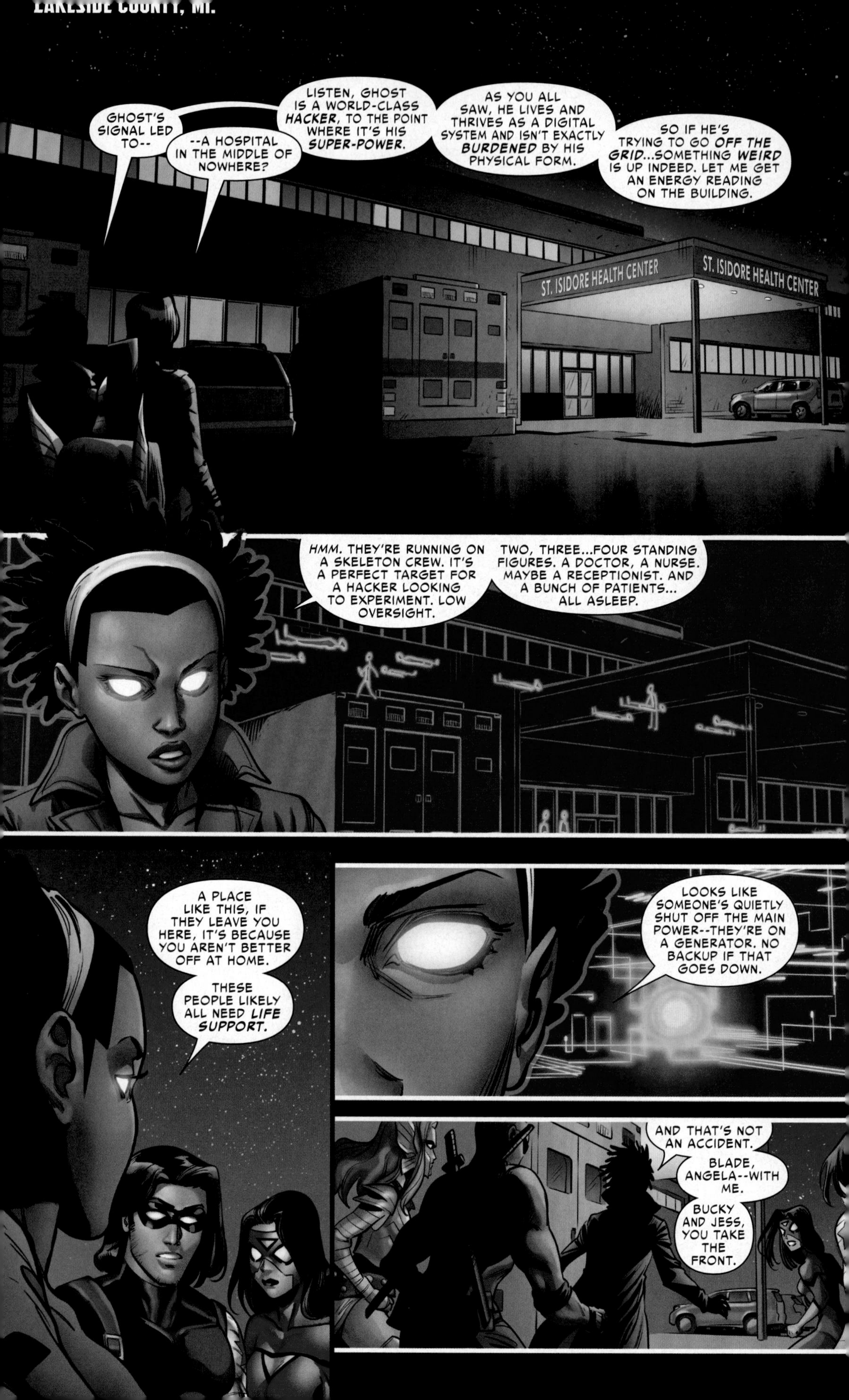
LAKESIDE COUNTY, MI.
GHOST'S SIGNAL LED TO--
--A HOSPITAL IN THE MIDDLE OF NOWHERE?
LISTEN, GHOST IS A WORLD-CLASS HACKER, TO THE POINT WHERE IT'S HIS SUPER-POWER.
AS YOU ALL SAW, HE LIVES AND THRIVES AS A DIGITAL SYSTEM AND ISN'T EXACTLY BURDENED BY HIS PHYSICAL FORM.
SO IF HE'S TRYING TO GO OFF THE GRID...SOMETHING WEIRD IS UP INDEED. LET ME GET AN ENERGY READING ON THE BUILDING.
ST. ISIDORE HEALTH CENTER
ST. ISIDORE HEALTH CENTER
HMM. THEY'RE RUNNING ON A SKELETON CREW. IT'S A PERFECT TARGET FOR A HACKER LOOKING TO EXPERIMENT. LOW OVERSIGHT.
TWO, THREE...FOUR STANDING FIGURES. A DOCTOR, A NURSE. MAYBE A RECEPTIONIST. AND A BUNCH OF PATIENTS... ALL ASLEEP.
A PLACE LIKE THIS, IF THEY LEAVE YOU HERE, IT'S BECAUSE YOU AREN'T BETTER OFF AT HOME.
THESE PEOPLE LIKELY ALL NEED LIFE SUPPORT.
LOOKS LIKE SOMEONE'S QUIETLY SHUT OFF THE MAIN POWER--THEY'RE ON A GENERATOR. NO BACKUP IF THAT GOES DOWN.
AND THAT'S NOT AN ACCIDENT.
BLADE, ANGELA--WITH ME.
BUCKY AND JESS, YOU TAKE THE FRONT.

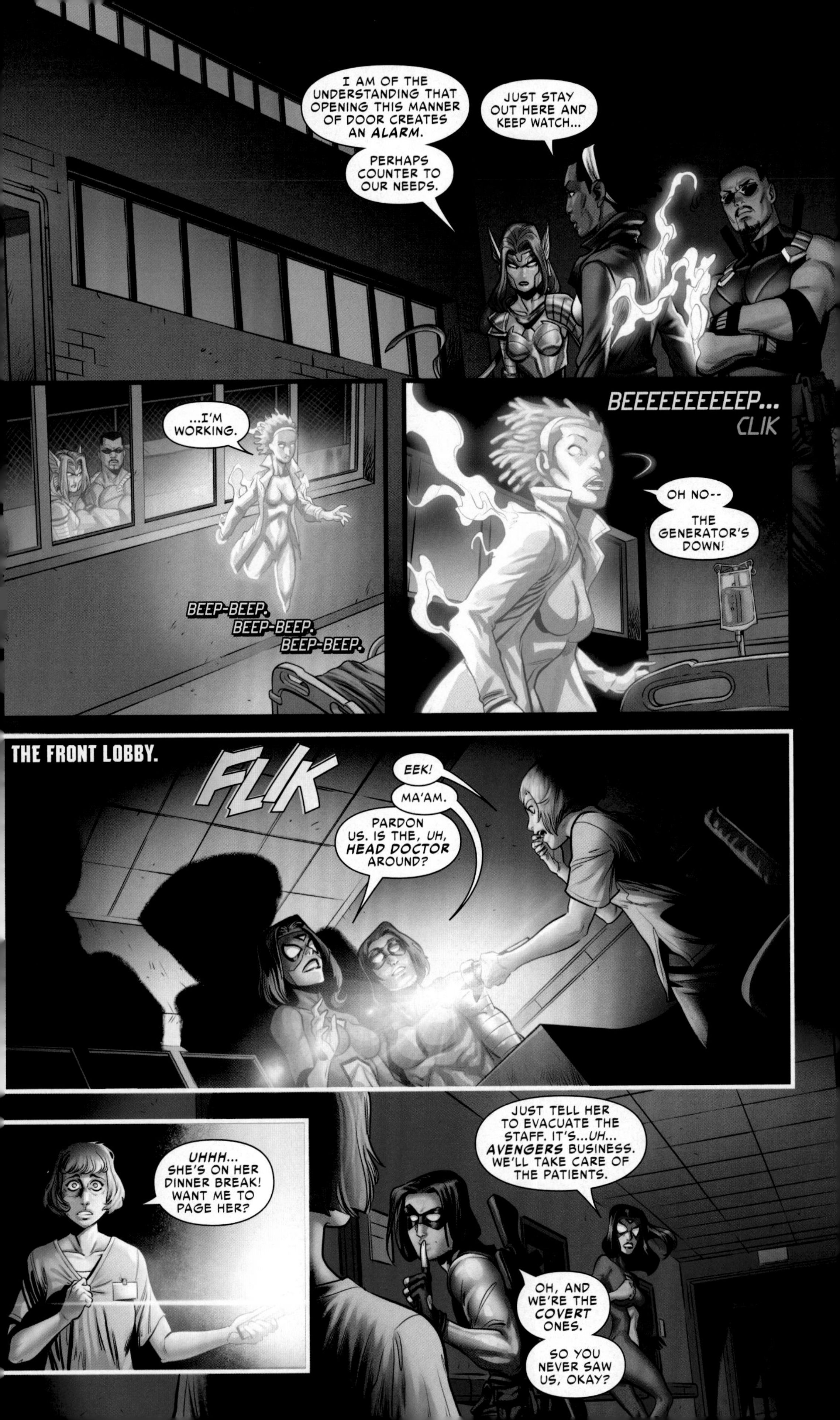
I AM OF THE UNDERSTANDING THAT OPENING THIS MANNER OF DOOR CREATES AN *ALARM*.
PERHAPS COUNTER TO OUR NEEDS.
JUST STAY OUT HERE AND KEEP WATCH...
...I'M WORKING.
BEEP-BEEP. BEEP-BEEP. BEEP-BEEP.
BEEEEEEEEEEP... CLIK
OH NO--
THE GENERATOR'S DOWN!
THE FRONT LOBBY.
FLIK
EEK!
MA'AM.
PARDON US. IS THE, *UH*, ***HEAD DOCTOR*** AROUND?
UHHH... SHE'S ON HER DINNER BREAK! WANT ME TO PAGE HER?
JUST TELL HER TO EVACUATE THE STAFF. IT'S...*UH...* ***AVENGERS*** BUSINESS. WE'LL TAKE CARE OF THE PATIENTS.
OH, AND WE'RE THE ***COVERT*** ONES.
SO YOU NEVER SAW US, OKAY?

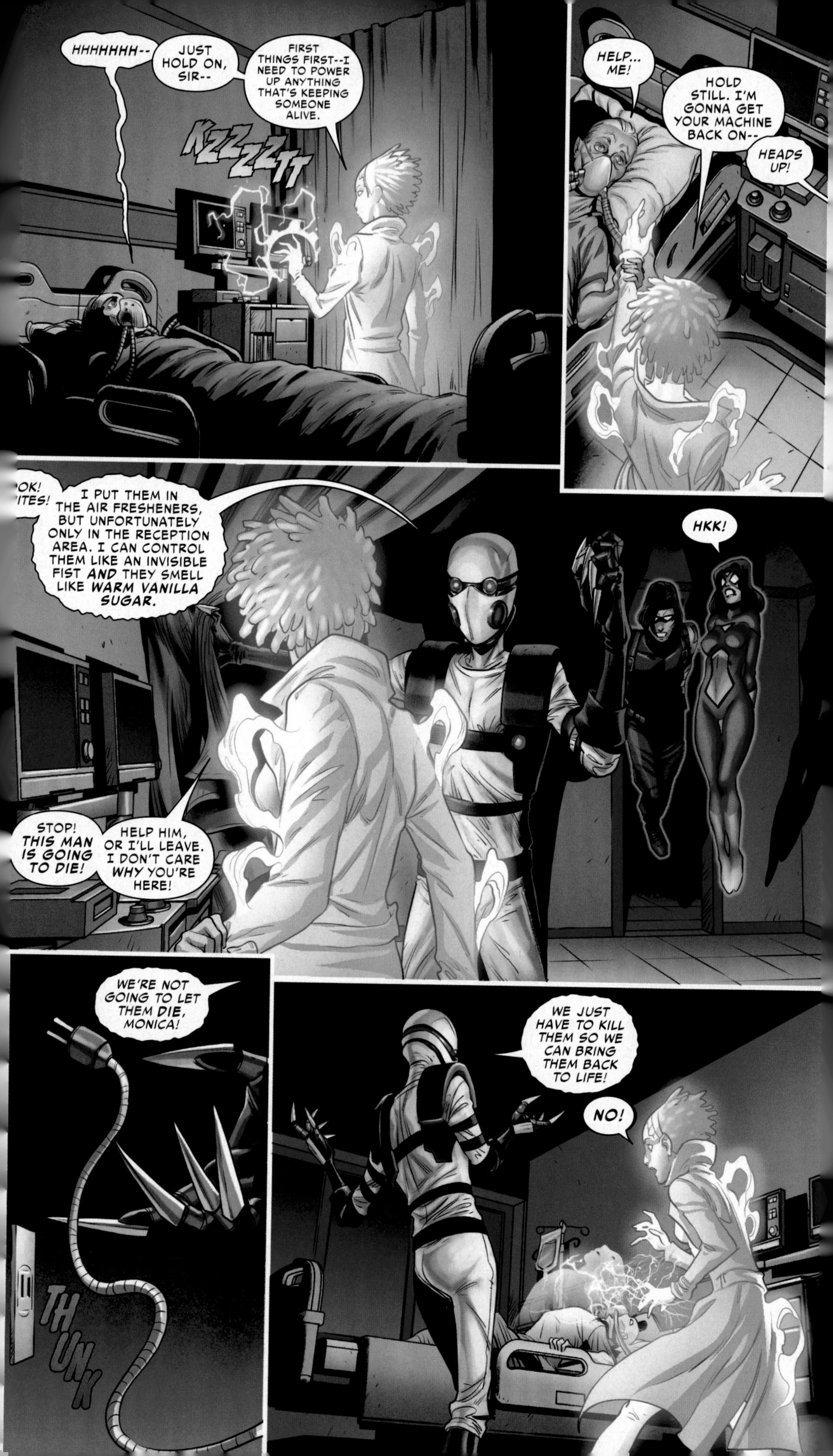
HHHHHHH--
JUST HOLD ON, SIR--
FIRST THINGS FIRST--I NEED TO POWER UP ANYTHING THAT'S KEEPING SOMEONE ALIVE.
KZZZZTT
HELP... ME!
HOLD STILL. I'M GONNA GET YOUR MACHINE BACK ON--
HEADS UP!
I PUT THEM IN THE AIR FRESHENERS, BUT UNFORTUNATELY ONLY IN THE RECEPTION AREA. I CAN CONTROL THEM LIKE AN INVISIBLE FIST AND THEY SMELL LIKE WARM VANILLA SUGAR.
HKK!
STOP! THIS MAN IS GOING TO DIE!
HELP HIM, OR I'LL LEAVE. I DON'T CARE WHY YOU'RE HERE!
WE'RE NOT GOING TO LET THEM DIE, MONICA!
THUNK
WE JUST HAVE TO KILL THEM SO WE CAN BRING THEM BACK TO LIFE!
NO!

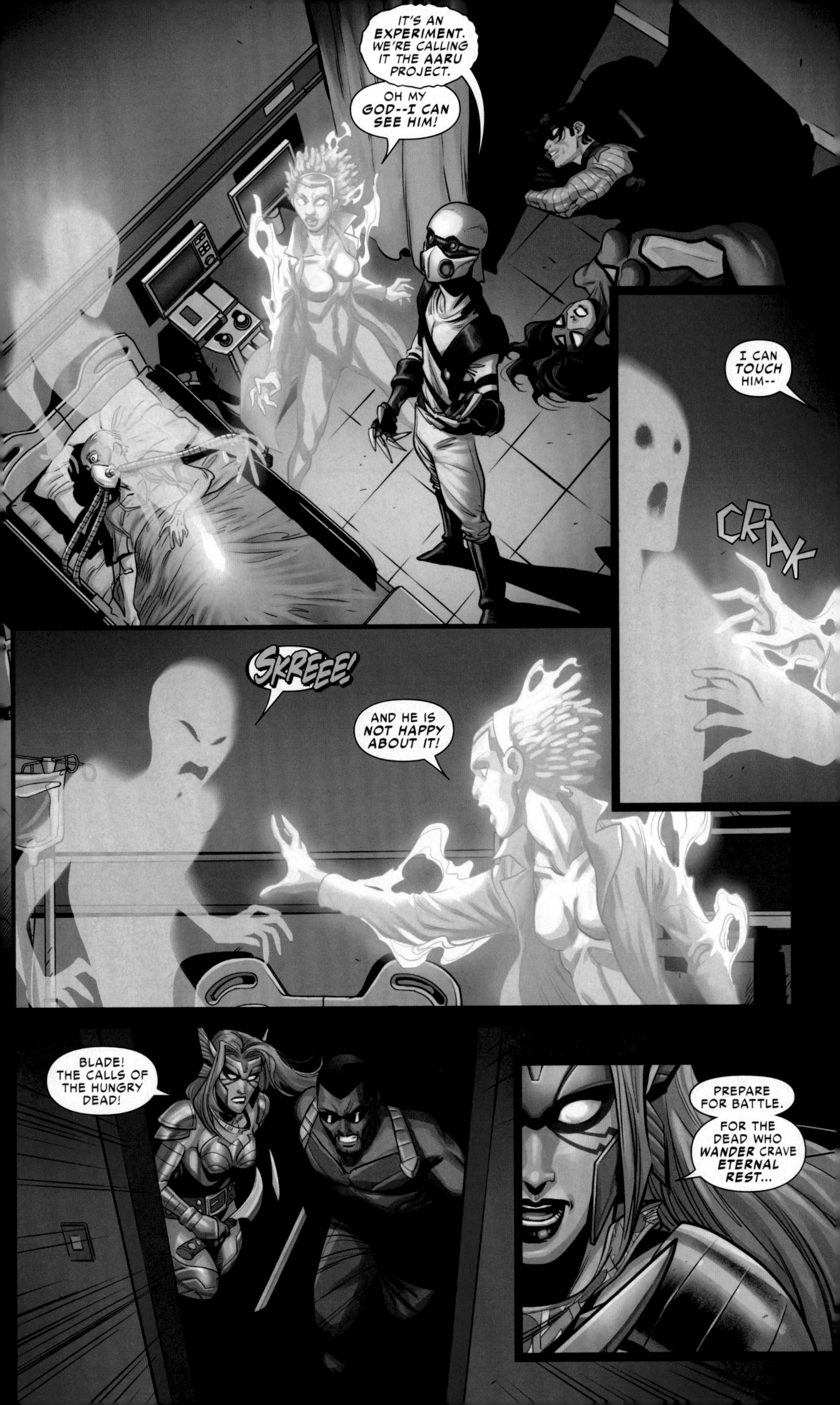
IT'S AN EXPERIMENT. WE'RE CALLING IT THE AARU PROJECT.
OH MY GOD--I CAN SEE HIM!
I CAN TOUCH HIM--
CRAK
SKREEE!
AND HE IS NOT HAPPY ABOUT IT!
BLADE! THE CALLS OF THE HUNGRY DEAD!
PREPARE FOR BATTLE.
FOR THE DEAD WHO WANDER CRAVE ETERNAL REST...

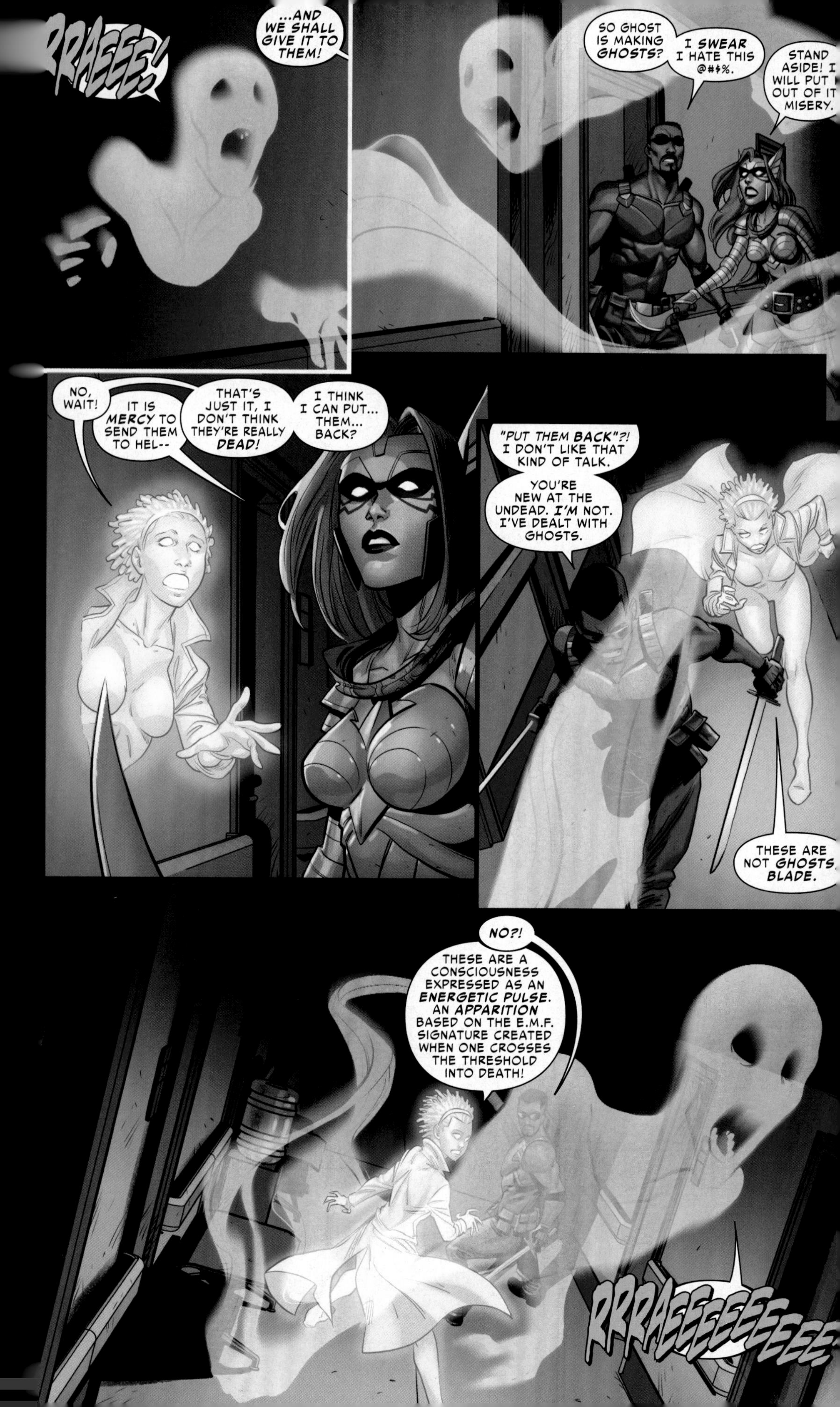
RRAEEE!
...AND WE SHALL GIVE IT TO THEM!
SO GHOST IS MAKING GHOSTS?
I SWEAR I HATE THIS @#$%.
STAND ASIDE! I WILL PUT I OUT OF IT MISERY.
NO, WAIT!
IT IS MERCY TO SEND THEM TO HEL--
THAT'S JUST IT, I DON'T THINK THEY'RE REALLY DEAD!
I THINK I CAN PUT... THEM... BACK?
"PUT THEM BACK"?! I DON'T LIKE THAT KIND OF TALK.
YOU'RE NEW AT THE UNDEAD. I'M NOT. I'VE DEALT WITH GHOSTS.
THESE ARE NOT GHOSTS BLADE.
NO?!
THESE ARE A CONSCIOUSNESS EXPRESSED AS AN ENERGETIC PULSE. AN APPARITION BASED ON THE E.M.F. SIGNATURE CREATED WHEN ONE CROSSES THE THRESHOLD INTO DEATH!
RRRAEEEEEEEEEEE

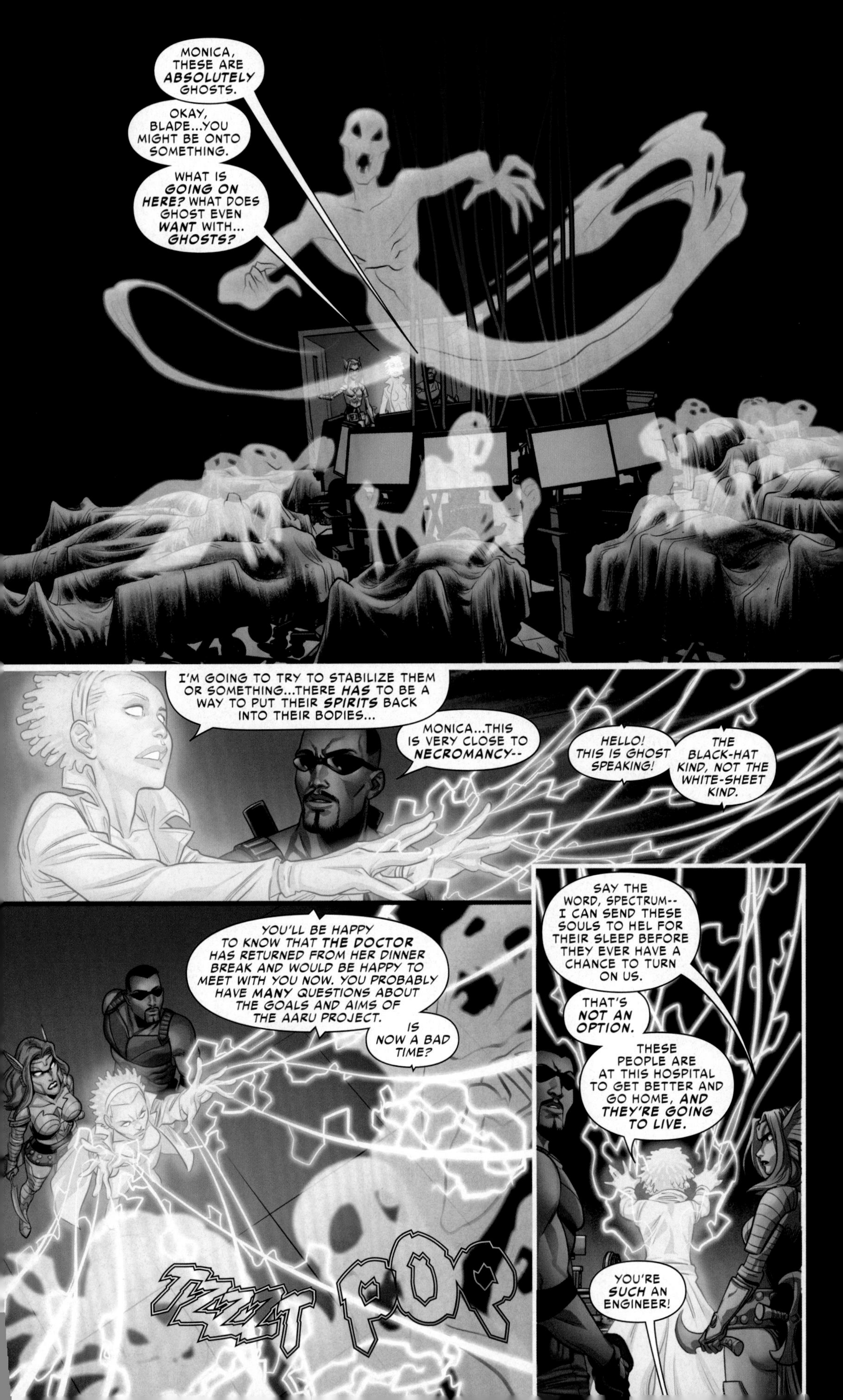
MONICA, THESE ARE ABSOLUTELY GHOSTS.
OKAY, BLADE...YOU MIGHT BE ONTO SOMETHING.
WHAT IS GOING ON HERE? WHAT DOES GHOST EVEN WANT WITH... GHOSTS?
I'M GOING TO TRY TO STABILIZE THEM OR SOMETHING...THERE HAS TO BE A WAY TO PUT THEIR SPIRITS BACK INTO THEIR BODIES...
MONICA...THIS IS VERY CLOSE TO NECROMANCY--
HELLO! THIS IS GHOST SPEAKING!
THE BLACK-HAT KIND, NOT THE WHITE-SHEET KIND.
YOU'LL BE HAPPY TO KNOW THAT THE DOCTOR HAS RETURNED FROM HER DINNER BREAK AND WOULD BE HAPPY TO MEET WITH YOU NOW. YOU PROBABLY HAVE MANY QUESTIONS ABOUT THE GOALS AND AIMS OF THE AARU PROJECT.
IS NOW A BAD TIME?
TZZZT
POP
SAY THE WORD, SPECTRUM-- I CAN SEND THESE SOULS TO HEL FOR THEIR SLEEP BEFORE THEY EVER HAVE A CHANCE TO TURN ON US.
THAT'S NOT AN OPTION.
THESE PEOPLE ARE AT THIS HOSPITAL TO GET BETTER AND GO HOME, AND THEY'RE GOING TO LIVE.
YOU'RE SUCH AN ENGINEER!

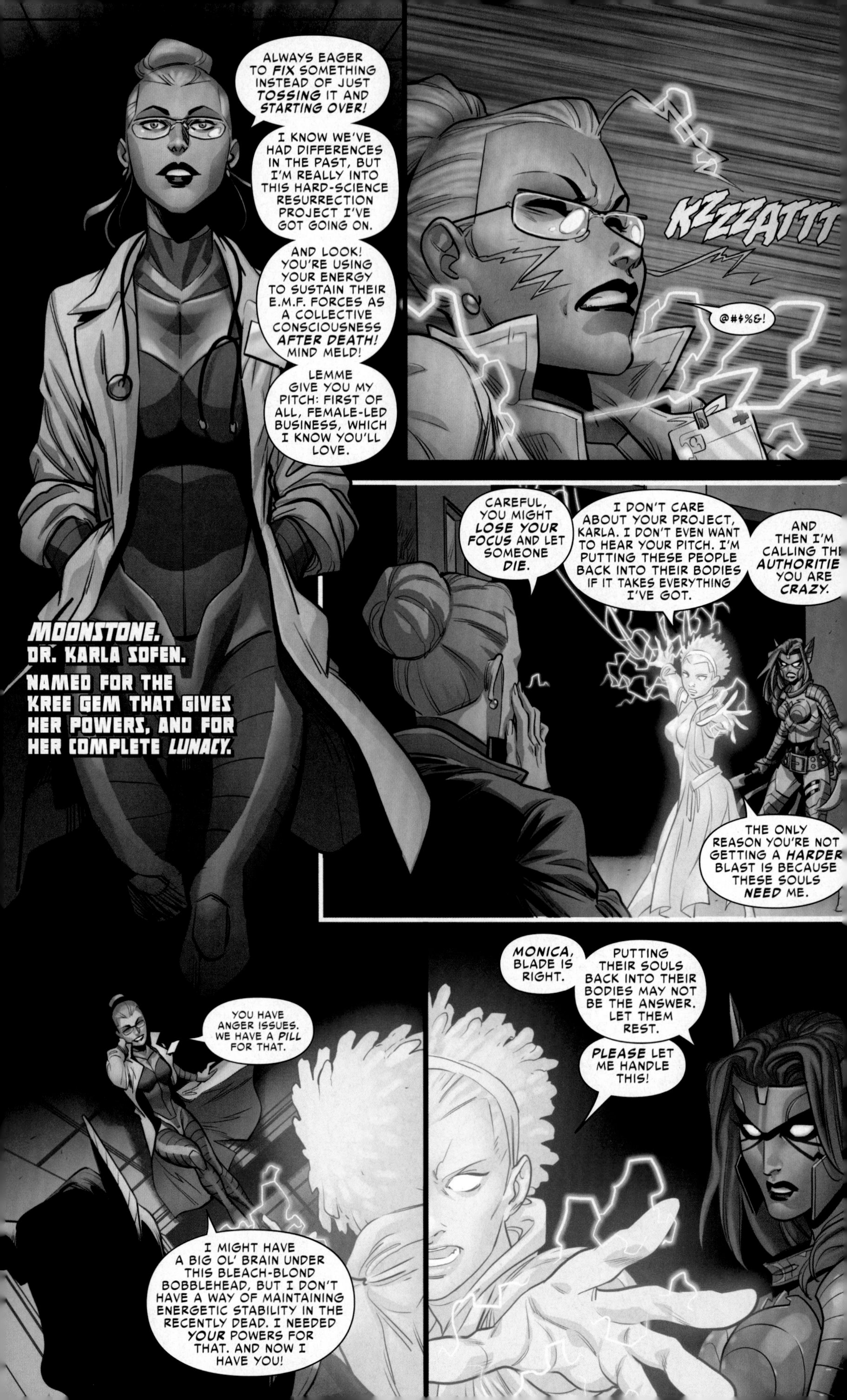

ALWAYS EAGER TO FIX SOMETHING INSTEAD OF JUST TOSSING IT AND STARTING OVER!
I KNOW WE'VE HAD DIFFERENCES IN THE PAST, BUT I'M REALLY INTO THIS HARD-SCIENCE RESURRECTION PROJECT I'VE GOT GOING ON.
AND LOOK! YOU'RE USING YOUR ENERGY TO SUSTAIN THEIR E.M.F. FORCES AS A COLLECTIVE CONSCIOUSNESS AFTER DEATH! MIND MELD!
LEMME GIVE YOU MY PITCH: FIRST OF ALL, FEMALE-LED BUSINESS, WHICH I KNOW YOU'LL LOVE.
MOONSTONE. DR. KARLA SOFEN.
NAMED FOR THE KREE GEM THAT GIVES HER POWERS, AND FOR HER COMPLETE LUNACY.
KZZZATTT
@#$%&!
I DON'T CARE ABOUT YOUR PROJECT, KARLA. I DON'T EVEN WANT TO HEAR YOUR PITCH. I'M PUTTING THESE PEOPLE BACK INTO THEIR BODIES IF IT TAKES EVERYTHING I'VE GOT.
CAREFUL, YOU MIGHT LOSE YOUR FOCUS AND LET SOMEONE DIE.
AND THEN I'M CALLING THE AUTHORITIE YOU ARE CRAZY.
THE ONLY REASON YOU'RE NOT GETTING A HARDER BLAST IS BECAUSE THESE SOULS NEED ME.
YOU HAVE ANGER ISSUES. WE HAVE A PILL FOR THAT.
I MIGHT HAVE A BIG OL' BRAIN UNDER THIS BLEACH-BLOND BOBBLEHEAD, BUT I DON'T HAVE A WAY OF MAINTAINING ENERGETIC STABILITY IN THE RECENTLY DEAD. I NEEDED YOUR POWERS FOR THAT. AND NOW I HAVE YOU!
MONICA, BLADE IS RIGHT.
PUTTING THEIR SOULS BACK INTO THEIR BODIES MAY NOT BE THE ANSWER. LET THEM REST.
PLEASE LET ME HANDLE THIS!

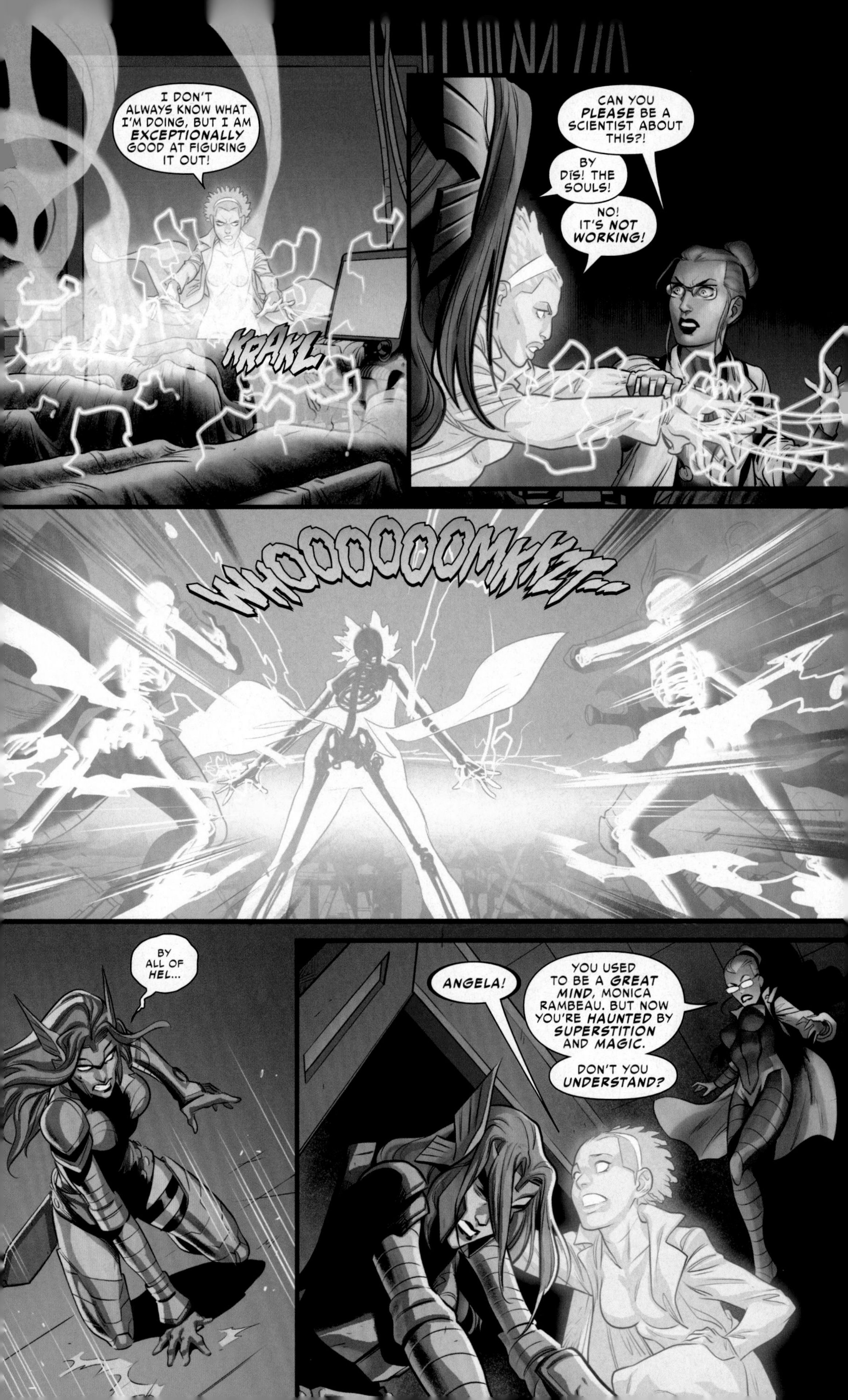
I DON'T ALWAYS KNOW WHAT I'M DOING, BUT I AM EXCEPTIONALLY GOOD AT FIGURING IT OUT!
KRAKL
CAN YOU PLEASE BE A SCIENTIST ABOUT THIS?!
BY DĪS! THE SOULS!
NO! IT'S NOT WORKING!
WHOOOOOOMKKZT--
BY ALL OF HEL...
ANGELA!
YOU USED TO BE A GREAT MIND, MONICA RAMBEAU. BUT NOW YOU'RE HAUNTED BY SUPERSTITION AND MAGIC.
DON'T YOU UNDERSTAND?

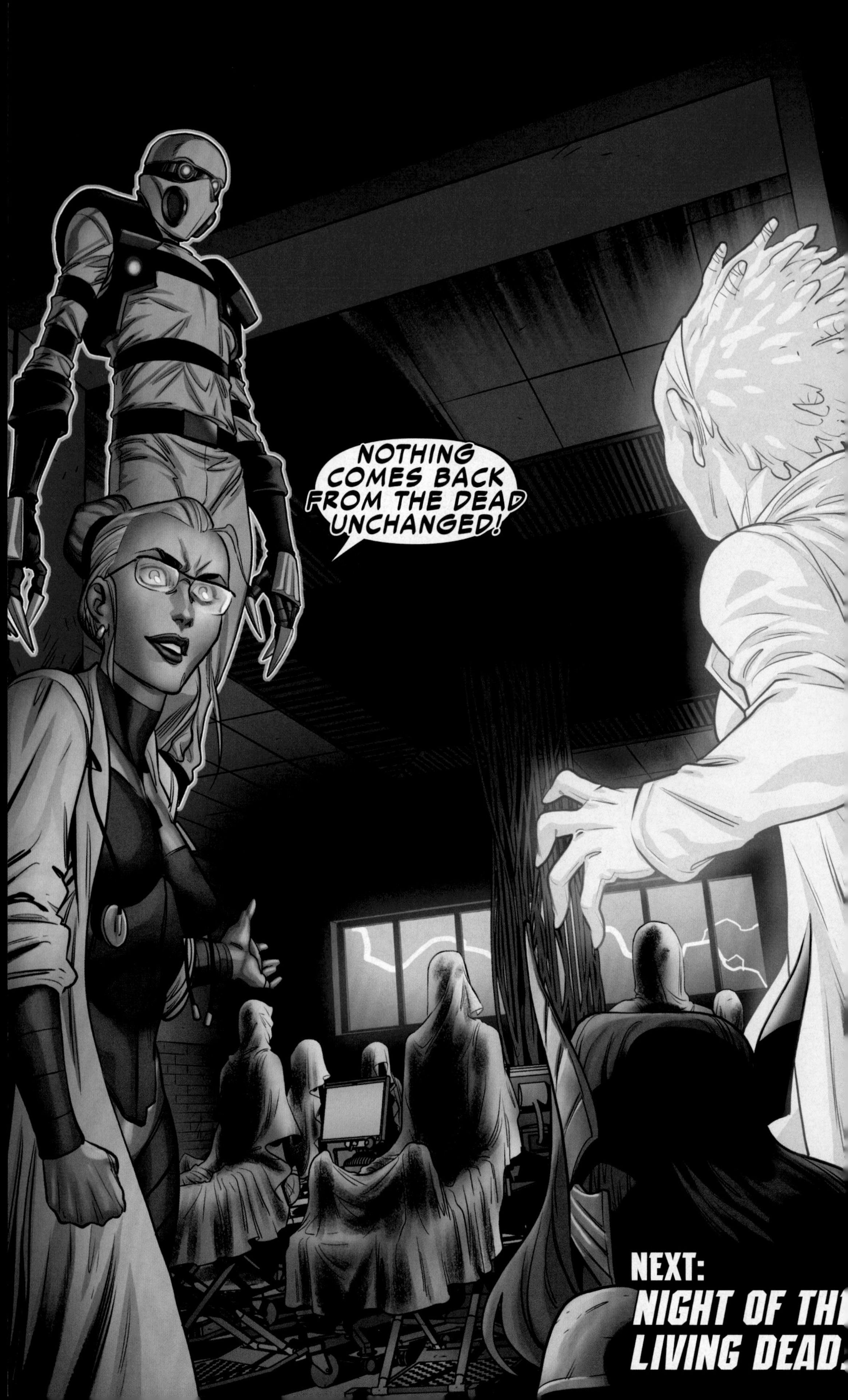
NOTHING COMES BACK FROM THE DEAD UNCHANGED!
NEXT:
NIGHT OF THE LIVING DEAD.

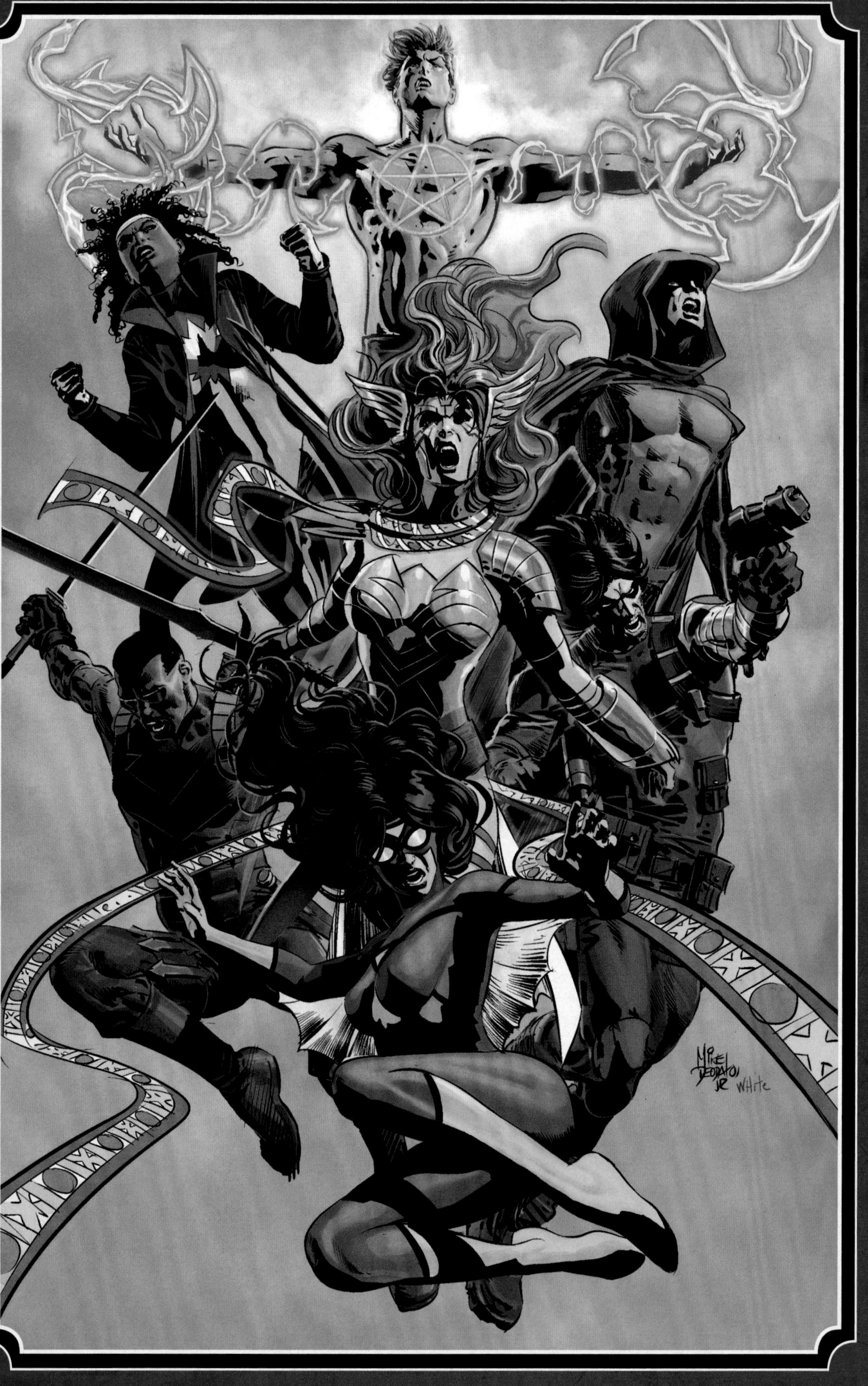
Mike Deodato Jr
White

#1 VARIANT BY **MIKE DEODATO JR.** & **DEAN WHITE**

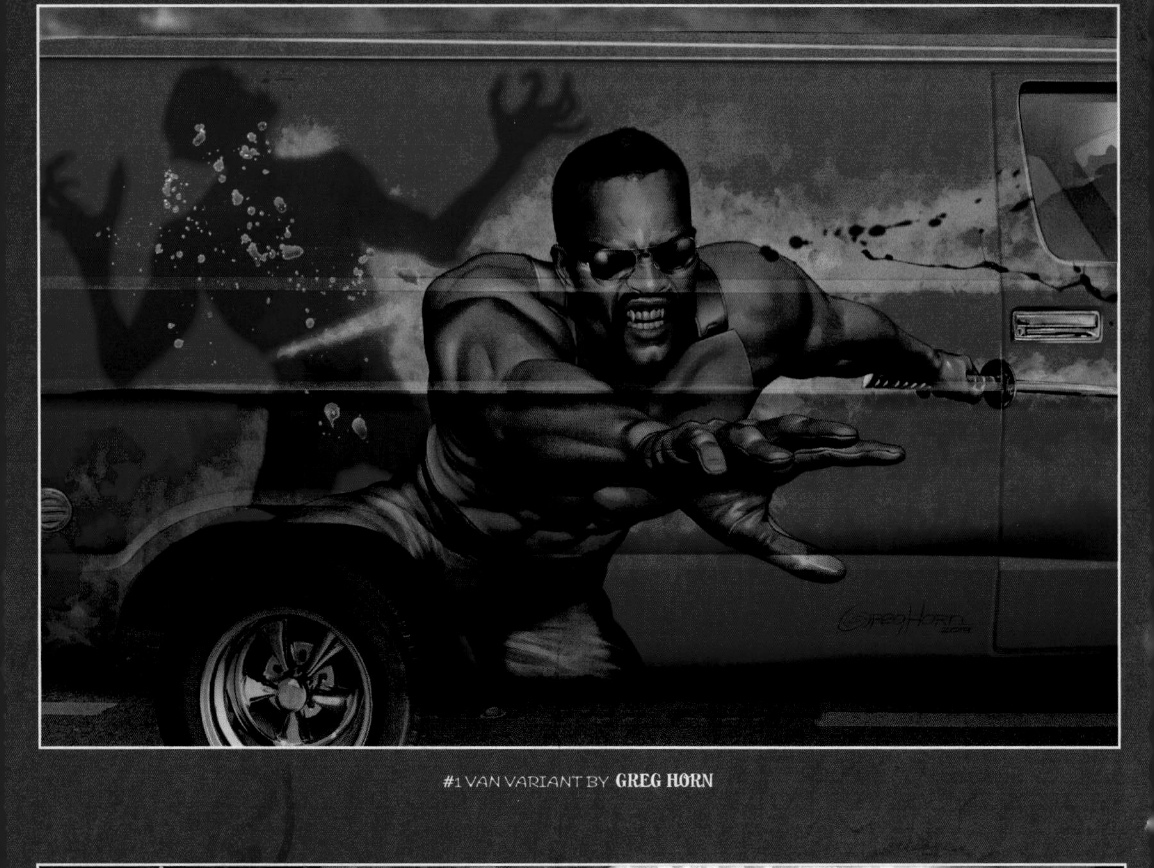

#1 VAN VARIANT BY **GREG HORN**

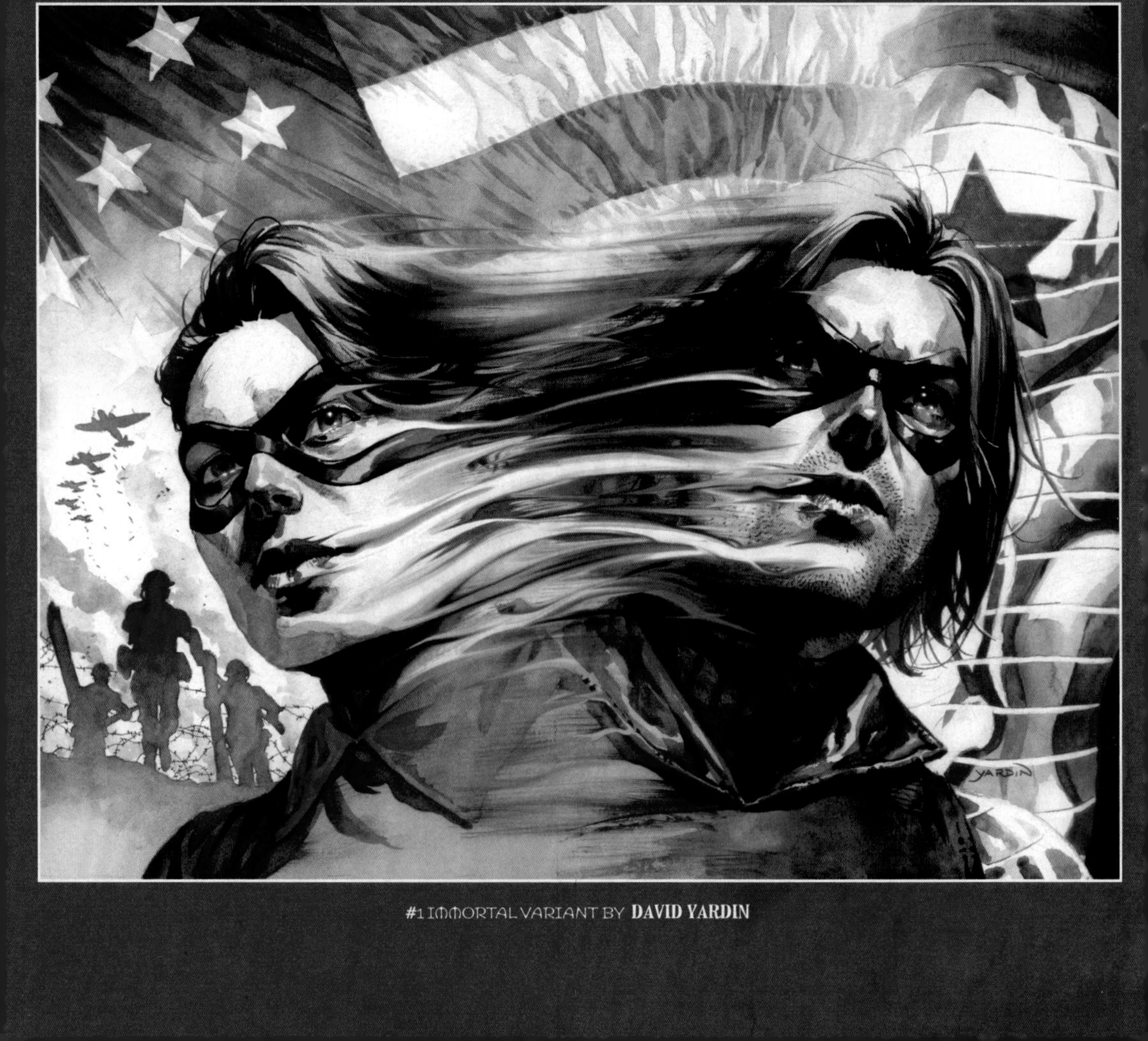

#1 IMMORTAL VARIANT BY **DAVID YARDIN**

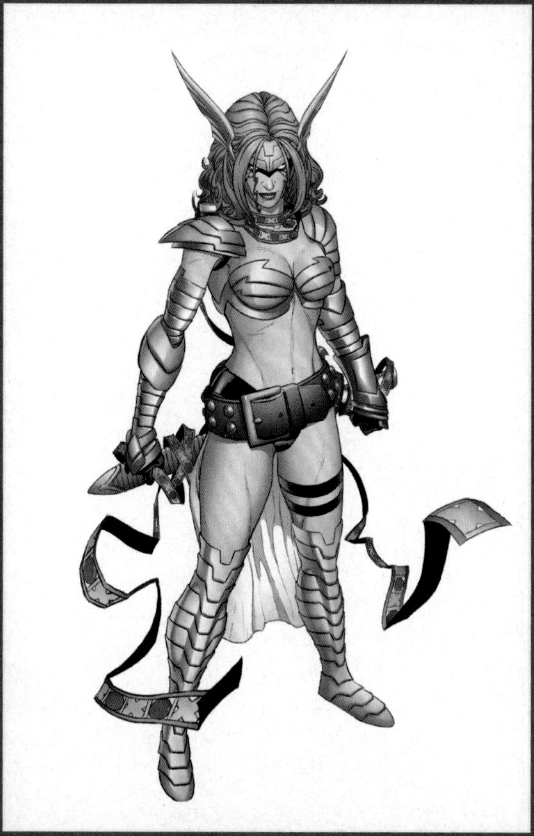

#1 HIDDEN GEM VARIANT
BY **JOE QUESADA & RICHARD ISANOVE**

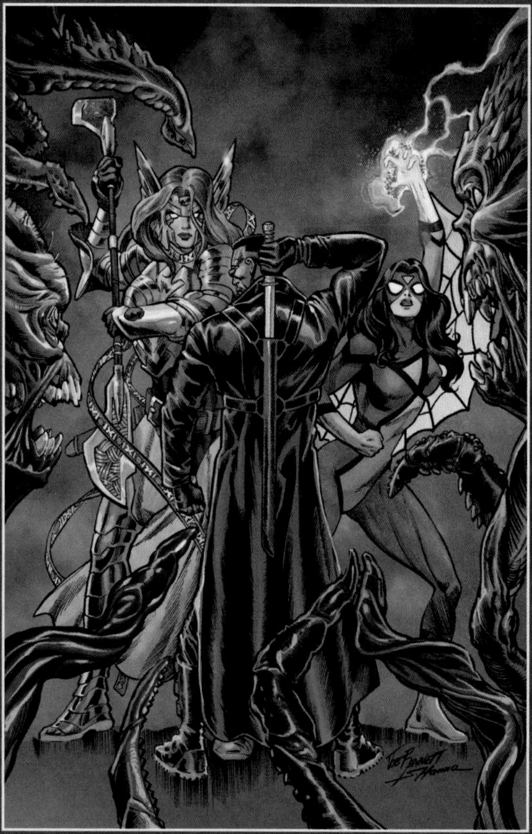

#1 VARIANT BY **JOE BENNETT, SCOTT HANNA & DEAN WHITE**

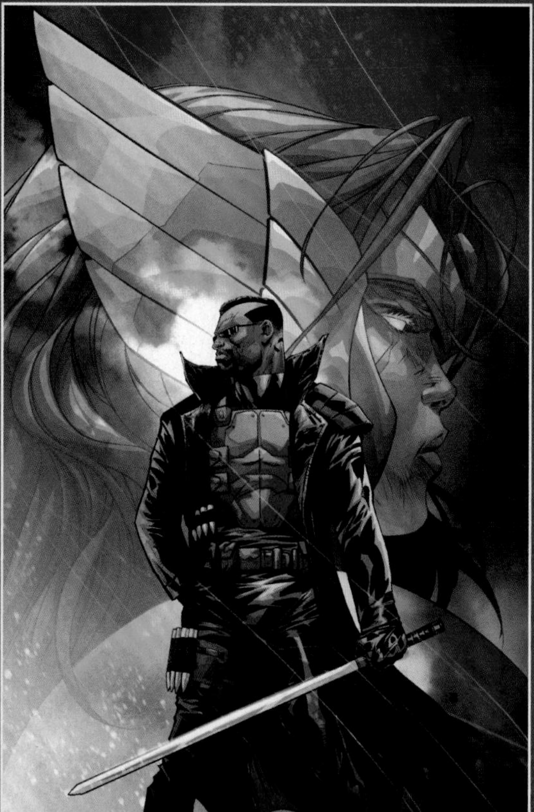

#1 VARIANT BY **RYAN BENJAMIN**

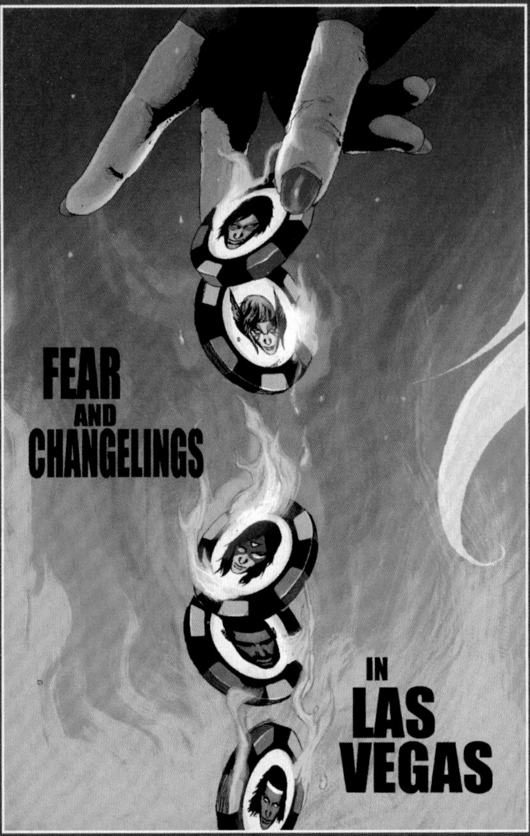
FEAR
AND
CHANGELINGS
IN
LAS
VEGAS

#2 VARIANT BY ANDREA SORRENTINO & DEAN WHITE

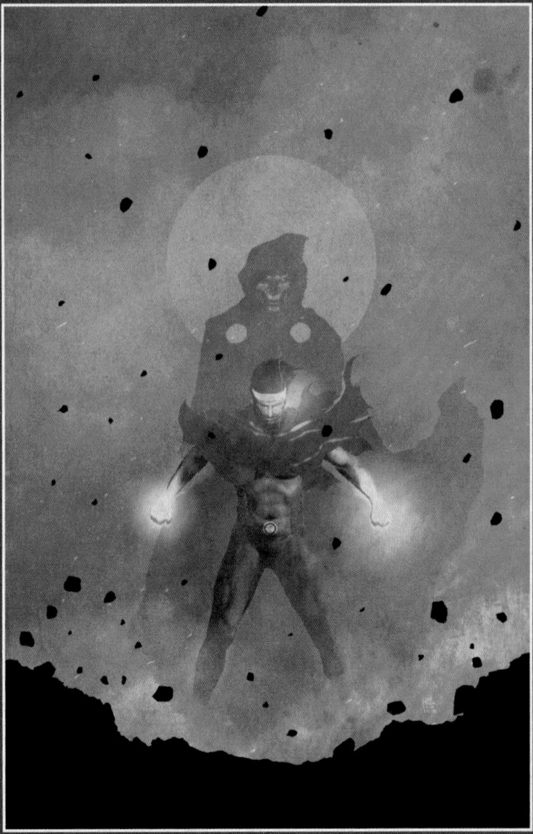

#3 VARIANT BY ANDREA SORRENTINO & MATTHEW WILSON

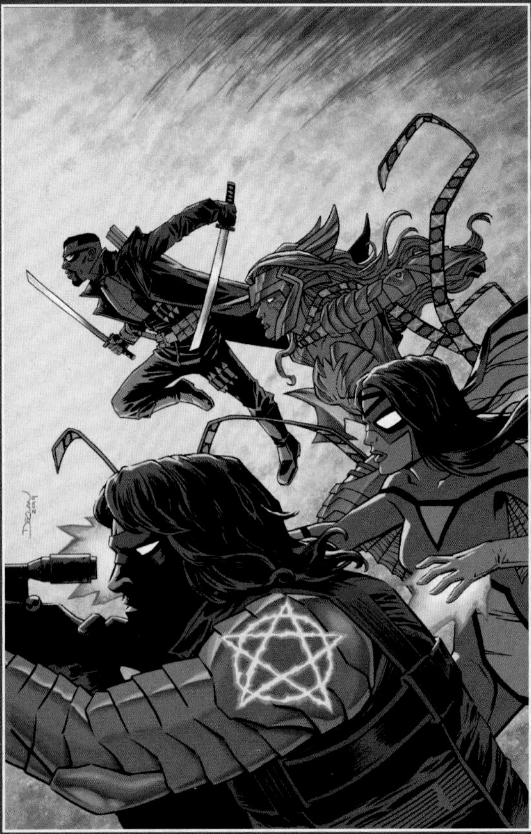

#3 VARIANT BY DECLAN SHALVEY